WHOLE AND FREE

NATO, EU Enlargement and Transatlantic Relations

edited by
John Leech

THE FEDERAL TRUST
for education & research

in conjuction with
The Trans European Policy Studies Association

This book is published by the Federal Trust in conjunction with the Trans European Policy Studies Association. The aim of the Federal Trust is to enlighten public debate on federal issues of national, continental and global governance. It does this in the light of its statutes which state that it shall promote 'studies in the principles of international relations, international justice and supranational government.' Up-to-date information about the Federal Trust can be found on the internet at www.fedtrust.co.uk

The Trans European Policy Studies Association is an independent organisation, established in 1974 at the initiative of a number of European institutes and aiming at the promotion of international research on European integration in order to stimulate discussion on policies and political options for Europe. TEPSA links affiliated national institutes from all Union member states and has associated members in the candidate countries of Central and Eastern Europe.

© Federal Trust for Education and Research 2002

ISBN 1 903403 34 0

NOTE: All contributors to this volume are writing in a personal capacity. Views expressed are those of the authors and do not represent the position of their institution.

The Federal Trust is a Registered Charity No. 272241
Dean Bradley House, 52 Horseferry Road,
London SW1P 2AF
Company Limited by Guarantee No.1269848

Marketing and Distribution by Kogan Page Ltd
Printed by MFP Design & Print

Contents

Whole and Free: European Union Enlargement and Transatlantic Relations

John Leech
Council Member, The Federal Trust
European Co-ordinator, West-West Agenda

Introduction

'A Europe whole and free.' Thus the Nato Council in its 1990 London Declaration. Simple, grandiose and with the still undimmed optimism of having witnessed the Iron Curtain rise upon a vigorous revival of democratic striving. In time, there followed the European Union's pledge in Copenhagen in 1993 that 'the countries in Central and Eastern Europe that so desire shall become members of the Union as soon as they are able to assume the obligations of membership by satisfying the economic and political conditions.' Pre-accession arrangements soon led to formal applications from ten of those countries: Poland, the Czech Republic, Slovakia, Hungary, Slovenia, Romania, Bulgaria, and the three Baltic states, Estonia, Latvia and Lithuania. Current accession negotiations also include two of the Mediterranean applicants, Cyprus and Malta, whilst Turkey is still considered short of having satisfied a number of key political criteria.

Nato's early leadership clearly testified that Europe and America were at one in their desire to embrace the whole of Europe within a zone of peace and prosperity. That common purpose was further emphasised, first by the Partnership for Peace programme, then by the full entry of Poland, the Czech

Republic and Hungary into the Nato structure in 1999. Yet the same developments began to reveal divergences in timespans and in the meaning of membership for the respective organisations. There emerged also the differing intents: the US concern with a security framework, the EU's with granting Central and Eastern Europe its right to share in the benefits of the Union and its decision making. Even if both systems spell security for the applicants, their criteria – and with them the sense of urgency – differ substantially.

A fuller understanding of these differences has yet to be achieved. But this represents only one of a multitude of points at which US and European interests intersect. They meet in the broad areas of political influence, trade advantages, economic management, security and a host of other self-evident as well as less obvious relations. Above all, they touch upon a multiplicity of private and corporate concerns, each exerting its specific pressures. Time was when these were graded within a more or less coherent diplomatic response. Today the protagonists meet directly in the field, their clash often heard loudly above more official pronouncements. The points of encounter are myriad, at will and without control or hindrance. Encouraged by a world system which favours open doors and free commerce, the levers of policy and diplomacy become engaged only when sufficient clamour is incited or commercial disadvantage dressed up as injustice. Transatlantic trade squalls have afflicted commodities such as chickens, wine, bovine hormones, sugar, rum and bananas, and now steel – hardly the stuff to affect the world's security balance. Yet at their height such disputes tend to seize a large proportion of the headlines, albeit that the total trade affected has been less than one per cent. Understandably then, potential loss of trade (and demands for compensation for it) are among the consequences of watching 100 million new consumers being incorporated into the EU economy.

As with the EU, it is simplistic to think of the USA as representing a monolithic singularity. Any polity exists at a multiplicity of levels, each with its own stake and agenda. Even at government level, divergences between the Pentagon and the State Department are as pronounced as those between the European Commission and the Council. There is no single, coherent vision on either side on how – and how soon – to bring all of Central and Eastern Europe into the 'western' comity. In the end, strategic issues may well override declared policies. US relations with Russia may become more compelling than a fixed timetable for membership of individual states. US insistence on National Missile Defense has already brought into the discussions a broader spectrum of issues – in the first rank the series of arms reduction treaties – which will open the way to an increasing elasticity of give and take. And even that may yield to the greater exigencies of the anti-terrorist coalition.

Slowly but surely, the world is beginning to adapt to accelerating change. Russia's full membership of Nato is a subject firmly on the table. In the end, therefore, instead of seeking to resolve the conflicting national interests of those within and those without, it is likely to be more rewarding to begin to consider a single Northern space in which these interests become 'domestic' instead of adversarial, and hence capable of being more easily requited. In essence, the world already accepts America's remit as a superpower; the task remaining is to find the golden formula that obliges it to accept not a *pax americana* but a *pax consociata* of united forces, or better still, a *pax foederata*. The present round of enlargement presents yet another opportunity for Europe and America to achieve that.

Convergent and divergent perspectives

This book is ambitious in that it examines both enlargement and the Union's external relations in an evolutionary way. Politically, it looks at the effects of enlargement as a future destination, but also at how it is likely to change the Union once the new members have been incorporated. Geographically, it surveys the great arc of the widened Union's close neighbourhood from the Baltic to the Barbary Coast.

These essays form part of a study conducted for the European Commission under the research and dialogue projects within its New Transatlantic Agenda. The objectives were to evaluate the impact of current and future EU enlargement on transatlantic relations; to assess the effects of political, economic, strategic and global changes on relations between the US and an EU of possibly 25-30 members; and to formulate appropriate policy options.

The contributors are a number of experts within the network of The Trans European Policy Studies Association (TEPSA) and their American colleagues. Their ideas were presented, analysed and contrasted at a series of meetings and academic conferences. This process showed on the one hand a strong identity or convergence of interests: strong US support for the overall drive towards enlargement as charted by the European Councils from Copenhagen (1993) to Göteborg (2001). The common core is a vision of European enlargement in its most challenging form as the best strategy for establishing a comprehensive region of stability combining political values, economic prosperity and peace. The 1999 Helsinki Summit reinforced the interest in such a security community, despite concerns about a possible EU overstretch. The Union's enlargement is thus a fundamental instrument of US strategy for Europe, akin to its strategy for Nato.

Behind this convergence, or even identity of policy objectives there are, however, some marked nuances over the EU's enlargement process itself, primarily those of timing and scope. The US considers its interest better served by a 'sooner and wider' strategy, whereas insistence within the European Union on strict procedures seems to argue for a 'later and smaller' strategy. This debate on timing and scope has highlighted quite fundamental differences, not in policy but rather in the nature of the two entities. On the one hand, the security concerns of the alliance acknowledge the EU as a vital instrument. Though in political matters Union intervention is rarely perceived as timely or effective, its outreach has become a highly convenient formula for reinforcing the overall stability of Europe, especially in view of uncertainties still surrounding the second round of Nato enlargement. On the other hand, an increase in EU membership represents, like marriage, a serious and irreversible step. Unless the marriage vows, the body of community policies known as the *acquis*, are accepted by all members – old and new – the contract cannot be honoured. The years since formal applications were lodged in 1998 and the earliest possible consummation by end-2004 bear witness to the complexity of the pre-nuptial agreements.

The first part of this study focuses on enlargement as a key issue in transatlantic relations. **Barbara Lippert** of the Institut für Europäische Politik examines how the EU and the US view their interests, roles, priorities and policies with regard to the enlargement process. Where are the differences and similarities? How will these affect transatlantic relations? These questions are contrasted with two US views. **Michael Calingaert** of The Brookings Institution addresses the economic implications both pre- and post-accession: the candidate countries may be of marginal economic importance to the US, but there are important adjustments to be made; and what role will the enlarged EU play in international fora – co-operation or competition? **Simon Serfaty**, Professor of US Foreign Policy and Director of the Center for Strategic and International Studies' Europe Program, examines the US political perspective and also raises the question of which position the enlarged EU will choose – counterweight or counterpart? How important are the economic aspects for the US? He also asks the key question whether Americans really understand the complexity of the enlargement process and its relationship with the enlargement of Nato.

There follows a geographic examination of the Union's likely relationships with its future neighbours, and its new role in the world after enlargement. **Bertel Heurlin** and **Jacob Ejlers** from the Dansk Udenrigspolitisk Institut look at the north-eastern region – a focal point for US policy – and relations with Russia. What contribution can the Northern European Initiative make to the development of an equitable relationship? What role will an enlarged Union play on the international scene? As to the south-eastern flank, **Christian Franck**, Professor at the Université Catholique de Louvain, questions whether Europeans – in contrast to America – take sufficiently into account the strategic importance of Turkey as a Western ally. And what contribution could Turkey make to a Cyprus settlement? To complete the Mediterranean arc, **Roberto Aliboni** of the Italian Istituto Affari Internazionali looks at the whole southern shore and its problems, invoking current EU policies as well as the EU's growing role in international diplomacy and peacemaking. In relative terms, will the so-called East-South balance continue to be respected, or will Mediterranean countries become less pivotal for the Union after eastward enlargement?

This sets the scene for **Wolfgang Wessels**, Jean Monnet Professor at the Forschungsinstitut für Politische Wissenschaft und Europäische Fragen, to examine the concepts and realities of the EU as an effective global actor. Is the trend towards becoming a civilian power balanced by progress towards an effective 'peace power?' Could implementation of the Amsterdam provisions on the Common Foreign and Security Policy become the test of the EU's capacity to fulfil such a role? This theme is developed further in the final chapter where **Hans Labohm** and **Alfred Van Staden** of Clingendael

(Netherlands Institute of International Relations) outline a number of possible scenarios for future transatlantic relationships, based on a range of assumptions from a 'weak' to a 'strong' Europe. Will the Union become inward looking and reveal itself as an impotent actor on the international stage? Will it become fragmented and divided and therefore too complex a partner to deal with? Or will it actually become a fully-fledged global actor and, if so, will it then choose to become a counterweight or a counterbalance to the USA?

Appended are two equally important contributions by **Laurent Van Depoele**, Professor at the Université Catholique de Louvain, and **Kalman Deszeri** of the Magyar Tudományos Akadémia Világgazdasági Kutatóintezet (Institute for World Economics of the Hungarian Academy of Sciences). They discuss the extent to which the EU's internal problems, of institutional reform and budgetary policy, impact upon the outside world and impede the EU's ability effectively to digest a substantial enlargement and still play a positive role in world affairs.

Overall, the EU's enlargement to anywhere between 25 and 30 members, in time possibly including parts of the former Soviet Union and Yugoslavia, will inevitably change its defining parameters. The weight of its profile and interests, a shift in its centre of gravity towards the East and a greater focus on Russia, closer proximity to crisis regions in Europe and the Mediterranean, all these should be balanced by an increasingly proactive role at international level. These changes will inevitably exercise an impact on the identity of Nato, with results which are not easily predictable. In their totality, these essays provide strong indicators for the range of policy options now available to the EU. Of greater significance to the world's medium term future are the opportunities charted for a constructive partnership between an increasingly strong and effective EU and a USA anxious for a partner to share the burdens of ensuring peace, freedom from terrorist attack, and sound governance.

Throughout, there are two recurring themes. The first is that the EU's prolonged integration process has burdened it with an accretion of legal texts and a proliferation of instruments whose combined weight threatens its own efficient governance. Together with its internal contradictions and systemic tensions, this structural confusion cannot but weaken the EU's ability to act decisively in world affairs. The second is that, whilst the direct effects of enlargement on transatlantic relations in terms of trade, investment and business activity are likely to be small, of much greater import will be the political outcomes. Of these, none will have more far-reaching consequences than the effect on the development of the Union itself. It is this which will ultimately determine the weight, reliability and compatibility of the power balance across the Atlantic.

There then remains the intriguing question, not even posed explicitly let alone answered, of the extent to which an invisible contest of wills between the two powerful entities has in any event been ineluctably shaping their decisions and fortunes.

These papers were substantially written before the events of 11 September 2001. Far from being invalidated, they have been given a sombre but sharper focus. There may also be effects on the pace and remit of enlargement. But supremely the terrorist attacks and their consequences have provided a jolting reminder that the transatlantic relationship exists not at will but is an inescapable fundament of our society. On the European side, the events have reawakened a sense of kinship long overlaid by the concerns of affluence and the relativities of power. But America, too, has woken to the imperative of seeking dependable allies, even though it is militarily fully capable of proceeding on its own. Suddenly, the true cement of the transatlantic community has been laid bare, and with it the realisation for Europe that the US is not the partner of choice but of an inextricable destiny. Like most other matters, EU enlargement has to be seen and pursued in that light.

Executive Summary

Eleven points for a new core partnership

1. *Together, the EU and the US conduct the most important economic, political and strategic relationship in the world.* Their shared values and interests – democracy, freedom, human rights and protection of minorities, security, prosperity – are clearly basic to this; yet perceptions of their relative importance and responsibilities also induce a perennial element of tension. The two continents are each other's main trading partners and investors, together accounting for around 40 per cent of world trade and 60 per cent of world output. Despite a number of well known and publicly often exaggerated trade disputes over commodities such as wine, hormones or bananas, whose total value does not exceed 1 per cent of total transatlantic trade, the EU and the US largely share the principles of trade liberalisation in a globalised world. There is now scope for agreement on a general framework to launch a new round of multilateral trade negotiations which would permit real progress towards sound international economic governance. In the political and security arena, the EU and the US have joined forces – as they are doing today – on numerous occasions to secure democracy, freedom and human rights, on the European continent and elsewhere. They have acted together in common institutions like the UN, Nato and OSCE, most recently throughout the disintegration of former Yugoslavia and even in Afghanisation. But the Balkan crises have also served to show the basic imbalance in the relationship: Europe's lack of military equivalence. Further development is needed of the EU's defence capacity to strengthen the European pillar of Nato, thus benefiting both the EU and the USA. For the most part Europeans and Americans have a common agenda but so far the responsibility for it has not been evenly shared. Yet this is precisely what the US expects from the Union: shared responsibility and burden sharing. New global challenges such as international terrorism and crime, drug trafficking, mass migrations, protection of the environment, nuclear safety and transmittable diseases have lent a fresh dimension to such joint responsibility. The EU and the US are compelled in their own interests to take the lead in the search for solutions to these challenges

through a set of adequate policies, instruments and institutions.[1] It is questionable whether the current institutional arrangements, where the EU has treaties with a host of countries but none with its most important partner, will be strong enough to face these challenges.

2. *After the fall of the Berlin Wall, the European Union started an enlargement process with the Central and Eastern European Countries (CEEC) to secure a smooth transition towards a market economy, political stability and security, and democracy and human rights.* This process was part of a joint effort by the Western partners and among other elements included widening of Nato membership, financial assistance through the EBRD and other institutions as well as through the EU's Phare programme. The appealing prospect of reuniting the continent is probably the most ambitious mission the EU has ever engaged in. Yet it brought in its train a multitude of political, economic, financial, institutional and social implications for both the EU and the CEEC which it had proved impossible to anticipate. To make this huge undertaking a success, it was necessary to find a balanced approach, combining adequate assistance for the CEEC without undue burden on the Union, and with time for careful preparation and adaptation. The Union's 'widening' was to be accompanied by a strategy of 'deepening' its common

---

[1] Official relations between the US and the then EEC date back as far as 1958. But the most important milestones of an ever more institutionalised relationship were reached in the last decade : the Transatlantic Declaration (1990), the New Transatlantic Agenda with the EU-US Joint Action Plan (1995) and the Transatlantic Economic Partnership (1998). After the fall of the Berlin Wall, voices in the first Bush Administration as well as in the European Commission further called for development of the relationship. In May 1990, the German Foreign Minister, Hans Dieter Genscher, called for a Transatlantic Declaration to strengthen bilateral relations but also to serve as a framework for assistance to the new democracies of Central and Eastern Europe. The Transatlantic Declaration contained four pillars: economic co-operation, co-operation in the field of education, science and culture, trans-national challenges and an institutional framework for consultation (bi-annual summits). These instruments soon appeared to be insufficient to handle problems efficiently and new forms of a strengthened institutional relationship were sought. But attempts to launch a transatlantic treaty or a transatlantic free trade area (TAFTA) encountered too many obstacles (disagreement on the content, limits of Community competence, incompatibility with GATT legislation, ...) and never materialised. In December 1995 efforts resulted in the New Transatlantic Agenda, a framework (though not a legally binding one) for closer co-operation built on four cornerstones: 1. Promoting peace and stability, democracy and development around the world. 2. Responding to global challenges. 3. Contributing to the expansion of world trade and closer economic relations. 4. Building bridges across the Atlantic. The Joint Action Plan that accompanied the NTA set out a number of priority areas for action. The Transatlantic Economic Partnership (TEP-1998) and the Bonn Declaration (1999) constitute the two most recent important steps in the relationship. The TEP is a framework for further bilateral and multilateral liberalisation, bringing together labour, business, environmental and consumer issues. The Bonn Declaration established a 'full and equal partnership' in economic, political and security matters.

policies and institutions. In addition to continuously increasing financial transfers from the Union (and its Member States) to the CEEC [Deszeri], guidelines for preparing the CEEC for membership were set out in Copenhagen (1993), in the Commission's White Paper (1995) and in Agenda 2000 (1999).[2] Based on these criteria and guidelines, the CEEC have been enabled to initiate a process of massive reforms, in the knowledge that the speed of their EU membership will be greatly dependent on the introduction of these reforms, and principally the speed of adopting the body of EU common policies, the *acquis communitaire*. For the EU, the major challenge of enlargement will be to ensure that a Union of more than 25 members remains workable, and to build up a high level of cohesion among its present and future members. To meet this challenge, institutional reforms and the adaptation of policies are indispensable. Whilst the Treaty of Amsterdam failed to produce the necessary dispensations to achieve this, the Treaty of Nice succeeded in positioning the candidate countries on the map of the EU institutions, so that at least the formal conditions for enlargement have been met [Van Depoele].[3] At the same time, it failed to engage the fundamental institutional reforms necessary to ensure optimal working of an enlarged Union, inter alia by maintaining veto rights over a number of important common policies. Moreover, to allow the Union to become a strong actor on the global scene – of major importance for its relations with the US – CFSP reform should have simplified the institutional framework and transferred the function of the High Representative to the European Commission. Hence the Nice Treaty cannot represent the last step in the institutional reform process. Its unsatisfactory result is evidence that the Union is still in the grip of an intergovernmental philosophy. For its future development, the EU will clearly need a more communitarian methodology, preferably as the result of a wide-ranging public debate [Van Depoele].

---

[2] Three criteria were put forward at the European Council in Copenhagen (1993): 1. stable institutions to guarantee democracy, the rule of law and respect of human rights; 2. a functioning market economy and the ability to cope with competitive pressures and market forces within the Union; 3. the ability to adhere to the political, economic and monetary goals of the Union. The Commission's 'White Paper on the Preparation of the Associated Countries of Central and Eastern Europe for Integration into the Internal Market' (1995) identified the most fundamental pieces of internal market legislation in twenty-three sectoral areas. Agenda 2000 adopted on 15 July 1997 evaluated the prospects of each of the applicant states in detail and the Commission identified perceived problems and noted areas of progress. It also provided its analysis of the anticipated effect of enlargement on the European Union itself.

[3] The indication that candidate countries which become members of the Union before November 2004 will participate in the 2004 elections for the European Parliament has raised the prospect of early accession. But this remains a political aspiration and does not constitute any legal commitment.

3. *The US has been supportive of the EU enlargement process from the outset, mainly out of political and security considerations.* An enlarged EU will offer the best guarantee of stability and security on the European continent. In addition, EU membership of the CEEC will prevent Russia from re-exerting its influence upon those countries, should it ever wish to do so. However, enlargement is more than a matter of US preferences; it is also a matter of the expectations of Europe itself. Failure to enlarge would be reckoned a fundamental failure of the whole EU construction, with possibly dire results: institutional reforms would stall, EU economies stagnate, the euro zone tumble, applicant states fail to keep up with rising EU demands, and member states become indifferent to the applicants' needs. Such failure would erode a rising US interest in the EU as a serious partner, and resurrect instead past patterns of privileged partnerships with one or more individual countries [Serfaty]. In this respect American fears do not differ substantially from the fears expressed during the enlargement debate in Europe. But Americans do not always fully understand the complexity of the enlargement process and of the Union's internal functioning. They would prefer that the EU moves on more rapidly with enlargement, without proclaiming deadlines that then fail to be met. US policy makers and the media have widely criticised the EU for its presumed dilatory handling of the enlargement issue. While the US seems to concentrate on achievement of the status of membership, the EU is concerned with the level of political and economic integration that is achieved prior to accession [Lippert]. However, the main point of controversy between the two sides remains Turkish membership, which the Americans strongly favour, as against the Union which retains considerable doubts (see also 7 below). On the economic level, enlargement will not entail vital considerations for the US and is not expected significantly to affect the economic relationship between the EU and the US. In contrast to the *transatlantic economic relationship* – the most important economic relationship in the world – the CEEC are of marginal economic importance to the US [Calingaert]. The economic problems that may arise from enlargement have little importance in the global picture. In the pre-accession period such problems as there are relate to access for exports from the US and to bilateral agreements which the US has concluded with the CEEC. Once enlargement has taken place, its implications for the economic transatlantic relationship will depend on the direction in which the EU itself develops [Calingaert]. The US would be well satisfied if enlargement

acted as a stimulus towards more efficient decision-making and market-orientated reforms, especially in respect of the Common Agricultural Policy [Lippert].

4. *EU enlargement will profoundly change the EU but will also affect its role in the global environment as well as in relations with its neighbourhood, principally the republics of former Yugoslavia, Russia, Ukraine and the Mediterranean countries.* During the nineties, the Union was able to show increasingly its desire to shape Europe's regional environment and to influence the global political system [Wessels]. The question of whether the Union should indeed be a global actor is controversial and gives rise to doubts over the appropriateness and desirability of the very idea. In some sectors of traditional trade policy (especially in negotiations within WTO and the UN environmental conferences), the EU has indeed become a global player, but on matters of security the picture still looks very different. At the regional level, as new external borders are drawn, relations with the European periphery will have to be intensified to secure a new geo-political coherence and the cohesion of the enlarged EU. Such cohesion will depend on balancing the allocation of resources for external and internal aims, and on a balancing of policy objectives in supporting external actions [Aliboni]. Enlargement will most probably tend to allocate greater resources for internal policies and coherence, whereas new common external interests can result in competition among different regional groups – the Mediterranean, the Balkans, Russia and the Ukraine – with shifting of funds from one external policy area to another. The Union's external actions are usually designed to create some form of inter-regional equilibrium with its neighbours. The Americans, however, are not yet convinced that such EU policies of inter-regional co-operation and integration (which could lead to enclaves of prosperity) are consistent with true globalisation [Aliboni]. Despite their common interests and challenges, the EU and the US frequently do not agree on the setting of priorities, nor on the policies necessary to tackle the challenges. The Union favours economic, social, cultural and soft-security co-operation – its global role being limited to that of an economic and civilian power. Indeed, the Union is still far from being a real political and military power, since it does not yet dispose over adequate instruments of foreign and security policy, nor over the ability rapidly to express a common political will so as to take the

lead in hard-security co-operation. Hence the key to a fully-fledged global power role for the Union lies in institutional strengthening; and enlargement in itself will not necessarily produce this. The US welcomes a stronger European security role, especially in international crisis management, but only to the extent that this role is consistent with US and Alliance interests as well as effectively carried out [Aliboni]. For the Americans, hard-security issues are to be dealt with in the Nato framework. The US attaches great importance to the structure of transatlantic relations, and particularly the nature of EU-Nato relations, and fears that enlargement and institutional reinforcement could lead to a strengthened EU political and security role outside the transatlantic framework and not necessarily in line with America's interests. Any such clash of interests could be further exacerbated by differences over burden sharing within the alliance.

5. *Since the early nineties, the EU has been concerned with the so-called East-South balance.* Member states declared at the Cannes Summit of 1995 that 'an ambitious policy of co-operation to the South forms a counterpart to the policy of openness to the East and gives the European Union's external action its geopolitical coherence.' The Barcelona Declaration of the same year launched the Euro-Mediterranean Partnership, a framework of bilateral and multilateral regional co-operation with 12 Mediterranean partners based on three baskets: (1) political and security partnership, (2) economic and financial partnership, and (3) social, cultural and human partnership. At the insistence of its Southern member states, the Union considers the 12 Mediterranean non-EU Member Countries (MNMC) to be one region for which it has developed a single policy. This concept of looking at the MNMC as a more or less coherent region is alien to the US, which has always distinguished between the Western and Eastern Mediterranean with their respective, very distinct areas of conflict [Aliboni]. The Americans believe that the problems of arms proliferation, terrorism, threats to energy sources concentrated in the Mediterranean and more particularly in the Middle East should be tackled by a policy of containment – economic sanctions and military pressure – and that Nato should be involved. The Union considers the Mediterranean threats to be the result of political, economic and social problems that require measures of an equivalent nature. For the EU the

appropriate instrument is the Euro-Mediterranean Partnership and not Nato. The EU and US inevitably have different views also on the Middle East Peace Process, because of their respective strategic involvement with Israel and the Arab States. The Union's Mediterranean policy is a good example of the thesis that the Union is an economic and social power, but not a politico-military one: the second and third baskets of the Barcelona Declaration are indeed much more developed than is the first. The MNMC appear to welcome and value the Europeans' economic involvement – the Union being their natural trading partner – but have also understood that the EU is politically weak and dependent on its alliance with the US to uphold an international role [Aliboni]. This is especially discernible in the Middle East Peace Process. Will enlargement strengthen Europe's role in the Mediterranean? The European Commission stressed in Agenda 2000 that 'enlargement of the Union should lead to an intensification of economic and trade relations between the European Union and its Southern partners.' But this will depend on the extent to which the member states will regard the Mediterranean as a priority area in relation to other regions such as the Balkans, Russia and the Ukraine.

6. *On the Northern flank, both the EU's Northern Dimension – a Finnish initiative – and the USA's Northern European Initiative were launched in 1997, aimed at creating stability in Northern Europe through promoting interdependence [Heurlin and Ejlers].* In this region, however, unlike in many others, the US does not regard itself as the principal actor. The former US Northern European Initiative Coordinator has stated that the US role is that of 'an actor whose activities can bring added political, symbolic, and financial value to the efforts of the countries in the region.' After the fall of the Berlin Wall, US policy towards North-Eastern Europe was characterised by three elements: a Northern component comprising the Scandinavian countries, a Baltic component and a Russian component. In the case of the Baltic States, the US – like the Union – supports Baltic independence and integration into institutions like Nato, the EU and other sub-regional networks. As for Russia, the US has three objectives: an improvement in Russia's relations with its neighbours so as to avoid future conflicts, ensuring that Russia has no veto with respect to the future of the Baltic States, and that Russia becomes a part of Europe and of the European integration process [Heurlin and Ejlers]. The policies of the

transatlantic partners towards the Northern region are therefore aimed at similar outcomes and appear essentially complementary.

7. *Among the applicant states, Turkey is undoubtedly the one case where the EU and the US have divergent views and interests.* For Turkey, EU membership is one of the most important foreign policy objectives. For the EU, Turkish membership has long been – and to a large extent still is – a controversial and sensitive issue. Although relations between Turkey and the EU have a far longer history – the Ankara Association Treaty was signed in 1963, the customs union entered into force in 1996 – relations between the Central and Eastern European Countries and the EU developed much faster and more smoothly. When the Luxembourg Summit of December 1997 granted candidate status not only to ten CEEC but also to Cyprus and Malta, Turkey was left in suspense. The situation was rectified when, in Helsinki in 1999, Turkey was formally recognised as a candidate country destined to become an EU member on the basis of the same criteria applied to the other states. But despite this recognition, EU member states seem hesitant, or even unwilling, to start negotiations with Turkey in the short term. Reasons for the EU's ambiguous attitude are manifold: human rights and minority protection issues, extension of the borders of the EU to countries such as Syria and Iraq, fear of massive migration, and for the maintenance of a religiously, culturally and ethnically diversified Europe. For the USA, on the other hand, Turkey is in the first place a vital Nato ally, located in an important geo-strategic region and destined to play an eminent role in potential conflict areas such as the Aegean, the Balkans, the Black Sea or the Middle East. Secondly, it is a secular nation and potential bridge builder with the Islamic World. The US wants to secure Turkish commitment to the transatlantic alliance and believes this is best guaranteed through inclusion in the enlargement process and eventual EU membership. Although the US appreciates the EU's fears that Turkish membership could provoke internal difficulties, it believes that such fears should not be overestimated and the importance of the global geo-political picture should prevail. The partners' views on *Cyprus* are more identical. EU member states placed Cyprus in the first group of candidate countries at the Luxembourg Summit and negotiations began in April 1998. Whilst these are firmly on track, the prospect of a widening economic and political gap between

its two communities will make Cyprus a test case for the EU's capacity as peacemaker. Expectations were that the prospect of EU membership would encourage the Greek and Turkish communities to settle their differences and collaborate. But despite EU hopes that both communities would at least take part in the negotiation, Turkish Cypriot representatives have so far refused to sit around the table. To resolve the complex Cypriot question, it is indispensable that all players – the EU, Greece, Turkey, the UN and the US – work together and develop supportive and constructive policies for reuniting the Island. Hence the EU and US are supporting attempts to settle the problem within the UN framework, possibly through the creation of a bi-communal federation. In any event, membership of only one of the communities – whilst not excluded – can hardly represent a desirable outcome.

8. *Should the EU and Nato enlarge along a similar pattern and timetable?* Such a notion of 'dual enlargement' gained ground, particularly in the US, because both processes were seen as complementary and based on shared values and principles [Lippert]. On the face of it, co-ordination of new accessions to the EU and Nato would enable both institutions to work together more effectively than under conditions that shut European Nato states that are not EU members out of EU initiatives, whilst EU states that are not Nato members cannot participate in Nato initiatives. Such a strategy of dual enlargement would keep the respective enlargement processes separate, but without the current pretence that EU and Nato decisions are separable [Serfaty]. The EU, on the other hand, is eager to keep the processes separate to maintain autonomous EU decision-making. But a US-led Nato did indeed define the pace and set points of reference for the selection and sequencing of candidates for EU membership [Lippert]. The first six countries with which the EU opened negotiations, the so-called Luxembourg group, was composed of the three new Nato members, Poland, the Czech Republic and Hungary, plus Slovenia, Estonia and Cyprus. Equally, the CEECs that become early EU members are likely to be leading contenders for Nato membership [Serfaty]. In the medium term, however, identical membership of both institutions seems unlikely, since the EU will probably incorporate more CEECs than Nato, whilst the present non-Nato EU members will not wish to join the organisation unless it changes its character materially.

9. *In conclusion, it appears that the transatlantic relationship will be largely determined by the way the Union develops.* This in turn will depend largely on two main factors: the speed and scope of the enlargement process and the ability to adapt the Union's institutional structure to new challenges. Depending on the Union's weakness or strength four *scenarios* can then be postulated [Van Staden – Labohm].

The first scenario is that of an *Impotent Europe*, based on an enlarged but less effective EU. Such a Union would be inward looking, unable to resolve its internal problems created by a premature and over-ambitious enlargement, and unable to play a serious role as a global actor. Under this scenario the Union might not only be a weak ally of the US but possibly even a nuisance power.

Under the second scenario, a *Kaleidoscopic Europe* would become a fragmented and divided Europe, consisting of different groupings and formations. Its institutional structure and external representation would be ever more complex and a number of member states could feel marginalised. The Union would again be a weak ally of the US, which for its part could be tempted to apply a policy of 'divide et impera.'

The third scenario, a *Muddling-through Europe*, would basically be a continuation of the current state of affairs. Institutional reform would be sufficient to prevent paralysis in decision-making but insufficient to allow the Union to be a global actor on the international scene, especially as a military power. The Union would maintain its present semi-dependent, semi-autonomous relationship with the US.

Europe as a global player is the fourth possible scenario. Enlargement and deepening would lead to a mutually reinforcing dynamic, making the Union a powerful global actor capable of external action. The EU would no longer be solely an economic power but build up the necessary military capabilities to become, with the US, an effective joint crisis manager on the world stage.

It is clearly this last scenario which would best suit the transatlantic relationship. But if it is to exploit fully the potential for strengthening the relationship, the Union should refrain from defining itself as a 'counterweight' to the US, challenging its hegemonic position and seeking an independent role in world politics. On the contrary, the Union would do better to seek to become an equal partner, a 'counterpart' of the US, offering its increased economic and military resources for the achievement of common goals. Enlargement might well have a beneficial impact on such a rebalancing of responsibilities because most candidate countries will be likely to favour security policies in close co-operation with the US. An enlarged EU, having the weight of numbers, the capacity to share responsibility on the world stage, and a predisposition for co-operation with the USA, thus promises the best hope for a new era in transatlantic relations.

10. Policy recommendations. The institutional structure of the Union needs to be reformed if Europe wants to be an equal partner of the US and fully play its role as a global actor. The strength and effectiveness of the Union's institutions will be crucial for managing the deployment of civilian, economic and military instruments and carrying out of complex interventions. The Union will have to build up and make operational the necessary military capabilities and develop a fully European Security and Defence Policy. Whilst its principal purpose must be to reinforce the European pillar of Nato to the benefit of both the EU and the US, it must also be designed to be capable of autonomous action where Nato does not wish to become involved.

In an enlarged Union, the need for a transatlantic agora will become greater since the political and civilian elements will become even more important. A new transatlantic institutional framework would require new agenda points such as migration and economic and monetary co-operation.

Migration is one of the main global challenges to be faced. Europe's new borders will not facilitate this problem but will provide the stimulus for dealing with it. To do so effectively, it is recommended that national immigration policies be harmonised and the necessary set of Community policies established within the *Third Pillar* [Aliboni].

Further co-operation is recommended in transatlantic economic relations. In the field of *trade and investment*, the EU and the US should strive together for further liberalisation in the framework of WTO. They should intensify efforts for a successful new round of multilateral negotiations [Van Staden – Labohm].

With the introduction of the euro, international *monetary* relationships have been profoundly altered. The new monetary constellation could now give rise to new institutional arrangements for which the EU and the US should act as driving forces. In the future it would be desirable that their monetary authorities co-operate more closely to achieve greater stability between the euro and the dollar. Such co-operation could in a first stage consist of common analysis of monetary developments and, where necessary, of joint support within the IMF framework in response to financial crises. In a further stage, study and establishment of a transatlantic currency union could be conceivable [Van Staden – Labohm].

The accession of the candidate countries requires profound adaptations within the Union and even more profound adaptations from the candidate countries themselves. In addition to the right set of technical measures, political support is of vital importance for the successful completion of enlargement. The Union should take account of the *perceptions* both of its own citizens and those of the US. Both partners would therefore benefit from a close and continuous economic and political dialogue in order to prevent possible misperceptions and their potentially damaging effects [Van Staden – Labohm].

11. *Enlargement Strategies have also to be seen in the context of 11 September 2001.* The original accession doctrine of the EU stressed the principle of 'each according to his merits' i.e. those able to implement the *acquis* should have the right to become members. From the start there were doubts about the viability of individual 'single accessions.' Group accession was seen as more politically correct and easier to ratify and manage than the processing of individual applicants.

The Luxembourg group of 1997 was thus more geared up to the 'sooner and smaller' strategy (strategy 1). The Helsinki decision of the European Council, envisaging a much larger group, then showed the tendency towards a 'larger and later' scenario. The claims of a 'big bang' strategy (strategy 2) had become more dominant. They meant delayed entry, with the Copenhagen criteria and individual progress assessment by the Commission still being taken seriously. The US position on the other hand was dominated by security objectives, with a benign neglect for the political and economic preconditions required by the EU. The demand to integrate Turkey is the most visible sign of an all-embracing US strategy.

For many, the events of 11 September 2001 have served to give the 'larger and sooner' (strategy 3) scenario a fresh impetus. They deployed the

Size of enlargement (number of new members)

		SMALLER	LARGER
Timing	SOONER	Strategy 1 'Luxembourg'	Strategy 3 US Position
	LATER	Strategy 4 EU risk minimalisation	Strategy 2 'Helsinki'

argument that by enlarging, the EU would promote and create a new security structure for Europe; by offering membership to Turkey it would give an important signal that the West is not anti-Islamic per se; and that the role of the EU as a global player would be correspondingly enhanced.

However, there are also arguments in favour of strategy 4. This looks at the vulnerability of western systems and their governance, and at the efficiency of policy-making and implementation that currently protect EU members. Worries about the performance of new members and their observance of the *acquis*, not least in respect of border controls, underline the risks of overtaxing the candidates. The enlarged Union's capacity for effective action must also be subject to a higher degree of uncertainty. The institutional reforms agreed in Nice have still to be tested in times of crisis. At the same time the EU system itself might begin to suffer from overload. Such imponderables may now prompt member countries to favour a more measured accession process.

'Business as usual,' or accession negotiations following the earlier schedule, is another possible outcome. This would put enlargement on a lower level of transatlantic priorities, with the process following its pre-determined path. But the rationale for US support and urging would remain the same.

EU Enlargement: Comparing US and European Approaches, Interests and Roles

Barbara Lippert
Deputy Director, Institut für Europäische Politik

Introduction

Enlarging the EU to the East has always been an uncontentious issue between the EU and the US. Compared with the debate over Nato enlargement in the US,[4] enlargement of the EU is far less topical and seems uncontroversial among experts and policy makers. On the contrary, in the US EU enlargement is taken more or less for granted and perceived as beneficial for the EU, the CEECs and therefore also the US. However, Washington's geopolitical outlook often underestimates the array of institutional, political, economic and financial burdens of EU enlargement and the threat it poses to consensus and cohesion inside the EU. The EU for its part has done much to confirm this American belief. Throughout the nineties the EU denied that deepening and widening were partly conflicting agendas and pretended that it could cope with both in a parallel process. In practice, and to the disappointment of the applicants as well as the US, up to the Nice summit the process of enlargement was fully dependent on the path of further integration, thus giving priority to deepening over widening.

---

[4] Cf. as a starting point see Knapp, M. 1997, *Europäische Sicherheit und die Osterweiterung der Nato aus Sicht der US*, in Pradetto, A. (ed.) 1997, *Ostmitteleuropa, Rußland und die Osterweiterung der Nato*, Westdeutscher Verlag, Opladen, pp.251-287; and Broer, M. 1997, *Die Entwicklung der Politik der Nato zur Osterweiterung*, also in Pradetto, A. 1997, pp.289-329; also Lewis Gaddis, J. 1998, *History, Grand Strategy and Nato Enlargement*, in *Survival 1*, pp.145-151; and Gallis, P. 1998, *Nato Enlargement: Pro and Con Arguments*, Congressional Research Service Report, Library of Congress, Washington.

At the end of the nineties, the institutional map of Europe was redrawn. In 1998 negotiations on EU accession started with five CEECs (plus Cyprus) whilst the other five 'pre-ins' (and Malta) followed swiftly in early 2000. Moreover, Nato completed its first expansion in March 1999 and welcomed the Czech Republic, Hungary and Poland as partners into the alliance. Both enlargements were hailed as overcoming the system of Yalta that had divided Europe after World War II.[5] Hence, enlargement would 'right the wrongs of the past'[6] and at the same time constitute a decisive step towards Europe's future as a continent 'whole and free.' Mostly in connection with Nato expansion, experts and policymakers alike have argued that there are considerable costs attached to a gradual inclusion of countries, which challenges those which are – at least temporarily – left out. As a consequence of its staged enlargement, the EU will also have to cope with peripheries. Sophisticated politics of inclusion and the breaching of boundaries beyond territorial borders are an imminent challenge for the EU and also the US.[7]

The logic of extending the core institutions of the Cold War, the European Union and Nato, to the East can be read as the final mastery of the West over the organisations in the Soviet hemisphere. It reflects the magnetism exerted by the institutions that helped secure peace, prosperity and democracy over the last 50 years. The projection of these attributes and merits to CEE, a region that is already undergoing transformation towards democracy and market economy and struggling with severe consequences of socio-economic modernisation, lies at the heart of the enlargement project. The rationale as well as the moral and historic legitimacy of the underlying motives are beyond doubt. However, the logic of enlargement is not self evident, but needs explanation and consideration of the likely implications for all parties involved. As the accession and enlargement process of the EU becomes more serious, bargains and policy choices that – at times – contradict the politically correct

---

[5] Although historically not correct, the Conference of Yalta has become a synonym for the decision to divide Europe into a Soviet and an Anglo-American sphere of influence, ceding CEE to Moscow's rule.

[6] Prepared Statement of US Secretary of State Madeleine Albright before the United States Senate Armed Services Committee, Washington, April 23, 1997.

[7] Lippert, B., Becker, P. 1998, 'Structured Dialogue Revisited: the EU's Politics of Inclusion and Exclusion,' in *European Foreign Affairs Review*, Vol. 3, pp.341-365.

pro-enlargement rhetoric are becoming more assertive inside the EU, threatening to create frictions in the whole process. At the same time, the US administration and business community, though not directly involved in the enlargement process, are pressing their specific interests – over the terms of accession and the internal reforms of the EU set out in Agenda 2000 and the new Treaty of Nice.

Although enlargement seems firmly on track, uncertainties remain all around: with regard to the future of Russia as a co-operative or potentially antagonistic European power, the pace and degree of further European integration, and the ability of the reformers and westernisers in CEE to stay the course.

This contribution will compare US and EU approaches, interests and roles in relation to EU enlargement and examine the implications for the future of EU-US relations.

Differing approaches to the 'Logic of Enlargement'

Enlargement of Euro-Atlantic institutions seems non-controversial among the political elites in the US and the EU. Peter van Ham even suggests that 'one of the few concepts that seems to be widely shared is the so-called 'logic of enlargement:' the idea that enlargement of the Euro-Atlantic institutions is a natural process, that prospective members have a 'right' to 'join Europe' now, and that obstacles which have kept them from doing so during the Cold War have finally been removed.'[8] The EU's CFSP did not make Nato enlargement an explicit topic of its policy towards the CEECs, yet the United States fully endorsed the new democracies' aspirations to accede to the EU in its own foreign policy vis-à-vis these countries.

From a US point of view EU enlargement is principally a challenge of political inclusion and of keeping pace with the changes in post-Cold War Europe. Unlike the US, the EU cannot cope with CEE as a foreign policy

---

[8] Van Ham, P. 1998, 'US Policy towards the Baltic States: An Ambiguous Commitment,' in Jopp, M., Arnswald, S. (eds.) 1998, *The European Union and the Baltic States: Visions, Interests and Strategies for the Baltic Sea Region*, UPI & IEP, Kauhava, pp.213-234.

issue in traditional terms of thinking. Its swiftly engaged and expanded bilateral relations with the CEECs rapidly turned towards enlargement. However, as Helen Wallace points out, the specific resonance and dimension of the EC/ EU as an embodiment of liberal democracies with functioning market economies challenges the Union to enlarge 'each time that newly democratic neighbours want to join the club.'[9] Both the US and the CEECs appealed specifically to this essential characteristic of the Union. Traditional foreign policy instruments of the EU, like trade and co-operation or association agreements, foreign assistance and political dialogue, were soon modified or redirected to meet the membership aspirations of the CEECs. In 1993, four years after the fall of the Berlin Wall and eighteen months after the signing of the first Europe agreements, the EU made a clear political statement offering membership to associated countries once they had met the essential criteria. This specific shift from a neighbour to an applicant had important implications which are still widely underestimated outside the EU and even in some applicant countries themselves. Despite the magnitude of the difficulties that a near doubling of its membership from 15 to 25 or more members will certainly create, US policy makers and the media widely criticised the EU for its presumed dilatory handling of the enlargement issue. While they acknowledge the positive impact of the EU's pre-accession and association policy on the economic and political development of the applicant countries, Brussels' alleged foot dragging on enlargement is regarded as a major shortcoming. Put differently, while the US, just like most CEECs, seems to concentrate on the status of membership, the EU points to the level of political and economic integration that is already being achieved prior to accession. That is why the EU focuses more on the process of enlargement. Process versus product is a well-known pattern of conflicting perceptions and priorities in US-EU relations. In a positive scenario these differences might co-exist without problems. If, however, enlargement were to have to take place in a far more turbulent context (implosion of Russia, slowing down of EU integration) these differences might severely limit a co-operative EU-US approach towards European stability.

---

[9] Cf. Wallace, H. 2000, 'The Policy Process,' in Wallace, H., Wallace, W. (eds.) *Policy-making in the European Union*, 4th edn, Oxford, pp.39-64.

Differing roles and policies

EU enlargement may be understood as a case where the US and the EU share a common agenda but in which their interests and commitments vary and sometimes conflict.[10] It is an area where the 'mutual acceptance of roles'[11] is crucial for long term success.

The immediate response of the 'West' to the revolutions in the East was to offer assistance, which started as a joint effort of the OECD countries.[12] The so-called G24 process signalled a division of labour which left the EU with the key responsibility for CEE up to the then Soviet Union. It was implicit that the EU would bear the strains of economic and other forms of assistance. This initial division was all the more plausible as the US was absorbed with the Gulf War and a revision of its strategic priorities in a post-Soviet world. From this perspective, EU enlargement, or at least intensive relations between the EU and the CEECs, figured as an essential element of the new order and was expected to progress swiftly and smoothly.

At the beginning of the nineties the EU was *the* key political organisation in Europe within reach of joining. The difference between, say, the Council of Europe or CSCE as opposed to the EC was well understood in the CEECs who publicly declared their aspiration for quick admission to membership of the EC as early as 1990.[13] Nato membership was not on offer as long as the Soviet Union and the Warsaw Pact existed, so that the politico-economic involvement of the US was far less prominent than the EU's. Moreover, it seemed to go without saying that the EU would play a similar role vis-à-vis the CEEC as the US had played in Europe after 1945.[14] So Christopher Hill

---

[10] Cf. Peterson, J. 1996, *Europe and America, The Prospects of Partnership*, 2nd edn, London, p.67.

[11] Gardner Feldman, L. 1998, 'The European Union's Enlargement Project and US-EU Cooperation in Central and Eastern Europe', in Burwell, F., Daalder, I. (eds.) *The United States and the European Union in the Global Arena*, Macmillan, London, p.6.

[12] Cf. Nicolaïdis, K. 1993, 'East European Trade in the Aftermath of 1989: Did International Institutions Matter?,' in Keohane, R., Nye, J., Hoffmann, S. (eds.) *After the Cold War: International Institutions and State Strategies in Europe:1989-1991*, Harvard University Press, Cambridge, p.218.

[13] Cf. Zellner, W., Dunay, P. (eds) 1998, *Ungarns Außenpolitik 1990-1997: Zwischen Westintegration, Nachbarschafts-und Minderheitenpolitik*, Nomos, Baden-Baden, p.129.

[14] Cf. Allen, D. 1998, 'Who speaks for Europe?' The search for an effective and coherent external policy,' in Petersen, J., Sjursen, H. (eds.) 1998, *A Common Foreign Policy for Europe? Competing visions of the CFSP*, Routledge, London, p.47.

concludes: 'after all, in the first months of the post-Cold War world it seemed that the EC's status as a civilian power, consisting of rich, liberal-minded states, made it perfectly suited to take the lead in an environment where military forces now suddenly seemed irrelevant. Moreover the United States, the world's indisputable dominant force, actively supported the idea of the Europeans taking on more responsibility (and paying more bills).'[15]

It has frequently been noted that the EU was prepared neither to deliver a master plan for re-ordering Europe after the end of the Cold War, nor fully to grasp the strategic consequences for European integration, and for its own role as an international actor, of a 'Europe whole and free.' In response to the 'turning of the tide,' the EU merely followed a cumulative approach combining traditional offers (market access, financial support, political dialogue) with new incentives or labels ('Europe agreements'). In light of the CEEC's ambitions for swift integration into the Euro-Atlantic organisations, the EU's approach was criticised as dilatory, technical and ad hoc rather than as determined and coherent. In retrospect, it did not add up to the seemingly coherent strategic steps of the one-time Marshall Plan or Truman Doctrine that created the post-World War II system and the Cold War defence.[16] The lack of dynamic and determination is clearly also due to a less threatening international context and the rebirth of multi-polar relationships. The EU nevertheless contributed to managing interdependence on the continent and to stabilising its periphery in an incremental way. The main instrument were the Europe Agreements, which already included a political perspective of EU membership.

However, the Europe Agreements were strategically ambivalent and bore all the signs of accommodating the diversity of interests inside the EU. They were born at a time of intense uncertainty, the anticipation of heavy financial burdens, challenges to the delicate consensus on further integration, and expectations of tectonic shifts in the EU as a political community – such as the

---

[15] Hill, C. 1998, 'Closing the capabilities-expectation gap?,' in Petersen, J., Sjursen, H. 1998, p.21.

[16] Chace, J. 1998, *Dean Acheson: The Secretary of State Who Created the American World*, Simon and Schuster, New York.

role of a unified Germany, the search for a new geo-political balance, and implications for decision-making, political identity, potential deepening of already existing cleavages between north and south, and the polemic of integrationists versus intergovernmentalists. Against such a backdrop, a timid approach was not surprising: 'Western Europe faces a growing number of problems. Most member states have double figure rates of unemployment. It has become impossible to finance the welfare services built up in previous decades. Global competition has burgeoned. The increasingly complex (and bureaucratic) system of Community regulation has become difficult to comprehend and is meeting resistance from society (a 'democratic deficit'). All these factors have increased the concerns surrounding future enlargement.'[17]

Throughout the 1990s the EU was preoccupied, in addition to its own internal problems, with questions of how to integrate the CEEC and to build a new European system. Answers and specific measures were manifold, but none included an instant opening of the EU and its institutions. Instead, the EU initially tried to modify and adapt its traditional legal and political models for co-operation and association. Friis and Murphy explain this conservatism on the part of the EU as conditioned by its system of multi-level governance.[18] This period produced a number of oddly fashioned proposals for a European Political Area, affiliate or partial membership and even a European Confederation.[19] All these would have had the effect, if not the objective, of weakening the boundaries between 'ins' and 'outs,' e.g. by granting observer status in the Council and the European Parliament. While reducing pressure to take definitive decisions on the enlargement issue, these proposals tried to shift the focus from 'full' membership to effective co-operation, but also integration in the economic and political spheres. Ideas of a 'third way' between

---

[17] Inotai, A. 1997, *What is Novel About Eastern Enlargement of the European Union?*, Institute for World Economics of the Hungarian Academy of Science, Working Papers, No.87, Budapest, p.9.

[18] Cf. Friis, L., Murphy, A. 1997, *EU Governance and Central and Eastern Europe – Where are the Boundaries?*, Paper presented to the ECSA Fifth Biennial International Conference, 29 May-1 June 1997, Seattle, Washington.

[19] Cf. Lippert, B. 1995, 'Shaping and Evaluating the Europe Agreements – the Community side', in Lippert, B., Schneider, H (eds.) 1995, *Monitoring Association and Beyond: The European Union and the Visegrád States*, Europa Union Verlag, Bonn, pp.227-228.

membership and non-membership recurred throughout the debate on shaping a strategy for stabilising the East. A set of political and economic criteria for membership was defined at the Copenhagen summit in June 1993. It reflected the minimum agreement of the then 12 Member States on a political commitment to widening the EU, on condition that candidates bound themselves fully to take on the *acquis* and that enlargement did not threaten the dynamics of further integration.

Apart from the rather broadly defined accession criteria expected of the applicants, it was the maintenance of a functioning community political system within a wider EU that caused concern in the CEECs, who by that time were afraid of running into the 'deepening or widening' trap the EU itself was trying to escape. All these obstacles can now be cleared only by ratification of the Treaty of Nice.

Different priority setting

Throughout the nineties, the path-dependence of enlargement became ever more obvious. While the EU intensified the deepening of integration by setting qualitative objectives and criteria linked to a timetable, the enlargement process was driven by a series of initiatives that omitted to impose clearly defined obligations on the EU. This one-sided approach reflected on the one hand that the EU defined the rules of the game and, on the other, that deepening would determine the pace of accession. The US would clearly have preferred a more balanced approach towards the parallel processes of deepening and widening. Although the US did not address the issue directly, it was increasingly worried about what it saw as delays to enlargement, be it on purpose or due to protracted internal bargaining on reforming the EU.[20]

Though an outsider to the pan-European integration process, the USA's superficial approach to a far-reaching enlargement of the EU challenges not only the EU's priority setting but also the key elements that hold the EU

---

[20] Cf. Council on Foreign Relations' Independent Task Force. 1998, *The Future of Transatlantic Relations*, Washington, p.17.

together. Although the US administration does not explicitly claim a change of objectives, its approach implies that the EU could yield on terms of membership, probably at the cost of a firm *acquis* and cohesiveness. The outright expectation that deepening and widening is like walking and chewing gum, 'something a healthy individual or community should be able to do,'[21] does not, however, mean that the US is totally ignorant of the problems of doubling the size of a 15-member EU, or rule out that the US views 'the right kind of deepening and right kind of broadening as mutually reinforcing.'[22] The emphasis of the US is, however, more on the EU's ability to politically structure, subsidise and 'control' its 'backyard.' Moreover, the US challenges the rigidity of being 'in' or 'out' of the EU, which effectively means that it also challenges the terms of accession and membership. This could imply some sort of paradigmatic change: post-1989, the EU should leave behind its *raison d'être* to organise peace and prosperity through co-operation and integration among its members and focus on projecting democracy and economic development beyond its boundaries. Its mission, then, is to 'consolidate Europe's liberal order and to spread it across the whole continent'[23] rather than to achieve unity and unification in one – albeit expanding – part. This would clearly constitute a weakening of institutional and legal boundaries, at the risk of splintering even the existing Union. At the European Council in Helsinki and in the aftermath of the recent Kosovo campaign, the EU – at least rhetorically – emulated this geo-strategic outlook. There is now a stronger undercurrent in the EU's approach to enlargement that tentatively realises the irreversibility of the process and its dynamic.

In general terms, the US has always wanted to see the EU in the vanguard of economic, social and soft security issues (preventive diplomacy through assistance and aid) and to do and pay more rather than less. Washington's main interest was to also make the East safe for democracy and free markets, with the EU best placed to do the groundwork. In essence, to halt

---

[21] Deputy Secretary of State Strobe Talbott. 1998, 'European Union Enlargement: An American Perspective', Address to the conference 'A Wider Europe: EU Enlargement and US Interests,' Washington, 12 March 1998.

[22] Ibid.

[23] Garton-Ash, T. 1998, 'Europe's Endangered Liberal Order', in *Foreign Affairs*, No.77, Vol.2, p.65.

disintegration in the East, with all its negative consequences, constituted one of the main tasks for both the US and the EU.

All in all, the US recognises its challenge to the status-quo mentality of the EU member states but regarded the timely settling of 'Agenda 2000' in March 1999 as a minimum condition for enlargement. US concerns over delays often have more to do with the EU's pace of reform than the candidates' pace of adaptation to the *acquis*. Both US administration and business favour a political target date for the completion of the first round of enlargement. The American Chamber of Commerce takes the position that 'the list of applicant countries to enter at this target date should be left open. The worst case scenario would be that the EU is not ready to welcome those applicant countries that have fulfilled the criteria for membership.'[24]

For the US, a resolution of the EU's institutional reform issues which the Amsterdam Treaty left behind would have been a more important goal. Beyond the numerative issues – re-weighting of votes in the Council, size and composition of the Commission, distribution of seats in the European Parliament – the extension of majority voting stood out as a high objective for the United States. Its expectation was a more efficient and coherent EU that could be more easily addressed by third parties. As well as dashing many of these expectations, the Nice Treaty did little by way of collective representation of member states in international trade negotiations, especially those dealing with trade in services and commercial aspects of intellectual property. The US also remains extremely sensitive towards the formation of a security and defence policy within the sole framework of the EU. However, it encourages the EU to act more collectively on internal security issues, since the US is purposefully looking for partners to support the fight against international terrorism, organised crime and other imported evils.

By and large, the US continues to pay little attention to the financial, institutional and political implications of enlargement for the EU itself. There is a profound trust that the EU will – through reorganisation and a move

---

[24] Cf. *Uniting Europe*, No.42, 1st March 1999, p.8.

towards greater flexibility and variable geometry – address and avoid the dangers of splintering. Washington views with equanimity the many ways in which the enlargement of the EU will result in internal change; it estimates that this task will absorb the EU for some time, so that its independent ambitions beyond the European theatre are likely to be reduced. The huge transfer of resources to the East and the costs of social and economic cohesion inside an enlarged EU might even push the EU towards an overhaul of its regulatory and distribution mechanisms. Moves to use the challenge of enlargement as a trigger for more efficient decision-making and market orientated reforms, notably in the agricultural sector, would be strongly welcomed by the US administration. Although there might be ulterior motives, the US does not seem to be following a hidden agenda of promoting change in the European socio-economic model. However, enlargement could add a twist towards greater flexibility and competitiveness which the US would welcome.

Shared interests and complementary roles

There is hardly another area where foreign policy interests of the EU and the US are more convergent or even identical than in the stabilisation of CEE.[25] Both the EU and the US rate EU enlargement in the first place as a political and security project. The extent of political and economic involvement in CEE – spearheaded by the EU – gives proof of the decisive geo-political role that the Union plays in Central and North Central Europe. The US fully supports a strong EU commitment and acknowledges the strategic value of EU enlargement. The Union is extending the zone in which conflicts are solved peacefully, where political convergence and socio-economic cohesion develop within a system of pooled sovereignty and where complex interdependencies hold together an increasing number of nation states. These are adequate reasons for the US to expect that the EU proceeds with enlargement at utmost speed and avoids delay as well as the dangers of mismanaging the deepening and widening process. Having initially been concerned at the

---

[25] Cf. the perception of EU member states reported in, Institut für Europäische Politik/TEPSA (eds.) 2000, Enlargement/Agenda 2000: Watch No.3/2000, Berlin/Brussels 2000, [online] available: www.tepsa.be.

slowness and ambivalence with which the EU opened its doors to the CEECs, those US experts and policy makers more familiar with the EU increasingly value the adherence to process of the EU's approach. Thus, the administration is not pressing for a target date for enlargement but rather for a steady and organic process that remains credible to the applicants.

Early on, the US was attracted by the potential that European integration offered to the new Europe. First, the EU was perceived as a successful source of solidarity for the West. This proved to be a political and psychological precondition for the unification of Germany and an antidote to potential German dominance, which was also shared by its Eastern neighbours. Secondly, in relation to CEE, the EU was expected to work as a magnet and model for the transformation of those countries. Moreover, the US hoped, as did many inside the EU, that the example of reconciliation and subsuming of historic enmities and conflicting interests through the pursuit of common objectives would inspire a similar development in the area of the former Warsaw Pact. While the EU model, allied to its policies of carrot and stick, had some impact on the Viségrad and Baltic countries, it failed in South-Eastern Europe. At the end of the nineties one can see that the EU had become an independent regional factor only in North-Central Europe. Here the EU is at least equal to the US in economic and political terms and in some cases even 'acts as its pathfinder.'[26] The picture is different in the area of turmoil and instability that is post-Yugoslavia and the Balkans at large. There, the US feels that the political clout of the EU is insufficient and that the US has to provide the traditional functions of pacifier as far as the intra-EU differences are concerned and of balancer and security guarantor in relation to the warring parties.[27] In the second half of the nineties, the US launched a series of initiatives that complemented EU activities in South-Eastern Europe. Once more the US administration perceived the EU as slow and cumbersome in taking effective action, specifically in the framework of the Royaumont process, and therefore

---

[26] Cf. Smith, M. 1992, "The Devil you know: the United States and a changing European Community,' in *International Affairs*, Vol.68, No.1, p.116; also Hill, C. 1998, 'Closing the capabilities-expectation gap?', in Petersen, J., Sjursen, H. 1998, p.25.

[27] A European lesson of Nato's intervention in Kosovo for EU-US relations was to upgrade and accelerate the building of autonomous military capabilities and crisis management of the EU.

launched a complementary initiative (SECI). The coincidence of traditional and post-Cold War foreign policy roles of the US and the EU clearly characterises the nineties as a period of transition and flux. Russia, the primary focus of US European policy, is treated in a separate category. Only at the end of the nineties did the EU begin to develop a common strategy towards that huge but politically and economically declining Eurasian power. *Thirdly*, all across CEE the EU is the largest *provider of assistance* and *long term aid* programmes. Although these programmes are now largely directed towards supporting preparations for accession to the EU, and so clearly reflect also the self-interest of the EU, the funds and technical assistance are a contribution to the retarded modernisation processes of the CEECs and designed to help them catch up. The US warmly welcomes the financial transfers from Brussels to the CEECs because of Washington's preference for more short term, selective and goal-orientated activities. In the area of aid and assistance US-EU co-operation gives ample examples of how both actions and policies can be co-ordinated. The nineties witnessed exactly that pattern of an EU-led focus on aid, economic stabilisation and soft security issues – political recognition, conflict prevention and mediation – with the US focusing on 'order, on control of nuclear and other weapons, and the preservation of the gains from a decade of arms control.'[28]

Competition and co-operation

There is little doubt that EU enlargement has become a cornerstone of US European policy. The US has no say in the formulation and implementation of the Union's enlargement strategy, but Washington pronounces an emphatic interest in the effectiveness and success of the Brussels policy. Although enlargement as such is not a ring-fenced topic of transatlantic relations, US policy-makers are regularly briefed on related developments. At the levels of the SLG, the NTA Task Force and clearly the meetings at ministerial and highest political levels, the US makes known its political and economic interests. Bilateral consultations with key EU member states offer an additional

---

[28] Smith, M., Woolcock, S. 1993, *The United States and the European Community in a Transformed World*, Pinter, London, p.74.

avenue to influence the process. The US has also established regular consultations with the applicant countries and prepares its ('negotiating') positions vis-à-vis both the applicants and Brussels on the actual terms of accession. Despite this strong political support for swift accession of the CEECs, the highly sensitive American business community and the imperatives of overall trade policy impel US policy-makers towards a circumspect but aggressive defence of their commercial and economic interests. As in previous rounds of enlargement, the administration will fight for compensation and non-discrimination in relation to Single Market actors. While US reaction to pre-accession phenomena is largely on a case by case basis, the State Department, the Department of Commerce and USTR are currently preparing a more coherent and far-reaching approach. US trade with CEE is marginal, but US capital has large stakes in the three new Nato countries. There is no way that the US is willing to cede CEE to the EU as its politico-economic backyard. The US is therefore highly critical of any EU attempt to exclude third parties. These US sensitivities show that the EU is taken seriously as an economic power, especially following the creation of the euro-zone. Even those who view enlargement as a huge EU foreign policy project still recognise that its potency relates mostly to the first (economic) pillar of the EU rather than the second pillar of its Common Foreign and Security Policy.

While the picture presented here shows a harmonious process of EU enlargement, encouraged rather than hampered by the US, some observers of transatlantic relations have come to the conclusion that the US is a far more powerful determinant of EU decision and policy making. Hill, for example, suggests that the EU's 'enlargement policy is a supine example of allowing outsiders to dictate the EU's own agenda, policy and pace of implementation.'[29] William Wallace points to the flaws of EU decision-making which he describes as 'disjointed incrementalism.'[30] This decision making style tends to hide strategic goals and camouflage the significance of the underlying cumulative political steps. Hence the enlargement approach lacks definition and fails to

---

[29] Hill, C. 1998, 'Closing the capabilities-expectation gap?', in Petersen, J., Sjursen, H. 1998, p.37.

[30] Wallace, W. 1996, *Opening the Door: The Enlargement of Nato and the European Union*, Centre for European Reform, London, p.4.

explain to the wider public the costs and benefits of this crucial foreign policy project. Moreover, Forster and Wallace criticise the asymmetries between the dominant position of the EU in CEE in terms of trade, assistance and frequency of political consultations and the sparse influence of EU policy makers over the basic decisions surrounding a new European architecture.[31] There has indeed been no transition of EU enlargement into the realm of high politics and strategic planning of foreign and security policy. The new dynamic in the CFSP/ESDP pillar came as a reaction to the EU's performance as the distinctly junior partner during the Kosovo crisis and the subsequent military intervention. The initial momentum of 1989, generated by the co-ordinating function of the EC for the G-24, soon withered away into haphazard decision-making of an ambivalent and self-centred EC trying to work its way out of the post-Maastricht malaise. Within this overall muddling-through approach, the impulse for enlargement was created in large measure by the stubborn insistence of the CEEC that they would not accept anything less than membership of the western clubs on equal terms.

1993/94 were watershed years. Nato and the EU abandoned the search for alternative solutions to enlargement and declared that arrangements falling short of enlargement, whether Partnership for Peace or (upgraded) association, were only transitional and should soon be replaced by membership in both organisations, which themselves were undergoing slow change. In the US the notion of 'dual enlargement' gained ground because both processes were seen as complementary, and based on shared values and principles of democracy, rule of law and market economy.[32] Between June 1993 and December 1994, whilst the EU was still haggling over the practical terms of a pre-accession strategy, the US took over the initiative to open up Nato, irrespective of the EU's schedule for enlargement. The EU and its CFSP were not in any event the primary organs for overseeing the development of security structures for the new Europe. Given that Nato had gained a lead over the EU, Brussels became eager to keep

---

[31] Forster, A., Wallace, W. 1996, 'Common Foreign and Security Policy,' in Wallace, H and Wallace, W. (eds.) 1996, *Policy-Making in the European Union*, Oxford University Press, Oxford, p.431.

[32] Cf. the contribution of Simon Serfaty in this volume and the official Nato documents referring to parallel enlargement of Nato and EU: Communiqué Nato N-NAC-2(94)116, issued at the Ministerial Meeting of the North Atlantic Council, Brussels, 1 December 1994 and Nato: Study on Enlargement, PO(95)177, point 18.

dual enlargement separate and to safeguard autonomous EU decision making. There is consequently a widespread feeling in the US that Nato has so far done better with enlargement, mainly because it happened faster. Czempiel's assumption that US policy makers unsuccessfully tried to monopolise the entire CEE policy of the West through Nato[33] ignores the failure of the EU to exploit its strong initial position fully. Under US leadership Nato did indeed set the pace and define points of reference for the selection and sequencing of candidates. On many occasions the US administration let the EU know that it saw itself as a powerfully interested non-member. With the exception of their differing positions over the inclusion of Turkey in the enlargement process,[34] a controversy that dates back to well before the CEECs began to queue up for membership, the US is in full accord with the structuring of the accession and negotiation process as set out at the Luxembourg summit in December 1997. The EU and US are therefore decidedly not working at cross-purposes in CEE. On the contrary, in this area a foreign policy partnership is developing between the EU and US in which the EU is a strong and indispensable actor. The US now argues that Nato enlargement is conducive to EU enlargement and hopes that ultimately both organisations will have identical memberships. Following the completion of the first round of Nato enlargement, the EU has taken over as leader in the enlargement processes. In keeping with its unlimited open door rhetoric, the US is likely to exert permanent pressure on the EU to play its part, particularly in relation to the Baltic countries. As it happens, Nato enlargement was high on the agenda of Nato's Spring 2002 summit – the same year in which the EU is to confirm the new members for its own first round of enlargement. It seems unlikely, however, that these two rounds will move in lockstep. There is no prospect of two of the Nato candidates, Bulgaria and Romania, joining the EU in the medium term. Only Slovenia and Estonia, but again not Slovakia, have a reasonable hope of joining in the EU's first round. The question of political compensation thus arises for Nato with regard to South-Eastern Europe, whilst the EU will face the same problem over the Baltic states.

---

[33] Cf. 1998, 'Hat die euro-atlantische Gemeinschaft eine Zukunft?: Ein 'Blätter-Gespräch' mit Ernst-Otto Czempiel', in *Blätter für deutsche und internationale Politik*, Vol.5, p.558.

[34] Cf. the contribution by Christian Franck in this volume.

Although the EU has restricted its membership commitment to the ten associated CEECs, in the medium term the EU will in all likelihood integrate more countries from CEE than Nato, but in very differently composed packages. For some time to come, identical memberships of Nato and EU thus seem rather unlikely, not least because of the present non-Nato EU members.

Implications for transatlantic relations

At first sight there has been a good deal of continuity in US-EU relations from the post-World War II period to the post-Cold War period.[35] In the early 1990s there was talk of the EC's 'meteoric rise in the post-Cold War international system, coupled with revitalisation and expansion of the EC economy that made the old world look new and has prompted US responses.'[36] The nineties therefore saw a considerable institutionalisation of transatlantic relations and a high frequency of consultations from summits to working levels. Despite all these contacts, a key concern of the EU remains to be consulted rather than confronted with unilateral faits accomplis by the US administration. In general terms, the political content of the relationship increased, though not the transparency of the ways in which the EU and US influence each other.[37] The US has stressed the leading role of the EU in stabilising CEE with all the means available to a civilian power; but it also acknowledged that in this region a step-by-step scaled approach was best calculated to attain the common objective of projecting stability and, where necessary, containing conflict.

While US rhetoric in transatlantic relations continues to be very positive, Washington's ambivalence with regard to European integration is fuelled by the coexistence of contradictory American perceptions of the EU. Elizabeth

---

[35] Cf. Petersen, J., Sjursen, H. 1998, 'Conclusion: The myth of CFSP?', in Petersen, J., Sjursen, H. 1998, p.182.

[36] Ginsberg R. H. 1991, 'EC-US Political/Institutional Relations,' in Hurwitz, L., Lequesne, C (eds.) 1991, *The State of the European Community: Policies, Institutions & Debates in the Transition Years*, Lynne Reinner, Boulder, p.387.

[37] Cf. Ginsberg, R, H. 1997, 'Transatlantic Dimensions of CFSP: The Culture of Foreign Policy Cooperation,' in Regelsberger, E., de Schoutheete de Tervarent, P., Wessels, W. (eds.) 1997, *Foreign Policy of the European Union: From EPC to CFSP and Beyond*, Lynne Reinner, Boulder, p.299.

Pond portrays a 'funereal' US perception of Europe that judges the EU's role largely by neo-realist standards and so decries the ineffectiveness and limitations of a consensus based civilian power. The conflicts and bloodshed in former Yugoslavia are emblematic of a dependent Europe with centrifugal tendencies which it is incapable of managing on its own.[38] Put into an historic perspective, these lamentable developments appear as residuals of a European century of wars between the ideologies of nationalism, communism and fascism. By contrast, optimists focus on the achievements at the heart of Europe which today also exemplify a different paradigm:[39] an unaccustomed reconciliation[40] and pooling of sovereignty. In this development, the EU is seen as *the* anchor, model and pilot, as demonstrated again by its comprehensive pre-accession and enlargement policy. However, the EU cannot be compared with and measured against the straw man of a would-be United States of Europe, so that the US will have to continue to live with frustrations caused by the EU's 'limited actorness.'[41] The US is ready to acknowledge that the EU has taken on the political and financial burden, at least in Central and North-Central Europe, with clear benefits to security and the overall US foreign policy agenda.[42] A successful process of enlargement is central to American expectations.

The US continues to challenge the EU to develop into a real post-Cold War organisation. That is taken to mean making its widening the determinant factor for its deepening. The Clinton administration was cautious enough not to make calls for a change of paradigm or advance its own reform proposals, for instance over Agenda 2000 or the Nice summit. The EU, however, wants to

---

[38] Cf. passim Pond, E. 1999, *The Rebirth of Europe*, The Brookings Institution, Washington D.C, pp.17-23.

[39] On these two co-existing paradigms cf. Foreign Minister Fischer before the European Parliament, in Auswärtiges Amt, Speech Outlining the Agenda of the German EU-Presidency by the President of the Council of the European Union Mr. Joschka Fischer in Strasbourg on 12 January 1999, Bonn 1999.

[40] Pond, E. 1999, p 23 and for an elaborate treatment of this concept see Gardner Feldman, L. 1999, 'Reconciliation and Legitimacy: Foreign Relations and Enlargement of the European Union', in Banchoff, T., Smith, M, P. (eds.) 1999, *Legitimacy and the European Union: The Contested Polity*, Routledge, London, pp.66-90.

[41] On this term see Hill, C. 1998, 'Closing the capabilities-expectation gap?', in Petersen, J., Sjursen, H. 1998, p.24.

[42] Cf. Wayne, The European Union, op.cit.

avoid running into a success-trap and prefers to enlarge only on the basis of a modified status quo and protection of the integrity of the *acquis*. Despite this, the decisions of the Helsinki European Council signalled a trend towards a more strategic or 'foreign policy' approach to enlargement which is closer to the US conception. The likelihood of a 'big bang' enlargement of between six and ten countries joining at the same time would also be in line with US preferences.

The US deems the present degree of integration inside the EU to be sufficient and is therefore urging the EU to adjust its priorities and satisfy the legitimate aspirations of the CEEC. Despite the shortcomings of the EU as a crisis manager, the US is seeking co-operation with the EU rather than with individual members like Germany or the UK also in South-Eastern Europe. This area has proved a test of the relative strengths of the partners; it has also revealed that the efforts of both actors have been neither convincing nor successful. A typically European approach to the problem was set out by the German EU presidency in its proposal for a 'Stability Pact for South-Eastern Europe.' This 'aims to bring under one roof the current initiatives to foster regional co-operation (such as SECI and the Central European Initiative) which have all hitherto been somewhat less than effective.'[43] In the framework of the Stability Pact the US has acknowledged 'the leading role and effort the EU is putting into the rebuilding of Kosovo and the region,'[44] with Europe pledging over 85 per cent of the costs. Today's EU-US co-operation in South-Eastern Europe appears as one of the 'very successful'[45] activities under the New Transatlantic Agenda.

From a pragmatic point of view the US expects the EU increasingly to become 'the other power' on the continent. As this also means that the EU will become a less comfortable partner, co-operation and competition will be seen to coexist and intermingle, a relationship which Pond calls 'transatlantic

---

[43] 'EU presidency proposal for a stability pact for South-Eastern Europe,' in Uniting Europe, Document No.29 and No.49, April 19 1999, p.12. The immediate American response was that this should be mainly a European project.

[44] Cf. Highlights of the Report of the Senior Level Group – EU-US Summit – Queluz, 31 May 2000, Conseil 100/193, p.7.

[45] Statement of the European Union and the United States on South East Europe, EU-US Summit, Washington, 18 December 2000.

co-opetition.'[46] Successful enlargement should eventually overcome present differences over its details and technicalities and no longer pose a source of conflict. The US call for an outward-looking EU that develops global and strategic instincts is often linked to the enlargement issue. Such instincts, however, can take different directions. While the EU's is to surrender sovereignty to larger units also in the international arena, the US remains eager to protect its own sovereignty. In time, the EU will strengthen the political component of transatlantic relations and aim to build collective security capabilities, starting with implementation of the Petersburg tasks and the absorption of the Western European Union structures and functions. The development of a distinct European pillar inside Nato and of its own capacity for power projection will be a defining point for future transatlantic relations. While the US welcomed the results of the Nice European Council on the institutional and practical development of a European Security and Defence Policy (ESDP), the new Bush administration will look closely at the EU's progress in building the necessary military capabilities and making them operational.[47] The ESDP could lead to a balancing of US power and tend towards a more symmetric relationship. However, as the EU is enlarged, its CFSP/ESDP profile could become even more diffuse than it is today. The new entrants from CEE may be expected to want to strengthen the role of the US as a European power and are likely to remain sceptical of the EU's security ambitions.

The horizon for future transatlantic relations still shows a broad spectrum of probable options.[48] The pragmatism which currently characterises both sides seems to favour the conclusion of neither a comprehensive partnership agreement nor a comprehensive economic integration agreement. Today's 'war on terrorism' with its global coalition cannot mask either the lack of any grand design, or the uncertainties of the foreign policy agenda of the new Bush administration, nor the struggles inside the EU over its own future.

---

[46] Pond, E. 1999, p.23, pp.183-205.

[47] Cf. Highlights of US-EU co-operation under New Transatlantic Agenda, EU-US Summit, Washington, 18 December 2000.

[48] Cf. Bail, C., Reinicke, W. H., Rummel, R. 1997, 'New Transatlantic Agenda', in Bail, C., Reinicke, W. H., Rummel, R. 1997, *EU-US Relations: Balancing the Partnership*, Nomos, Baden-Baden.

Thus the most likely options for transatlantic relations are the politics of continued fine tuning and a gradually renewed security relationship. In any event, the importance of the EU as a foreign policy partner for the US will grow. Vacillations between a co-operative and competitive relationship – and hence tensions – with regard to different components of transatlantic relations will continue. For the foreseeable future the EU will focus on Europe and remain a reluctant junior partner of America's global policy outreach. For that reason the options of enhanced co-ordination of responses to global challenges are unlikely to represent the glue for the transatlantic relationship. Despite Nato's leadership in military security relations, the wider EU will upgrade its own role also in other neighbourhood regions, in particular the Mediterranean and the Middle East.[49] After enlargement, Russia and the Europe left out of the 'integration-through-membership' circle will constitute the biggest challenge and concern for the EU. It is quite clearly in Europe where the fate of the EU as 'the other power' will be decided.

---

[49] Cf. Denton, G. 1999, *A New Transatlantic Partnership*, Report by the Trans European Policy Studies Association (TEPSA), Kogan Page, London, p.25.

Economic Implications of EU Enlargement for Transatlantic Relations

Michael Calingaert
Guest Scholar, The Brookings Institution
Executive Director, Council for the United States and Italy

The focus of Americans – government and non-government alike – on EU enlargement is largely political and geopolitical. It revolves around the absorption of the previously subject countries of Central and Eastern Europe into the democratic, market-based system of the West, and the enhancement of stability and security in what had been a buffer zone between the two Cold War superpowers. Similarly, the accession of Cyprus and possibly Turkey is considered largely in the context of their contribution to peace and security in the Eastern Mediterranean (Malta does not seem to appear in any calculus). Thus the economic implications for the United States are clearly viewed as being of secondary importance. The prospective accession even of such a number of states to the EU is not expected to change the fundamental nature of the transatlantic economic relationship in any significant respect: neither in its breadth, in the issues requiring attention, nor in the modes of interaction – be they co-operative or conflictual. Changes will occur, of course, but they will essentially be ones of degree, reflecting a shift from dealing bilaterally with independent, sovereign countries to the 'mixed' relationship that characterises US relations with the present EU Member States – part bilateral, part multilateral.

An assessment of the implications of further EU enlargement on the EU-US relationship must take as its starting point the nature and extent of the economic relationship between these two major economic actors, both pre- and post-enlargement. This relationship is without doubt the most important economic relationship in the world. Together, the EU and the United States account for over half of the world's GDP [1997 statistics in IBRD, *World Development Indicators*, 2000] and foreign direct investment [1999 statistics in IMF, *International Financial Statistics*, January 2001] and for about two-fifths of global trade [2000 statistics from Eurostat, quoted on EU Delegation/Washington website]. Each accounts for about one-fifth of the other's trade, and, more importantly, for about one-half of foreign direct investment in the other [European Commission, *US Trade Barriers Report*, 1999]. As policy-makers like to boast, it is the world's first trillion dollar relationship.

Pitted against that, the EU candidate countries are of marginal economic importance to the United States (since accession negotiations have not begun, Turkey is not considered in this paper). Even though trade and investment is growing sharply, the levels are barely visible in the EU-US context, let alone the global. US exports to the 15 countries of Central and Eastern Europe (which include some non-candidates such as Albania and the former Yugoslavia, while excluding Cyprus, Malta, and Turkey) amounted to $3.2 billion in 2000 (double the 1991 level) and imports to $7.4 billion (four times those of 1991) [US Census Bureau, *World Trade Atlas* 1992 and U.S. Department of Commerce]. This compares with 1999 bilateral EU-US merchandise trade of about $385 billion [US Trade Representative, *2001 National Trade Estimates and Report on Foreign Trade Barriers*]; thus US trade with these countries was equivalent to about 2 per cent of the total. At the same time, the United States is not a significant supplier to them. In none of them (other than Cyprus and Malta) do US imports account for more than 3 per cent of total imports (compared, for example, to Germany's 24 per cent share and the EU's 61 per cent share of the Polish market) [IMF, *Direction of Trade Statistics Yearbook*, 2001]. The situation as regards direct foreign investment is similar. At the end of 1999 the stock of US investment in these countries totalled about $16 billion [derived by the US Department of Commerce from US Embassies' *Country Commercial Guides*], compared to over $500 billion in the EU as a whole [U.S. Trade Representative, 2001] and about $1 trillion globally.

The transatlantic economic relationship consists, of course, of far more than trade and investment flows. It also includes a myriad business relationships, interactions involving technology and R&D, dialogue and at times disputes among governments over policy issues and specific problems affecting individual enterprises or economic sectors, and intersection in a multitude of international economic and financial organisations and institutions. Similar kinds of relationships now exist bilaterally between the United States and the candidate countries, though necessarily on a far narrower basis.

How, then, will EU enlargement affect the United States and its relationship with the EU? An assessment of this question must take as a starting point several unique features of this particular enlargement:

- the large number of candidate countries, there being almost as many potential candidates as existing members;
- the lengthy gestation period from the first presumptions of membership soon after the fall of the Berlin Wall in 1989, through various stages leading toward membership (notably the Europe Agreements), until final accession, the date of which is still indeterminate even for the first successful candidates; and
- the prospect that the EU will be engaged for the foreseeable future in an on-going process of dealing and negotiating with would-be and actual candidates for admission – in fact, 'enlargement' is likely to remain an open-ended process well into the next decade.

Under these circumstances, the implications of enlargement can be assessed in two different ways, distinguishing (a) between the pre-accession and post-accession periods (i.e. between the present and the date(s) at which various countries will over time accede to the EU), and (b) between the effects on the US relationship with the candidate countries and that with the EU itself.

Pre-accession

The long and rather indeterminate period leading to accession presents two kinds of problems for the United States, one specific and one general. The specific problem – the most immediate and troublesome one relating to enlargement from the US perspective – relates to access for exports from the United States. In most cases, US exports face higher tariff barriers in the candidate countries than in the EU, in some cases significantly so. Thus the

United States will benefit from enlargement on balance and in the long term. However, during the pre-accession period Europe Agreements provide for reciprocal (though not balanced) trade preferences between the EU and the candidate countries, generally involving duty-free entry of exports from the candidate countries into the EU. As a result, exports into these countries from EU enterprises face lower tariffs than those from firms in the United States, in effect bringing in advance the benefits of enlargement. One striking example is automobiles, with US exports facing a 43 per cent tariff into Hungary compared to a zero tariff on EU-produced cars. While the economic and political rationale for these preferences is understood, there is a strong feeling that it is unfair for US exporters to have to bear this disadvantage over what will necessarily be a prolonged period.

The Europe Agreements are also the source of related concerns in the field of agriculture. In the case of most candidate countries, the agreements provide 'zero-for-zero' tariff treatment for specified commodities – in effect a trade-off involving the EU forswearing export subsidies and the candidates providing tariff preferences or duty-free entry. This clearly affords EU agricultural exports an advantage over those from the United States (and other third countries). At the same time, US exporters of beef and poultry are concerned that candidate countries are moving towards adoption of phytosanitary restrictions (on the use of hormones and chlorine processing respectively) presently imposed by the EU.

The general problem relates to the range of bilateral arrangements and agreements the US has concluded with the candidate countries. While they will, of course, eventually need to conform to or be subsumed under EU law and policy, there is a strong suspicion within US officialdom that the EU – in particular the European Commission – is pressing candidate countries in many cases to back away from existing arrangements with the USA, and certainly not to enter new ones, and instead to adopt 'EU policies.' Understandably, whenever candidate countries face competing pressures from the EU and the United States, they can be expected to submit to the former.

One case in point is bilateral investment treaties (BITs), which the United States has negotiated with many countries around the world. BITs have proved to be a critical element in establishing a satisfactory investment climate, thus serving the interests of both US enterprises and the investment-receiving countries. As an important element in its policy of assisting the new democracies of Central and Eastern Europe in their transition to a market economy, the United States has negotiated BITs with all the candidate countries except Cyprus, Hungary, and Malta (all of which were deemed already to offer sufficient incentives and protection for investors). Negotiations with Slovenia have come to an impasse because of Slovenian concerns over granting national treatment to US investors, which it fears might create difficulties in its negotiations for EU accession.

In similar vein, the Commission has reportedly sought to dissuade the Baltic countries from negotiating bilateral civil aviation agreements with the United States. In so doing, it has made these countries pawns in an internal EU struggle, that between the member states and the Commission over competence for civil aviation relations with third countries. The Commission has long - and unsuccessfully – sought to persuade member states to cede their authority to negotiate such agreements, as it believes that EU-wide negotiations would achieve greater benefits than individual negotiations with the United States. Thus it has discouraged negotiations on 'open skies agreements,' similar to those the United States has concluded with most countries of Western Europe, and which the United States believes accord with the interests of both sides.

In a related area, there are concerns in the United States that the recently concluded EU mutual recognition agreements with certain candidate countries (Czech Republic, Hungary, and Latvia) will permit the export of goods from the EU to these countries bearing the CE mark (indicating that testing and certification have taken place in accordance with EU procedures), while US exports bearing the same mark which, under the terms of the EU-US mutual recognition agreement, can enter the EU without further testing, will have to undergo additional assessment before gaining entry to the candidate countries' markets.

Post-accession

Once new members join the EU and become part of its customs union, the one issue that will undoubtedly arise between the United States and the EU is what compensation, if any, is due the United States for increased tariffs on goods entering the newly-acceding Member States. This is an issue that arose on the occasion of each previous enlargement.

As mentioned above, most US exports to these new members will face lower, rather than higher tariffs once they adopt the EU's common external tariff. Nonetheless, for some products US exports will face higher tariffs – in the Czech Republic and Hungary for example – and in those instances the United States will claim compensation. However, the EU will argue, as it has in the past, that compensation would be due only if the *net* effect of the tariff revaluations – up and down – were to increase (which is not the case). The EU may also be expected to argue that the United States should be prepared to pay a price – and a modest one at that – for a major step in the re-integration of the former Soviet bloc countries into the West, a development that is quite as much in the interest of the United States. The 'theological' debate over the interpretation of the WTO Agreement (carried over from the GATT) is most unlikely to be resolved, but a negotiated settlement will be reached between the EU and the United States, though probably not without a struggle even though the volume of trade affected will be smaller than in previous enlargements.

Beyond the near-certainty that this specific issue will need to be addressed, the economic implications of enlargement for the transatlantic relationship are difficult to discern. They will depend in large part on the ways in which the EU develops and is transformed by enlargement. Areas of potential significance are the following:

The Common Agricultural Policy (CAP) has long been a bone of contention between the EU and the United States. It is difficult to envisage that situation changing, irrespective of the outcome of the enlargement process. However, enlargement creates an enormous problem internally for the CAP because the EU is being forced, in essence, to choose between two unpalatable alternatives: (a) extending the provisions of the CAP in full to new members, thereby substantially adding to the costs to be financed by the EU; or (b) extending the provisions of the CAP to the acceding countries only in part or on a phased basis, thereby relegating new members to second-class status, which would run counter to the basic principles of EU membership. The need to face this choice derives from EU budgetary pressures dictating a significant reduction in expenditures for agriculture and forcing a continuation of CAP reform already begun in the early 1990s. At the same time, the EU will face the constraints of having to accept the disciplines imposed by the Uruguay Round as well as the renewed negotiations on further trade liberalisation which the Round mandated. The combination of pressure to reduce agricultural expenditures and the obligations imposed by WTO commitments points to further movement by the EU towards a less subsidised internal regime and participation in a more open external regime. Both are clearly in the interest of US agriculture. On the other hand, the absorption into the CAP of the large agricultural sectors of the acceding countries, with the resultant increase in production incentives (direct and indirect), will serve to hinder the EU's ability to adopt a more liberal agriculture regime. In any event, the United States can be expected to monitor developments closely and to oppose EU actions and policies it considers contrary to its interests and to the EU's international obligations.

Decision-making: The implications of enlargement on decision-making were, of course, the motivating force behind the Intergovernmental Conference that ended with the European Summit in Nice in December 2000 [see Appendix A – 'The Political and Institutional Dimension']. The key question is the extent to which the resultant 'institutional reform' on voting weights and procedures and the extension of qualified majority voting will affect the speed and efficiency of EU decision-making in an enlarged Union. Transatlantic relations could be affected by a significant shift, if there were to be one, from the status quo. A further slowing of the process would make the EU more difficult to deal with and a less active collaborator internationally; conversely, a speeding-up would have more positive effects.

One specific imponderable for the future of the EU-US economic relationship is how the addition of several Member States to the 133 Committee will affect *decision-making on trade issues*. Will the dynamics within the committee change? Will the sheer number of participants add to the difficulty of arriving at decisions? Will the Treaty amendment at Nice providing for qualified majority voting on issues of trade in services and trade-related aspects of intellectual property result in a significant difference in EU positions and actions in this area? While it is hazardous to speculate, it seems more likely that the additional membership of the 133 Committee will increase the difficulty of reaching an internal consensus. It also remains to be seen whether the Treaty amendment at Nice will facilitate decision-making or whether member states will continue to decide issues largely on the basis of consensus (where it is easier for a member state to block action) rather than by formal votes. On balance, an enlarged EU will find it at least as difficult as at present to adopt positions on trade issues. In that sense, enlargement will not contribute to the ease of resolving the ever-present potential for trade disputes between the EU and the United States.

Trade policy: In future, as in the past, trade will be a major focal point of the interaction between the United States and the EU. Apart from the implications of enlargement on EU decision-making, there is the question of how it will affect the EU's trade policy, both bilaterally and multilaterally. In general, the new member states will probably lean more towards protectionist and other policies disadvantageous to the United States because of their relative economic weakness and the heritage of strong state participation in the economy. Some new members, such as Estonia and Hungary, will nevertheless bring a more liberal economic orientation into the EU. In either case, disputes will continue to arise, and the United States may find that it has less leverage with the new members than it did when it was able to deal with them bilaterally.

The same will presumably apply to negotiations on a new trade round. Here, too, the influence of the new member states is unlikely to become a significant factor in the determination of EU trade policy.

Extension of the single currency: As part of the accession conditions, the new members of the EU will be obliged to join the Economic and Monetary Union as soon as they meet the established criteria (i.e. there will be no provision for an opt-out). Thus, over time – and it may be lengthy – they will join the single currency area and adopt the euro. The implications of this extension relate largely to the EU itself rather than to third countries. The main imponderable is what the reaction of the markets will be. To the extent that enlargement is viewed as increasing not only the size but also the strength of Euroland, it will tend to enhance the value of the euro, and presumably the competitiveness of the EU. By contrast, if the markets interpret the enlargement of the euro zone as weakening the existing currency area (by adding weaker economies and possibly greater potential for inflation), the effect could tend in the opposite direction. While the implications for the United States will vary according to the particular circumstances, on balance a weaker rather than stronger euro will probably benefit the United States by impinging less on its freedom of monetary manoeuvre. However, whatever the outcome, an expanded euro-zone is unlikely to become an issue of contention between the United States and the EU.

Representation: As the membership of the EU grows, will the EU tend to use its increased numerical advantage in voting in international institutions? That would cause transatlantic strains, as the United States would object to being outvoted by a more numerous, but still weaker EU. This possibility would not be new: a case in point was the election of Renato Ruggiero as Director General of the WTO in 1995. In essence, the EU, using its individual votes plus its special relationships with the ACP countries and others, presented the United States with a *fait accompli*. As it turned out, the United States was highly pleased with the choice, but it was certainly annoyed by the EU's tactics. With a potential doubling of the EU's membership, such actions could in future become an irritant in EU-US relations.

International projection: How will enlargement affect the EU's ability and willingness to play an active international role? While some ambiguity surrounds the US position, on balance the United States seeks and would benefit from greater involvement by the EU on the international stage. That is all the more true since the events of 11 September. To a considerable extent, the EU and United States share common economic and political objectives and interests. However, the US bears the preponderant burden in promoting and protecting them around the world. The EU has shown an increasing desire and willingness to play a more active role in a number of areas previously considered beyond the scope of EU interests or falling within the province of member states. It is likely that that will continue, if and as integration progresses within the EU. However, enlargement might have the opposite effect by adding to the already existing variety of member states' interests and perspectives, thus impeding the EU's ability to take actions that would otherwise have been possible.

Co-operation/competition with the United States: There is a tendency in the United States to assume, or at least imply, that an internationally active EU would act in ways that accord with US thinking. While generally that is more likely to be the case, it is not necessarily so (and that should come as no surprise). It is difficult to forecast how such choices might be affected by enlargement. To some extent, and at least initially, new entrants may be expected to try to show solidarity with the existing members and thus not to interfere with their efforts to undertake various courses of action. In any event, because of their size and despite their number, the new entrants are unlikely to impinge significantly on the existing balance of forces within the EU. Nonetheless, they will have to consider their own interests – as do all member states – and that could retard what the United States would consider to be steps in the right direction.

Conclusion

EU enlargement will necessarily bring both economic advantages and disadvantages to the United States. However, the pluses will clearly outweigh the minuses. Over the long term, enlargement will increase the number and strength of countries subscribing to an open market system within a common framework of institutions, law, regulations, and ways of doing business. While the United States will lose certain benefits it enjoys from its bilateral relationships with the candidate countries, on balance it will gain overall from their entry into the Western system. The new member states will undoubtedly provide more competition to US enterprises, but the benefits will accrue to both sides.

That said, the United States can be expected to defend forcefully what it perceives to be its economic interests in an enlarged EU, as it does with the current 15 EU members. In so doing, it will have strong support from Congress, affected groups, and the general public, even as they maintain their support for the further integration of Europe.

Bigger is Better: A US Political Perspective on EU Enlargement

Simon Serfaty

Professor of US Foreign Policy, Old Dominion
University
Director, Europe Programme
Center for Strategic and International Studies

The division of Europe after World War II was not preordained. Rather, the United States envisaged a whole and united Europe that would rely on the Grand Alliance, including the Soviet Union, to achieve a quick and lasting reconciliation with the former enemies, including Germany. All too sensitive to the conflicts that had followed the end of the previous World War, the Truman administration reasoned that past divisions in Europe would be best overcome within an integrated, democratic, and prosperous space. In the spring of 1947, the US offer of Marshall aid was extended to the East as well, but Moscow's refusal was imposed also on her neighbours who were to start a 'community' of their own a few years later. Yet, as the Cold War gathered momentum, the United States seemed often more determined and even more eager to build a united, strong, and ultimately independent Europe than the Europeans themselves.[50]

Entering the 1950s, French efforts to launch the European Coal and Steel Community (ECSC) and develop a European Defence Community

---

[50] The argument is developed at greater length in Serfarty, S. 1997, *Stay the Course: European Unity and Atlantic Solidarity*, Praeger, Connecticut; and 'Memories of Leadership,' *Brown Journal of World Affairs*, Vol.5, No.2, Summer 1997, pp.3-16. Also, Ickenberry, J. 1989, 'Rethinking the Origins of American Hegemony', *American Political Science Review*, Vol.104, No.3, p.394.

(EDC) were actively endorsed by the Truman administration, notwithstanding Secretary Dean Acheson's scepticism over a scheme that he privately viewed as extravagant.[51] To an extent, the EDC was designed to postpone the enlargement of Nato to the newly established Federal Republic of Germany – not only because of its impact on Soviet attitudes towards the West but also because of its effects on Germany's status in Europe. But when the collapse of the EDC seemed to point to Europe's failure to enforce its commitment to unity, Nato became destined to expand even faster than might have been necessary otherwise: out of area and into central Europe, or out of business and without America. In May 1955, following the earlier accession of Greece and Turkey (hardly the geographic epicentres of the North Atlantic area), Nato integrated the Western half of Germany. A few days later, the Warsaw Pact Organisation completed an institutional 'iron wall' that was to keep Europe divided for the next three decades. After that, expectations of European unity were confined to the West, in opposition to the East. In June 1957, a small European Community (EC), started in Rome by six Nato allies, was applauded by President Eisenhower in the expectation that it would eventually be enlarged to other West European countries, including Great Britain.

Neither Nato, Europe's idea of security based on an entangling relationship with the United States, nor the EC, America's idea of security based on the end of national rivalries in Europe, reflected the earlier history of its sponsors. Returning to Europe was hardly America's vocation. Even less was unity a vocation for a core group of European nation-states that had made war a historic way of life. After 1945, the *choix communautaire* was based on a shared vision of a failed past – two major wars waged since the turn of the century. Subsequently, the rise of a relatively new Soviet threat from the East, ideological as well as military, confirmed their choice. Additional strength, at home and abroad, would be gained by more unity within Europe and with the United States – meaning further military integration within a US-led Nato, wider economic integration within an expanding US-less EC, and close anti-Communist alliances in all West European countries. If there was a vision, which there was, this vision was defined by these two institutional

---

[51] Harper, J. 1994, *American Visions of Europe*, Cambridge University Press, Cambridge, p.301.

commitments – the latter with a social design and the former with a clearer security function. Unlike Nato, Europe grew horizontally at first, and delays in adding new members proved beneficial regardless of their intent: the fewer the better, because bigger would have been harder. Between 1973 and 1986, however, vertical expansion was to double the size of the emerging community, with four of its new members (and altogether 10 of the 12 EC states) also in the by then 16-member Nato: the bigger the better because of a fear of remaining otherwise too small.

Entering the 1990s, the end of the Cold War briefly appeared to threaten both ideas and both institutions. By then, however, Europe's and America's earlier choices had become irreversible. Now, talk of dissolution of Nato (for the United States) or withdrawal from 'Europe' (for any of its members) had become meaningless. For both institutions, enlargement to the East now became the favoured option. As had been the case earlier, enlargement would move both Nato and 'Europe' out of their established Cold War areas to avoid that either be moved out of business. In 1995, Europe's fourth enlargement – to Austria, Finland, and Sweden – involved nearly all the Western European states that had chosen to be, or been compelled to remain, neutral during the Cold War. In 1999, Nato's fourth enlargement to the Czech Republic, Hungary and Poland involved three of the four countries in Central Europe that had previously constituted the dividing line between East and West.

Enlarging the EU to 15 and Nato to 19 members was also the first institutional expansion that widened the membership gap between the two Western organisations that America had founded or sponsored during the Cold War. Yet, even as the Clinton administration remained committed to further Nato enlargement, it was sensitive to the commitment made by the European Community, now the Union (EU), to expand to the East as well. The same focus was expected from the new Bush administration as Nato and the EU were preparing for their blind dates with new members – respectively at the Nato Summit in November 2002, and the next EU Intergovernmental Conference set for December 2004.

Stable, democratic, peaceful, and whole

EU enlargement is a central expectation of US policies in Europe, and a main pillar of its evolving relationship with the EU. The United States could not easily accept the prospect, let alone the fact, that EU enlargement might be aborted or needlessly postponed. This is not a matter of false sentimentalism or Europe's moral obligation to do for its sister states in the East what America had done for its European cousins in the West. Rather, it has to do with concerns that failure to expand the EU's democratic and affluent space would renew instabilities in Europe, including a *de facto* Russian sphere of influence extending to former Soviet republics and some former Warsaw Pact members that might find themselves denied EU membership. In short, enlargement has become a yardstick for Europe's commitment to attend to its share of the post-Cold War burdens. Nor is enlargement only a matter of preference in the United States. It is also a matter of expectations for Europe. As EU enlargement goes, so does Europe. Indeed, failure to enlarge expeditiously would suggest an even broader failure of the EU: that institutional reforms stall, EU economies stagnate, the euro zone tumbles, applicant states fail to keep up with rising EU demands, and member states ignore applicants' needs.

In effect, the criteria for EU enlargement defined by the European Council in Copenhagen in June 1993 are American criteria, or at least criteria that match those of the United States especially well. The first three criteria – stable democratic institutions, a functioning market economy, and the capacity to compete within the Union – reflect what the EU states themselves gradually became during the Cold War rather than what they had been at the start of the Cold War. Even the fourth criterion, which has to do with adopting the discipline of the *acquis communautaire* accumulated during the first 40 years of community building, would for the most part suit the United States as well as, or better than most current members, let alone applicants.

That the same was generally true with regard to the criteria for economic convergence set at Maastricht in December 1991 suggests that the deepening as well as widening EU tends to narrow the gap between its members and the United States. Launched in May 2000 by Germany's Foreign Minister Joschka Fischer, the renewed debate over Europe's finality is therefore an intra-European debate that need not raise serious apprehensions for the United States.

Whatever the end point may prove to be, the member states of a European Union that nears completion will be closer to the United States than the European mosaic of nation-states which is likely to be facing extinction. The emerging integrated European space is an unfinished American project that has already served US interests well. Its completion, including further enlargement, will respond to vital US interests equally well, or better still.

First, a larger and stronger EU is the most effective way to ensure the democratic stability and Western identity of the entire continent. What else is there? The transformation of Europe's hard core – France, Germany, and Italy – is a case in point. It is within a united Europe that France was able to end its wars of the republics, Italy to complete its unification, and Germany to exhaust its appetite for more living space. Examples of domestic upheavals within the European community have been few and have become even fewer.[52] At the margins of Europe, first Ireland, then Spain and Portugal, and subsequently Greece, also gained unprecedented democratic stability and affluence thanks, in large part, to the advantages of EU membership: economic gains, political centrism, and Western legitimacy. That Ireland would now be as prosperous as Britain, Spain and Portugal as democratically stable as France, and Greece as financially reliable as Germany is no small achievement. Settled at the historic centre of Europe, or moving farther to other parts of the continent, the EU has built a civilian space that makes war among its members unthinkable.

Second, enlargement also widens the internal zone of security in Europe. Indeed, the sheer prospect of future membership is enough to encourage reconciliation in areas where there might otherwise have been discord. Can today's EU really have been home to the Great Powers whose brutality shamed the history of the first half of the twentieth century? During the Cold War, while Nato prevented confrontation with countries outside the emerging community, reconciliation was achieved within the EU. Pointedly, after the Cold War the ghosts of the past are still sighted only outside the EU area, especially in the Balkans and the former Soviet Union (other than the Baltics)

---

[52] In 2000, the EU reaction to the appearance of democratic instabilities in one of the EU countries, Austria, confirmed, perhaps to an excess, the democratic identity of the new Europe.

where few countries seem poised for an early membership. Neither the peace of the bullies nor the peace of the braves, the peace achieved by the EU is a peace of contentment and assimilation as no gain, however construed, can compensate for the losses that would result from a war, whatever its origins. In truth, there is no threat of a return to past conflicts. The main risk is that EU members would become so content within their institutional boundaries as to refuse to fight an external enemy for good cause.

Unlike Nato, the EU cannot protect its members from external aggression but it can contribute to making peace between them. In several primary areas of conflict, including the Balkans and the Aegean, prospects of EU enlargement are helping to promote stability even if not all states in the region are included in the initial EU decisions. Arguably, some of the horror that plagued the former Yugoslavia in the early 1990s could have been avoided had the EU been involved earlier. Credible prospects for membership invite moderation, and, conversely, the absence of such prospects can be a licence for continued excesses. While no country in South-Eastern Europe, with the exception of Slovenia, can realistically expect to enter the EU before the end of the decade, every country in the region should still be able to view the EU as part of its future.

The same complementarity of goals and action between the United States and the EU countries is to be found in the Aegean. Especially in relation to Cyprus, EU membership may become the catalyst needed to end the *de facto* division of the island. Currently, a constellation of the growing economic gap between Greek and Turkish Cypriots, the EU's semi-formalisation of Turkey's status as an applicant country, the inclusion of Greece in the euro-zone, and renewed US involvement with negotiations pursued within the UN framework have offered some modest grounds for optimism.[53]

With regard to Turkey and its place in Europe, the transatlantic dialogue suggests an ironic reversal of roles between an America that thinks in geopolitical terms and a Europe that responds with semi-formulated cultural

---

[53] As EU Commissioner Verheugen put it, 'We have a well-co-ordinated policy. The EU, the UN, the US, the UK are co-operating close[ly]' and with a 'supportive Greek ... [and] Turkish government.' *Europe*.

or ethical arguments. Geography, as well as history, explain each side's position. For the EU countries, Turkey is an unwanted community partner likely to threaten their own internal balance, both culturally and in other directions.[54] For the United States, it is a vital strategic peg whose identity as a strong and reliable Western ally would be reinforced with the secular, democratic, and affluent rewards of EU membership. Turkey's accession would make Europe stronger, and extend its borders to Syria, Iraq, and Iran, as well as the Caspian states. While the EU states may view this proximity as a threat, the United States welcomes it as a promise. Admittedly, prospects of early membership are slight. At best, the EU might reach out to Turkey at the very end of the decade – but even that is unlikely: asking an applicant to reform its institutions is a lesser demand than its conversion to another religion. In the meantime, however, Turkey should at least be able to reinforce its ties with the EU as a non-member member state. But the US desire to reduce the distinction between European countries that belong to only one of the two Western institutions could have serious consequences, as it opens a backdoor to a widening of US commitments to individual European states.

Ultimately, Europe cannot escape its geopolitical, economic, and historical connectivity with neighbourhoods which affect its interests: a vital dependence on the Persian Gulf, an emotional involvement with the Arab-Israeli conflict, a demographic stake in stability in North Africa, and a cultural sensitivity to the revival of Islam.[55] Even in the long term, however, EU involvement with the Greater Middle East will remain curtailed by cultural issues that keep these countries politically abroad even when they are geographically near. For them, including countries of North Africa and Israel, EU membership is not part of the future, and pretending otherwise will not serve their interests.

---

[54] For example, Tsuoakalis, L. 1999, 'Greece: Like Any Other European Country,' *The National Interest,* Issue 55, Spring, p.72.

[55] See Marr, P. 2000, 'The United States, Europe and the Middle East: Cooperation, Co-optation or Confrontation,' in Robertson, B, A. (ed.) 2000, *The Middle East and Europe: The Power Deficit,* Routledge, London, pp.74-103. Also, Serfaty, S. 2000, 'Europe, the United States, and the Middle East,' *Journal of Defense Quarterly,* No.24, Spring, pp.56-61.

The expansion of the EU neighbourhood is especially significant as it approaches Russia. There, new EU members can also help to widen the outreach of European stability and Western influence as their newly gained affluence and newly reformed institutions spread over their own borders to their bigger neighbour.[56] This is particularly true of Europe's northern tier, an institutional mosaic of seven countries including the three Baltic states which the EU is likely to embrace more quickly and (relative to Russia) more easily than Nato. The issue with Russia and other former Soviet republics is not membership but an associate status that permits progressive assimilation with the rest of the continent. The specifics of such a status can remain vague, and the initial steps to achieve it can be small. But however vague that status and however small these steps, an institutional commitment from an expanding EU would confirm that Russia is a country in Europe even if it cannot become a European country. Conversely, EU neglect of Russia and other non-EU countries that used to form the Soviet Union (including Ukraine) would do damage to Europe, and by implication to US interests in Europe.

Counterweight or counterpart?

The political costs to the United States in relation to these advantages are real but small. The urge to seek counterweights to American power is the defining trend in international politics at the turn of this millenium, because it is the most traditional response to any uni-polar system.[57] Accordingly, what may matter most in the future is not an American 'giant' that might become 'uneasy' about the burdens of its condition, but other countries that become increasingly uneasy about the consequences of US predominance. Within Nato, European qualms about their followership would erode the effectiveness of American leadership, while US doubts over its leadership would erode the will for Europeans to follow. Not the least legitimate of American expectations is to avoid the rise of a Europe with which differences in values and interests would

---

[56] Van Ham, P., Grudzinski, P. 1999/2000, 'Affluence and Influence,' *The National Interest*, Issue 58, Winter, pp.81-87.

[57] Rodman, P. 2000, *Uneasy Giant: The Challenges to American Predominance*, The Nixon Centre, Washington, p.2.

tend to shape official policies, condition public attitudes, and ultimately motivate European actions that clash with US policies, attitudes, and actions.[58]

In short, the US commitment to an ever wider and more united Europe does not extend to any kind of Europe. An illusive European counterweight to US power and leadership is a price that the United States would find too high. By definition, a counterweight is adversarial, as it comes at the expense of the power that is to be countered, balanced, and ultimately exceeded. By comparison, the idea of a serious counterpart is more realistic as it suggests EU countries that resolve their own differences and accept the United States and its role in Europe. The point here is that America's debate over its renewed European identity is ahead of Europe's debate over its emerging American personality. Or, to put it differently, entering a new century America readily accepts the fact that it has become more like Europe while European countries still struggle with the dilemmas of becoming more like America.

The major decisions made by the United States since the end of the Cold War – including Dayton, Nato enlargement, and action in Kosovo – deepened the US commitment to Europe. In the years to come, the states of Europe and their Union will also have to confirm their commitment to going along with the United States outside Europe. Who, in other words, is trying to decouple from whom? For example, European neglect of security issues in the Far East, including China, combined with a European attempt to supplant US influence in the Middle East, including the Persian Gulf, would cause resentment in the United States and discord across the Atlantic. In this context, one risk of enlargement is that it might extend Europe from the Atlantic to the Urals, possibly with Great Britain but without much dialogue with the United States. That picture is not likely, but it is plausible.

A sense of failure resulting from unfulfilled or perpetually postponed promises of enlargement would also be destabilising. EU timetables for enlargement should be robust and credible; deadlines that serve short-term

---

[58] The risk is especially acute in the area of defence procurement and its political-industrial base. 'If Europe tries to go it alone,' warn John Deutsch, Arnold Kantor and Brent Scowcroft, 'the inevitable outcome will be inefficient defence companies, squandered defence resources, a growing gap between American and European military capabilities, and a fatal weakening of the alliance' ('Saving Nato's Foundation,' *Foreign Affairs*, November/December 1999, p.67).

political interests at home but cannot be met within the EU are self-defeating. In the 1990s, too many target dates for enlargement were postponed, from 2000 to 2003, even to 2005 or beyond. In each case, the informal commitment was qualified with the warning that institutional reforms would first have to be in place before enlargement could actually proceed, thus imposing criteria on the member states that proved to be even more difficult to meet than the criteria imposed on applicants.[59] In December 2000, the Nice summit, too, postponed many significant reforms till 2004 – after the next round of national elections in 2001-2002 (in Italy and Great Britain, and in France and Germany) but also after the launch of Europe's single currency in 2002 and the 2003 Headline Goals. Yet welcoming the applicant states as virtual member states – settling how many votes in the Council, how many seats in Parliament they should have – made the EU commitment to enlargement by a given time more tangible and credible than at any time since the 1993 summit. The next Intergovernmental Conference in 2004 now constitutes a credible timetable for the first accessions whose origins go back to 1993.

The failure to enlarge can take many forms, however, and no less significant would be a failure to make membership work after it has been granted. Like Nato, the EU is the victim of its own success but, unlike Nato, the EU's success is quantifiable. After the Cold War the countries of Central and Eastern Europe (CEE) endured several years of recession.[60] While most of them returned to growth by the mid-1990s, the need to prepare country and institutions for the *acquis* denied the peace dividends expected by their people. Now, the sacrifices and even the pain of the past decade must be healed not only with the status of membership for those that have met the admission criteria, but also with the rewards associated with membership – that is the rewards of economic affluence and democratic freedoms.

---

[59] As written by an exasperated Viktor Orban, the Hungarian prime minister who led anti-Soviet demonstrations in 1989, 'In 1993 we [heard] Hungary may become an EU member around 1995; in 1995 it turned out we may be a an EU member around 2000. Now in 2000 it comes out that we may join in 2004. We are well-trained and educated in disappointment.' (Orban, V. 2000, 'Hungary Frustrated as talks stall,' *The Times of London*, July 26 2000.

[60] Sgard, J. 1996, *The Transition Economies and the European Union's Eastward Enlargement*, Newsletter No.5, Centre d'Etudes Prospectives et d'Informations Internationales, Paris.

New applicants, mainly the poor, look at such other poor latecomers as Greece and Spain as examples of the gains that membership can bring. What is more difficult to appreciate, however, is the time it took for those gains to emerge. For nearly a decade before the political changes ushered in by General Franco's death in 1975, and two more decades before and after membership in 1985, Spain struggled to enforce the reforms which its people could enjoy as citizens in their own land rather than as immigrants in a foreign land. As for Greece, whose interest in joining Europe was made explicit almost from the beginning, it took 20 years after it had entered the EC in 1981 before membership in the euro-zone, in 2001, seemed to confirm its identity, at last, as a truly European country.

Dual enlargement

Bidding for Nato membership does not help aspirations for EU membership. For one thing, each institution can use the other as an alibi for its own inaction – either because negotiations are under way or because they are stalled. In addition, each institution, especially the EU, can rely on the experience of its sister institution, especially Nato, to assess the effectiveness of the decision it is contemplating – including the new member's ability to deliver on its pre-membership commitments. Admittedly, the linkage between the two processes is, and should be kept, implicit. Both Nato and the EU are distinct institutions. But because neither is a full service institution, each of them can do much that cannot be done by the other and both together can do more than either one of them alone.

To complicate matters, Americans still comprehend poorly, if at all, the complexities of EU enlargement. Accordingly, the slow pace of EU enlargement has caused exasperation and grief in the United States.[61] While much was learned during the Cold War about individual EU states, little is known of the EU itself. Indeed, explanations of EU enlargement in the United States must be presented by comparison with Nato enlargement rather than

---

[61] Pond, E. 2000, 'Come Together: Europe's Unexpected New Architecture,' *Foreign Affairs,* March/April, p.11.

with direct reference to the EU itself.[62] Thus, The 1949 Washington Treaty, which was drafted in simple language, is flexible and relatively undemanding, whereas the European treaties, a body of much more complex documentation, define a more rigorous discipline that has become increasingly exacting for current members, let alone new ones.

Nato enlargement is a decision that can still be driven by the United States, without whom the organisation could not endure. By comparison, EU enlargement cannot be achieved without the explicit approval of all 15 members because each member can exercise a right of veto for every one of the 13 steps that define the process. In other words, for Nato, the United States holds the key to enlargement, but for the EU, the key remains the *acquis*.

Unlike with Nato, the financial costs of EU enlargement cannot be easily fudged, either for the Community as a whole or for each of its members separately. Unlike with Nato, too, the political costs of EU enlargement cannot be easily assessed or justified before accession has taken place. In other words, EU enlargement is a process that demands not only that applicant states be prepared for the obligations of membership but also that member states be willing to extend its privileges as well.

Nato enlargement has aroused so little public passion among its members that a proposal for the big bang enlargement of Nato to all applicant states, offered in Vilnius, Lithuania in May 2000, was deemed necessary to re-launch a fading debate prior to the 2002 Nato summit. By contrast, EU enlargement affects national and even local interests that cannot be easily ignored: it is a central feature of the EU agenda. The passions it generates may be especially decisive if the decision to enlarge were to be subjected to formal public approval by one or more EU members or applicants (as the Irish referendum on the Nice Treaty was to demonstrate).

Because of the *acquis* imposed by the EU on its new members, entering Nato is less painful than joining the EU. The warlike conditions that surrounded Nato's enlargement in 1999 might have suggested otherwise, but

---

[62] Serfaty, S. 1999, 'Dual Enlargement,' in author's *Memories of Europe's Future: Farewell to Yesteryear,* CSIS, Washington, pp.47.

the war proper proved to be more painful for non-Nato countries like Bulgaria and Romania than for the newly inducted Nato countries, including Poland and Hungary. Yet, because of the affluence EU membership is expected to bring, being left out of the EU is more significant than being kept outside Nato, in which case non-membership need not entail less security. Indeed, the economic costs – or benefits foregone – of non-membership are even higher than the costs of membership. They include, above all, the strong risk that economic activity, spearheaded by foreign direct investment, might concentrate on the first members within a given regional cluster.

Wider disparities between EU and Nato membership would create a serious problem for Europe and the transatlantic relationship – including charges of deception from disappointed applicant countries and perhaps some temptations of external challenges from local powers including Russia.[63] Yet the schedules of enlargement of the two institutions no longer differ significantly. Thus, before 1999, the case for Nato enlargement was limited to Central Europe, and the rationale for enlargement appeared to be the institution itself – grow or perish.[64] Hints that countries in South-Eastern Europe like Slovenia and Romania might be in the first wave of new members were dismissed as the Clinton administration reasoned that going outside Central Europe would prove too controversial in the United States as well as in some other Nato countries. After 1999, the institutional case for enlargement was based on a free and whole democratic Europe that the 19 Nato members could complete more quickly than the EU's 15. An institutional right of membership became the basis of the so-called 'big bang' declaration meant to achieve Nato's wholesale enlargement in 2002, even if implemented only incrementally over subsequent years. Meanwhile, the initial EU short list of five countries (the Czech Republic, Hungary and Poland, as well as Estonia and Slovenia) was extended to all applicants from the East, plus Cyprus and Malta (and Turkey, though less convincingly).

A big bang by the EU and Nato would help to achieve a convergence of European membership in both institutions. Irrespective of its schedule, such

---

[63] Brzezinski, Z. 1998, 'The Dilemmas of Expansion,' *The National Interest,* Fall, pp.13-17.

[64] Kay, S. 1998, *Nato and the Future of European Security,* Roman and Littlefield, Boston.

convergence would prove more effective than conditions that keep European Nato states that are not EU members away from EU initiatives, and EU states that are not Nato members away from Nato actions. Moreover, membership convergence is what occurred between 1949 and 1986, when the EEC grew from 6 to 12 members. During that period, only one of the six new EC states (Ireland) failed to enter Nato. By then, too, only three of Nato's 14 European countries were not EC members (a status not desired by Norway or Iceland, but only by Turkey, admitted to Nato with Greece in 1952). By 1999, however, the gap had widened again as the three neutral states that joined the EU in 1995 were not in Nato, while none of the three countries to join Nato in 1999 was as yet in the EU, though all of them had applied for membership and been included in the short list of EU applicants.

A strategy of dual enlargement would keep the two processes of enlargement separate, but it would no longer pretend that EU and Nato decisions are separable. To achieve this goal and their respective ends, each institution would continue to reach out to the European states that belong to the other. Thus, after 2002, some non-Nato EU countries would also be candidates for Nato membership, including Austria in 2003-2004, but also Sweden and even Finland, later in the decade. Conversely, as EU enlargement to Central Europe and the Baltic countries begins in 2004, one of the non-EU European Nato states, Norway, might seek EU membership, subject to another referendum around 2006-2009, possibly in the context of an expanding euro-zone.

Thus, by the close of the current decade, 12 of the 14 European countries of Nato's pre-1999 membership of 16 could be EU members, with the three newest Nato members about to enter the EU as well. By that time, too, at least 12 countries (and possibly 14) of the EU's present 15 could also be Nato members, including Austria (and, arguably, Sweden and Finland). Thus, the convergence between Nato and EU membership would have been restored. Dual enlargement would expand the security zone of the North Atlantic area to regions of renewed importance to their respective members, in the East and the South, thereby building new common ground for compatible and even complementary strategies in these areas.

A Process with a purpose

The former French president Valéry Giscard d'Estaing once noted America's tendency to 'imagine' Europe rather than analyse it. Americans, wrote Giscard, 'see [Europe] in the context of their global ... geo-strategic vision [within which] they hope for the existence of zones,' including two converging Nato and EU zones.[65] That is true, but what is wrong with such geopolitical simplicity? Failure of the EU to enlarge, or the failure of EU enlargement, would not end the US commitment to Europe. It would, however, erode a rising US interest in the EU as a serious partner, and resurrect instead past patterns of privileged partnerships with one or more European countries. EU enlargement may go more or less quickly, and it may be more or less tedious, but it cannot be reversed. Expanding EU membership, and making it work, is an inescapable part of the EU's future, even though, admittedly, the pain of adaptation will often be high for current members and occasionally close to unbearable for the new members.

The process is not open-ended, to be sure, and one of the most formidable questions raised by enlargement concerns its limits. These limits reflect a complex mixture of geographic and historical, cultural and political aspects. Geographically, the 'E' of Europe is more decisive than the 'U' of the union. In other words, countries that are not part of the European geographic mass are not likely to enter the EU. Exceptions, beginning with Britain and soon to include Cyprus and Malta – not to mention the insular dependencies of continental members like France and Italy – are few. But who could tell the history of Europe without reference to its islands?

Moreover, south of the Mediterranean the dividing line is not only geographic or historical but also cultural. What is true at the level of the individual is even more compelling for countries or regions. Europe and Islam still define themselves in opposition to each other rather than in association with one another. Each defines its own identity in terms of what the other is not and cannot become. There is a Cartesian logic turned inside out: I am, therefore you are not. Each affirms its specificity in order to escape the other's – 'foreign, different, if not

---

[65] 'L'Europe met la Turquie en porte-à-faux: An Interview with Valéry Giscard d'Estaing', *Géopolitique*, No.69, April 2000, p.6.

barbarian, fundamentalist or fanatic' are words that can define both Europe's worst vision of Islam and Islam's worst vision of the West.[66] In sum, there is much debate over where enlargement begins in Europe, but there is little debate over where it ends.

For enlargement as for every other aspect of the broad EU agenda, the main US fear is over failure rather than over success. The EU is not yet a 'power with a mission' but it is still a mission without power. Much of the mission that was assumed by six European states in June 1957 has been fulfilled: 'Europe' now covers a space that is largely and irreversibly civil, democratic, and affluent. That mission, and the vision it embodied, is not transferable, however – meaning that the idea itself has no power since it cannot be effectively emulated. To be sure, EU influence has been growing and it has even been going global. Yet, on the whole, EU commitments and aspirations are not commensurate with its structure and capabilities.

As the EU enters its end game, the need for more structure and more reliable capabilities has a vital transatlantic dimension.[67] Just as Nato enlargement must face up to the need to accommodate a more united and stronger EU – and not just Nato but also every other regional or global institution – EU enlargement must face up to the need to accommodate the US presence and interests in Europe. Entering the twenty-first century, America has a relationship with Europe that is also no longer reversible. It may not be, and not wish to become, a European power, but it is, and is doomed to remain, a power in Europe. Such a conclusion is not a covert invitation to debate America's membership in the EU, but it is an open plea to debate the consequences of America's *de facto* presence as a non-member member state within the EU. In short, a vital but carefully hidden dimension of EU enlargement has to do with the structure of US relations with the EU, as well as with the nature of EU-Nato relations.

Implicit in such American satisfaction with a larger Europe is an understanding of the European idea as a process that challenges both the

---

[66] Ramadan, T. 1999, *To Be A European Muslim*, The Islamic Foundation, Leicester. p.1.

[67] More on the end game in Serfaty, S. *Europe 2007: From Nation States to Member States*, CSIS Report, January 2000.

history and the geography of Europe. The construction of Europe ends the long history of instabilities and conflicts that conditioned America's entangling relationship with the continent in the context of the three global wars endured in the twentieth century. It has also ended a history of US disengagement from a continent in opposition to which the American Republic was born, and matured for more than 150 years. That may well be the most endearing legacy of a century that brought Europe closer to America and America back into Europe.

The EU'S Northern Dimension: US Policy Towards North-Eastern Europe

Bertel Heurlin
Research Director
Dansk Udenrigspolitisk Institut

Jacob Ejlers
Research Assistant
Dansk Udenrigspolitisk Institut

Introduction

'During the Cold War, North-Eastern Europe was a strategic backwater and received relatively little attention in US policy. Since the end of the Cold War, however, the region has become a focal point of US policy.'[68]

During the Cold War the US did indeed lack a specific policy towards North-Eastern Europe. This part of the world was subsumed in the Cold War security dynamics and therefore an integral part of overall American policy towards the USSR.[69] Following the end of the Cold War and the dissolution of the USSR in 1991, it might therefore have been expected that

---

[68] Council on Foreign Relations. 1999, *U.S. Policy Towards North-Eastern Europe.* Council on Foreign Relations, p.1.

[69] Van Ham, P. 2000, 'Testing Cooperative Security in Europe's New North: American Perspectives and Policies' in Trenin, D., Van Ham, P. (eds.) 2000, *Russia and the United States in Northern European Security,* The Finnish Institute of International Affairs, Helsinki, pp.60-61.

the US would end any concern with North-Eastern Europe. However, as the above quotation indicates, the US is today even more engaged in northern Europe than it was during the Cold War. In an article from the magazine *Baltic Defence Review*, Edward Rhodes claims that American policy towards North-Eastern Europe since the end of the Cold War 'represents one of the most exciting conceptual departures in US international security policy undertaken during the Clinton years.'[70] One could even argue that the US, as a part of its global regionalisation strategy, has constructed a new sub-regional unit – Northern Europe. Why then is the US more engaged in North-Eastern Europe today than it was during the Cold War?

The purpose of this chapter is twofold: first, briefly to discuss the US role in the post-Cold War international system and the recent developments in North-Eastern Europe; and secondly to analyse the new American policy towards North-Eastern Europe and discuss its background. The first part of the chapter is essentially an analysis within the framework of neo-realist theory, emphasising the notion of uni-polarity.

The second part advances the claim that American policy was and is characterised by three components: a Baltic component, a Russian component and finally a Nordic component. The aim of the Baltic component was to make it clear to both Russia and the USA's European allies that the US perceived the Baltic States as part of a new politically, economically and militarily integrated Europe. In the years 1996 and 1997 it became a common understanding that the Baltic States would not become members of either Nato or EU in the short term. The US therefore wanted to ensure that the Baltic Sea area would not become a grey zone in terms of security politics. By establishing the Northern European Initiative and the US-Baltic Charter of Partnership, the US tried to forestall such a scenario.

Through the Russian component, the US policy was intended to make it possible that, in the longer term, Russia could become part of a new co-operative and more integrated Europe, and thereby to reduce Russian resistance towards Nato´s North-Eastern enlargement.

---

[70] Rhodes, E. 2000, 'The American Vision of Baltic Security Architecture: Understanding the Northern European Initiative' in *Baltic Defence Review*, No.4, pp.91.

Lastly, the aim of the Nordic component was to give the American engagement in North-Eastern Europe a regional dimension, at the same time as making sure that North-Eastern Europe did not become disconnected from the overall integration process in Western Europe.

A few definitions have to be made. In this chapter the term 'North-Eastern Europe' describes the geographic region consisting of Denmark, Sweden, Norway, Finland, the Russian *oblast* Kaliningrad and the North-Western part of Russia, as well as the three 'Baltic states' Estonia, Latvia and Lithuania. The term 'the Nordic countries' comprises Denmark, Sweden, Norway and Finland.[71]

The theoretical point of departure: unipolarity and regional integration

First the basic, almost ceremonial claims: After the end of the Cold War a new situation arose in Europe and in the international system in general. The US remained as the sole superpower, implying that there is no prospect of a counterbalance from any potential superpower or an anti-US coalition.[72] The present international system is characterised by its unipolarity and exhibits the following characteristics:[73]

- There are no alternative superpowers.

- The unipole sets the agenda.

- Balancing behaviour vis-à-vis the unipole is reduced.

- The unipole is privileged in the pursuit of its interests.

---

[71] For more definitions see Perry, C., Sweeney, M., and Winner, A. 2000, *Strategic Dynamics in the Nordic-Baltic Region: Implications for U.S. Policy,* Brassey's, London, Chapter 2.

[72] The neo-realist theory of unipolarity is based on Waltz (1979), but as adduced by Birthe Hansen. See Hansen, B. 1998, *The Unipolar World and its Dynamics,* 1998 Working Papers, No. 2, DUPI, København and Hansen, B. 2000, *Unipolarity and the Middle East,* Curzon Press, London. See also Waltz, K. 1995, 'The United States and the New World Order', in Hansen, B. 1995, *European Security 2000,* Copenhagen, Political Studies Press, København. An important discussion of the US' role in the unipolar international system has been adduced by Kupchan, C. A. 2000, 'After Pax Americana: Benign Power, Regional Integration and the Sources of a Stable Multipolarity', in Hansen, B., Heurlin, B. (eds.) 2000, *The New World Order – Contrasting Theories,* Macmillan, London, pp.134-167.

[73] See Heurlin, B. 1998, 'Contrasting and Disposing Structural Forces: The Role of the United States,' in Wivel, A (ed.) *Explaining European Integration,* Copenhagen Political Studies Press, Copenhagen, p.201.

- States flock to the unipole side.

- Inability to tilt the balance implies that they have to align with the unipole or become isolated; possibilities of free-riding are limited and effective co-operation is needed to maintain their influence.

- There is a world-wide unipole 'overlay,' differing in intensity, and a general disposition to regionalise.

The imperatives of US policy towards Europe are that it primarily wants European integration to proceed. For the US an unstable Europe characterised by balance of power politics is negative, since instability in the new European regions would affect the whole international system. For the dominant power, integration is an effective way to exert influence and the US therefore encourages the European powers to integrate in order to establish internal stability in Europe. This strategy could be called 'rule-and-integrate.'[74] As the system's manager, the US wants to share its global and regional responsibility with the European powers. By encouraging the integration process the US also avoids that the European states start to free-ride.

Looking at regional integration in the Baltic Region one could expect that the US (1) would encourage regional integration as a way of distributing its responsibility for the international system to other regional powers, e.g. the Nordic states in the Baltic Region; and (2) would encourage sub-regional integration as a further way of securing stability. In the case of the Baltic region the US may be expected to encourage the admission of the three Baltic states into institutions like Nato and the EU as well as sub-regional organisations.

The theory would also make one expect the small states to flock around the unipole, that is to try to keep up good relations with the unipole, and to work hard to optimise their security. Looking at the three Baltic States, it is clear that since their independence in 1991 they have all worked hard to optimise their security and flocked around the unipole, the EU and Nato.[75] In December 1999 the EU opened negotiations with them for membership

---

[74] Heurlin, B. 1998, p.202. The idea of the strategy rule-and-integrate is inspired by Lundestad, G. 1998, *Empire by Integration,* Oxford University Press, Oxford.

[75] For a longer discussion of the recent developments in the Baltic Region see Mouritzen, H. 1999, 'High politics in Northern Europe: Recent Developments and their interpretation,' in Hedegaard, L., Lindström, B. 1999, *The NEBI Yearbook 1999,* Springer Verlag, Berlin, pp.259-275.

of the Union.[76] They have also been taking part in Nato's Partnership for Peace programme (PfP) from its beginning in 1994 and become applicant States of Nato. As such, the Baltic States all participate in Nato's Membership Action Programme (MAP).[77] Since independence they have made considerable efforts to build up their defence systems and have been supported in this not least by the Nordic States and the US. The result of this co-operation is among other things the creation of a common peacekeeping battalion (BALTBAT), the foundation of a common Baltic defence college (BALTDEFCOL), of a regional Baltic Sea squadron (BALTRON), and finally the creation of an air surveillance network (BALTNET).[78] In order to co-ordinate donor contributions to the Baltic States the Baltic Security Assistance Group (BALTSEA) was created in 1998.[79]

Looking at the other states of North-Eastern Europe, Sweden, Finland, Denmark and Norway have all changed their foreign and security policy since the end of the Cold War, even if some more fundamentally than others. The Nordic countries, too, have 'worked hard' and flocked around the unipole and the European institutions. In the nineties, both Sweden and Finland became much more activist in their foreign policy compared with the Cold War period. Since 1995, both have been members of the EU, and especially Finland has utilised its membership to a high degree. It was on a Finnish initiative that the EU's 'Northern Dimension' was created in 1997/1998. In the Finnish perspective the purpose of the 'Northern Dimension' was to make North-Eastern Europe a more distinct region.[80] Besides being members of the EU, both Finland and Sweden have been taking part in the Nato initiatives PfP and EAPC, and Finland has been a contributor to SFOR and IFOR in Bosnia.[81] In both countries there has also been a debate whether membership of Nato is desirable, but as yet there is little practical prospect of this in either country.

---

[76] Lykke, F. 2000, *Den populære ekspansion – EU's udvidelse mod Øst [The Popular Eastward Expansion]*, Paper Number 2, DUPI, København.

[77] Perry, C., Sweeney, M., and Winner, A. 2000, Chapter 2.

[78] Ibid, p.13.

[79] Ibid, p.13.

[80] Finnish Ministry of Foreign Affairs. 2000, *A Northern Dimension for the Policies of the European Union*, Marts, Helsinki.

[81] Perry, C., Sweeney, M., and Winner, A. 2000.

The two other Nordic countries, Denmark and Norway, have also adapted their foreign policy to the new conditions, but in very different ways. Denmark's has since the end of the Cold War been marked by considerable activism.[82] Danish policy towards the Baltic States underlines this. At the CSCE conference in November 1990 Denmark presented the sharpest formulations in support of independence for the three Baltic states and in December 1990 a Baltic information office was opened in Copenhagen.[83] Following this policy, Denmark has during most of the nineties been one of the strongest supporters of Baltic Nato and EU membership and has actively supported the foundation of BALTBAT both economically and by donations of uniforms and weapon systems. Finally, Denmark has integrated Baltic forces in the peacekeeping forces DANBAT and NORDBRIG which both served in former Yugoslavia.[84]

On the other hand, it can be argued that, compared with the other states in the region, Norway has changed its foreign policy less than dramatically since the end of the Cold War.[85] Norway has decided to stay out of the EU and still seems to be the strongest supporter of the Atlantic security co-operation in the traditional Article 5 sense, generally appearing reluctant to adapt to the 'New Nato.'[86]

US policy towards north-eastern Europe

During the Cold War US attitudes towards North-Eastern Europe were dominated by overall strategic competition with the USSR. In the East-West conflict perspective, North-Eastern Europe was strategically important to the US for two reasons: first, it was a pivotal area for early-warning and

---

[82] See Heurlin, B. 1997, *Dansk forsvarspolitik – en ny verden – en ny forsvarspolitik* [Danish Defence Policy – a new World a new Defence Policy], Paper Number 5, DUPI København. See also: Jakobsen, P, V. 2000, 'Denmark at War: Turning point or business as usual?', in Heurlin, B., Mouritzen, H. (eds.) 2000, *Danish Foreign policy Yearbook 2000*, DUPI Press, Copenhagen.

[83] Mouritzen, H. 1998, *'Theory and Reality of International Politics,'*Ashgate Publishing, London, p.70.

[84] Perry, C., Sweeney, M., and Winner, A. 2000.

[85] See Heurlin, B. 1997. See also: Knutsen, B. O. 2000, *The Nordic Dimension in the Evolving European Security Structure and the Role of Norway,* Occasional Paper No.22, WEU, Paris.

[86] On Norwegian foreign Policy in the 90s see Knutsen, B. O. 2000.

intelligence;[87] and secondly, it constituted in most US military conflict scenarios a strategic flank to the central front.[88] Furthermore, it was divided between the two blocs of the Cold War. Denmark and Norway, with their Nato membership, were part of Western Europe, whereas the Baltic States formed part of the USSR. Finland and Sweden were in principle neutral, orientated towards the East and West respectively.[89]

Since the end of the Cold War the geopolitical landscape in Europe's North-Eastern region has undergone fundamental change. For the US this demanded a new policy towards the whole geographical area. To quote the Council on Foreign Relations report:

> 'The Clinton administration has given North-Eastern Europe high priority and has sought to develop a coherent overall policy towards the region. That policy has been designed to enhance stability and security in North-Eastern Europe and help overcome Cold War divisions by promoting greater regional co-operation.'[90]

The report gives a number of specific reasons why it was important for the Clinton administration to create a coherent policy towards the region. First, this policy was part of overall US policy towards Europe, with the aim of creating a Europe whole and free.[91] Secondly, the region was important in American endeavours to include Russia in the regional integration taking place in North-Eastern Europe. The report states:

> '...North-Eastern Europe is also a test case for the administration's policy towards Russia. One of the key elements of the administration's policy has been its effort to reach out to Russia to include Russia in regional co-operation schemes in North-Eastern Europe.'[92]

---

[87] Van Ham, P. 2000, in Trenin, D., Van Ham, P. (eds.) 2000, pp.60-61.

[88] Ibid, p.60.

[89] For a discussion of the Nordic States and their foreign policy during the Cold War see Wæver, O. 1994, 'Between Balts and Brussels: The Nordic Countries After the Cold War,' *Current History*, Vol.93, No.586, pp.390-394. Also, Wæver, O. 1992, 'Nordic Nostalgia: Northern Europe after the Cold War,' *International Affairs*, Vol.68, No.1, Royal Institute for International Affairs, London.

[90] Council on Foreign Relations. 1999, p.5.

[91] Browning, C. 2001, *A Multi-Dimensional Approach to Regional Cooperation: The United States and the Northern European Initiative,* Copenhagen Peace Research Institute, Copenhagen.

[92] Council on Foreign Relations. 1999, p.4.

Thirdly, the report confirms that North-Eastern Europe is an area in which a conflict between Russia and the US could emerge and therefore a US policy towards the region was necessary. Finally, such a policy development was important to define relations between the US and the Nordic States.[93]

There are thus a number of reasons why the US in the nineties was driven to formulate a policy towards North-Eastern Europe. As stated in the introduction, three components can be identified in this policy, addressing respectively the Baltic, Russia and the Nordic countries. These three components have been expressed primarily in three 'Baltic policies' which the US introduced during the nineties, namely 'The Baltic Action Plan' launched in 1996, the 'Northern European Initiative' introduced in 1997, and 'The Charter of Partnership' between the US and the Baltic States concluded in 1998.

The Baltic component

The point of departure for the Baltic component is US support for Baltic independence and integration into institutions like Nato, EU and sub-regional networks. The Baltic States' inclusion in Nato has thus been one of the main goals of US policy towards North-Eastern Europe. It was therefore an important political signal when in 1996 an Office for Nordic and Baltic Affairs was opened in the State Department.[94] Shortly after its opening, the Baltic Action Plan was adopted. Its three-track approach aims (1) to embed the Baltic States firmly in the European and Euro-Atlantic institutions, (2) to encourage the development of normal relations between Russia and the Baltic States, and (3) to promote development of the political and economic infrastructures of the three states.[95] Despite the fact that the Plan mentions the integration of the Baltic States into the Euro-Atlantic institutions, their admission to Nato is not mentioned specifically. However, by 1997/1998 the perspective of admission to Nato became one of the main elements in US policy towards the region.

---

[93] Ibid, p.4.

[94] Meyer, K. 2000, 'US Support for Baltic Membership in Nato: What ends, What Risks?' *Parameters, US Army War College Quarterly*, Winter 2000-2001, Pennsylvania, p.2.

[95] 1996 Baltic Action Plan [Homepage of Nato], 8 September 1999 - last update, [Online] Available: http://www.nato.int/usa/info/baltic_action_plan.htm [12 March 2002].

For a number of reasons it was obvious that the Baltic States would not be invited to join Nato in the 1999 enlargement. At Nato's 1997 Madrid summit Germany, France and the UK were against Baltic Nato membership.[96] A prime concern of US policy towards North-Eastern Europe after 1997 was therefore to ensure that the Baltic States' integration into Western Europe was not questioned. Among the tools for this policy were the launching of the Northern European Initiative (NEI) and the Charter for Partnership.[97] An important clue to these initiatives is an article written by the two RAND scholars, Ronald Asmus and Robert Nurick, published in the magazine *Survival* in 1996.[98] Shortly after its publication Ronald Asmus became Deputy Assistant for European Affairs in the US State Department Office of Nordic and Baltic Affairs. It was hardly a coincidence that most of the recommendations that Asmus and Nurick presented in 1996 were incorporated into US official policy during 1997/1998.[99]

Asmus and Nurick stated that the Baltic States' integration into Western Europe should be considered as part of the overall US policy towards Europe. If the Baltic issue was mishandled the US vision of a Europe whole and free would never be a reality. According to them,

> 'History has shown that events in the Baltics often have repercussions well beyond the region. If mishandled, the Baltic issue has the potential to derail Nato enlargement, redraw the security map in North-eastern Europe and provoke a crisis between the West and Russia.'[100] They further argued that a specific American strategy towards the Baltic Region was necessary. Their argument proceeded in four steps. First, a Baltic strategy was necessary to avoid a so-called 'Korea-syndrome'[101] in the Baltic Region.[102] They explain the 'Korea-syndrome' as 'the fear among many in the region that a Nato

---

[96] Asmus, R., Nurick, R. 1996, 'Nato Enlargement and the Baltic States,' *Survival*, Vol.38, No.2, p.123.

[97] Browning, C. 2001, *A Multi-Dimensional Approach to Regional Cooperation: The United States and the Northern European Initiative*, Copenhagen Peace Research Institute, Copenhagen.

[98] Asmus, Nurick, op.cit., p.123.

[99] The role of Ronald Asmus is also noticed by Peter van Ham and Christopher Browning. See Van Ham, P. 2000, in Trenin, D., Van Ham, P. (eds.) 2000 and Browning, C. 2001.

[100] Asmus, Nurick, op.cit., p.121.

[101] The term refers to the Korean War (1950-53).

[102] Asmus, Nurick, op.cit., p.121.

enlargement policy that excluded the Baltic States might be regarded by a hard line regime in Moscow as an invitation to take coercive action against those countries.'[103]

Secondly, a strategy towards the Baltic States was needed to assure the Nordic Countries that the Baltic Sea region would not become a zone of instability. To the Nordic Countries the independence of the Baltic States was very important. The argument was: 'in strategic terms, Baltic independence is to Finland and Sweden what the liberation of East Germany has been to Germany. And just as Germany made integrating the new democracies into organisations like the EU and Nato a main priority, the Nordic states see it as their top priority to preserve that gain in security and strategic depth as well.'[104]

Thirdly, an American strategy towards the Baltic Region was necessary to ensure that the Baltic States retained their chance to be admitted to the EU. Asmus and Nurick stated that 'EU officials admit that it will be impossible to enlarge the EU to any countries in the East without clarifying the security and defence implications of enlargement.'[105] Finally they argued that a strategy towards the Baltic Region was required because of the relationship between Russia and the West: 'the Baltic issue will be one of the most delicate in Nato's future relations with Russia, as well as in US-Russia relations.'[106]

It seems obvious that the main purpose of US policy towards the Baltic region in the nineties has been to avoid the security problems Asmus and Nurick discussed in their *Survival* article.[107] In a speech on the NEI at Vilnius University, former Secretary of State, Madeleine Albright, explained why integrating the Baltic States into the Euro-Atlantic institutions was so important to the US:

---

[103] Ibid., p.126.

[104] Ibid., p.126

[105] Ibid., p.128.

[106] Ibid., p.128.

[107] See Browning, C. 2001, for a discussion of Asmus and Nurick's article. A discussion of NEI and the Charter for partnership is in: Gfoeller, T. 2000, 'Diplomatic Initiatives: An Overview of the Northern European Initiative,' *European Security*, Vol.9, No.1.

'Our challenge is to build a fully integrated Europe that includes every European Democracy willing to meet its responsibilities. That goal embraces the Baltic nations. History has taught us that your freedom is our freedom. Europe will not be secure unless we work with you and others to make sure you are secure.'[108]

In the Charter for Partnership between the US and the Baltic States signed in 1998, Baltic integration into Nato and the EU was also one of the main elements. Among other things, it says that 'the United States of America welcomes the aspiration and supports the efforts of Estonia, Latvia and Lithuania to join Nato.'[109] The Charter also states firmly that the US and the Baltic States share the same vision of a Europe whole and free: 'as part of a common vision of a Europe whole and free, the Partners declare that their shared goal is the full integration of Estonia, Latvia and Lithuania into the European and transatlantic political, economic, security and defence dimensions.'[110] Finally, the Charter firmly says that Russia has no veto when it comes to Nato enlargement.

In essence, the main purpose of the Baltic component was to emphasise that the Baltic States were still considered a part of Western Europe; despite the fact that they were not included in Nato's 1999 enlargement, the door remained open. With the Northern European Initiative and Charter for Partnership the US signalled that the Baltic States were not forgotten. In addition to this symbolical aspect of US policy, the US has also assisted them in their defence planning policy. The American 'Kievenaar' study was made for this purpose, and the US has also been involved in the Baltic Security Assistance Group referred to above.[111]

---

[108] Remarks by U.S. Secretary of State, Madeleine Albright to students at Vilnius University, July 13, 1997. Read more about the NEI in, *Overview of the Northern European Initiative*, [Homepage of the U.S. State Department, 5 May 2000 - last update, [online] Available: http://www.state.gov/www/regions/eur/nei/fs_000501_nei.html, [12 March 2002].

[109] *A Charter of Partnership among the United States of America and the Republic of Estonia, Republic of Latvia, and Republic of Lithuania*, [Homepage of the U.S. State Department], last update 16 January 1998, Available: http://www.state.gov/www/regions/eur/ch_9801_baltic_charter.html, [12 March 2002].

[110] Ibid.

[111] In the Kievenaar study the Baltic Defence planning process was analysed.

US policy towards the Baltic States has to be understood in the light of this overall US vision for Europe.[112] The purpose of the NEI and the Charter for Partnership was therefore to avoid that Nato's deferral of their admission would create new borders and conflicts in Europe. To quote Christopher Browning:

> 'This notion of building a 'Europe whole and free' is at the heart of the NEI. ...the US goal of creating a Europe 'whole and free' has been explicitly linked to questions of the re-envisaging of Nato's role after the end of the Cold War in civilisational terms, and the consequent decision to open Nato to future enlargement...'[113]

Pursuing this position, Peter van Ham has argued that to the US,

> 'The aspiration of becoming a full member of Nato and the EU (and to a lesser extent WEU), is considered a necessary and natural element of being a European country, of not just being an integral part of *geographical* Europe, but also of a *political* Europe.'[114]

The Russian component

The Russian component of US policy towards North-Eastern Europe is closely connected to the Baltic factor. Its main thrust has therefore been to improve Russia's relationship with its neighbours in order to avoid conflict but at the same time to ensure that Russia is unable to exercise a veto over the future of the Baltic States.

Following the end of the Cold War, the relationship between Russia and the US has undergone dramatic changes, to the point at which partnership is now the favoured phrase. Although Russia is recognised as the successor state of the USSR, Russia has the potential also to be considered as a kind of an antidote, a negation of the Soviet Union. To the US, Russia is now a

---

[112] Browning, C. 2001.
[113] Ibid., p.5.
[114] Van Ham, P. 2000, in Trenin, D., Van Ham, P. (eds.) 2000, pp.60-61.

regional power and a part of the European region.[115] Russia's relationship with its neighbours is therefore a matter of great significance. To the US, good relations between Russia and its Baltic neighbours serve two purposes: first, to make Russia's long term integration into Europe possible; and secondly, to reduce Russia's opposition to Baltic Nato membership.[116] Looking back at US policy towards North-Eastern Europe, one of the aims of the NEI was to encourage Russia's integration into regional organisations like the Barents Euro-Arctic Council (BEAC) and the Council of the Baltic Sea States (CBSS).[117] A fact sheet on NEI from the US Department of State said that one of the aims of the initiative was to 'integrate North-Western Russia into the same co-operative regional network to promote democratic, market-oriented development in Russia as well as to enhance Russia's relations with its northern European neighbours.'[118]

Following this statement, Edward Rhodes argues that the US wants to revive the so-called 'Hanseatic community' which existed in the Baltic Sea Region between the 14th and 16th century: 'explicitly recalling the Hanseatic tradition of the region, the NEI's objective is to create a northern European community within which state and national boundaries mean relatively little.'[119]

How then can we best explain the Russian component? Like the Baltic policy, the Russian policy has to be understood in the light of the American vision of a Europe whole and free. The US wants Russia to be a part of Europe and a part of the European integration process. To quote Ronald Asmus in the capacity of the US State Department's Deputy Assistant for European Affairs: 'our mission in coming to Europe was not just to 'fix'

---

[115] See Heurlin, B. 1998, 'Contrasting and Disposing Structural Forces: The Role of the United States' in Wivel, A (ed.) 1998, *Explaining European Integration*, Copenhagen Political Studies Press, Copenhagen, p.201.

[116] Council on Foreign Relations, 1999, p.6.

[117] Herd, Graeme (2000): *EU Enlargement in the North: Security Dynamics in Nordic Baltic-EU-Russian Relations into the New Century.* Working paper from the Conflict Studies Research Centre, February 2000, pp.11.

[118] U.S. State Department, *Overview of the Northern European Initiative*, [12 March 2002].

[119] Rhodes, E. 2000, 'The American Vision of Baltic Security Architecture: Understanding the Northern European Initiative,' in *Baltic Defence Review*, No.4, Vol.2000.

western Europe but to 'fix' Europe as a whole. We wanted to be part of and contribute to Europe's effort to redefine itself and to extend integration from Western to Eastern Europe. We wanted to help Europeans build a vision of Europe whole and free as well as help to ensure continued democracy, prosperity and security.'[120]

The Nordic component

Two objectives can be identified in the Nordic component of US policy towards North-Eastern Europe. The first was to give overall policy a regional focus; the second to ensure that the Nordic Region would not be neglected in the European integration process. Due to these two objectives it is not surprising that US policy towards North-Eastern Europe strengthens the EU's policy, the so-called Northern Dimension.[121] Peter van Ham argues that: 'the US policy of co-operative security overlaps and even strengthens the Finnish initiative to create a Northern Dimension to the European Union, aimed at developing co-operation in Northern Europe.'[122]

Furthermore, there seem to be a number of similarities between the US Northern European Initiative and the EU's Northern Dimension: both originated in 1997, both profess the aim to create stability in northern Europe, and both envisage achieving this through promoting interdependence.[123] To support the point, NEI as well as the EU's Northern Dimension contain very similar security aspects. Chris Patten, the Commissioner responsible for the Union's external relations, summarises the Northern Dimension's security philosophy in this way: 'the basic aim must be to promote security, political stability and sustainable development through enhanced cross-border co-operation between the countries in Northern Europe. The Commission is convinced that the Northern Dimension can contribute to improved relations

---

[120] Asmus, R. 1999, *Address at the 4ᵗʰ annual Conference on Baltic Sea Regional Security and Cooperation*, Stockholm 4 November.

[121] An elaboration on the Northern Dimension in the EU is *En nordlig dimension i unionens politikker [A northern dimension in the policies of the Union]*, Meddelse fra Kommissionen, Bruxelles, 25 November 1998.

[122] Van Ham, P. 2000, in Trenin, D., Van Ham, P. (eds.) 2000, p.58.

[123] Browning, C. 2001, p.24.

and mutual dependence between Russia, the countries of the Baltic Sea Region and the European Union.'[124]

Dr Graeme Herd has also argued that there are three security strategies in the Northern Dimension.[125] The first, a strategy characterised as 'soft security,' is based on the assumption that an increase in wellbeing reduces the risk of conflict. As Herd puts it,

> 'One central assumption of the initiative is based on a traditional functionalist analysis which treats the promotion of welfare as an indirect approach to the prevention of warfare.'[126]

The second is a strategy which focuses on the security of the individuals in the region. Herd states: 'what is it that makes people feel insecure? If the answers are nuclear accidents, heavy air and water pollution, drugs on the streets and in schools, the spread of communicable diseases, then any increase in the authorities' ability to deal with these problems is a positive contribution to security.'[127] Lastly, Herd identifies a security strategy in the Northern Dimension based on the concept that if Russia and the Baltic States were to start to trade more with each other, then their relationship might improve. The argument runs, 'let's not talk about border issues, let's trade.'

As Peter Van Ham has claimed, the NEI and the Northern Dimension appear to complement each other, since the latter makes it easier for the US to achieve the purposes of its Nordic component. Following this argument, Christopher Browning has identified three reasons why the US has such a pro-active attitude towards the EU's Northern Dimension. To begin with, the partnership between NEI and the Northern Dimension defines a US role which the EU then assumes as a coherent executant in the international system. In other words, the US wants the EU to be a partner but not a competitor in

---

[124] Patten, C. 1999, A *Northern Dimension for the policies of the Union: current and future activities*, Speech given at the Foreign Ministers' Conference on the Northern Dimension, Helsinki, 12 November 1999.

[125] Herd, G. 2000, *EU Enlargement in the North: Security Dynamics in Nordic Baltic-EU-Russian Relations into the New Century*, Working Paper, Conflict Studies Research Centre, Sandhurst, p.14.

[126] Ibid.

[127] Ibid.

that system. The NEI therefore seems to be a vehicle which offers the chance for the US to remain engaged in Europe. As Browning argues,

> 'Through the NEI the US finds space and a forum within which it can retain a constitutive voice in European affairs, and more particularly in the developing relationship between the EU and Russia.'[128]

Secondly, Browning argues that the positive attitude of the US towards an NEI and Northern Dimension link can be explained in terms of the relative responsibilities of the US and its European allies. An ongoing theme in the speeches on NEI by US officials is that the US regards itself as a 'junior partner' in North-Eastern Europe. To quote Conrad Tribble, the former US NEI Coordinator:

> 'In the grand project underway here to create a new Baltic Sea Region, the US does not see itself as the main actor. We have neither the money nor the capacity to be this. Rather, the US sees its role as that of an actor whose activities can bring added political, symbolic, and financial value to the efforts of the countries in the region.'[129]

Finally, Browning argues that the US takes a positive view of the Northern Dimension because the partnership between the EU and US is down-playing the US role in the region. By linking NEI to the Northern Dimension, the US can avoid the accusation of being a hegemon in North-Eastern Europe.[130]

Conclusion

From its predominant position, the US chose during the nineties to encourage integration between the former East and Western Europe. The point of departure in US policy towards North-Eastern Europe therefore expressed itself in a tacit support for Baltic Nato membership. Three components could

---

[128] Browning, C. 2001, p.27.

[129] Tribble, C. 2000, *NEI and the Northern Dimension*, Address at the conference: The Northern Dimension: An Assessment and Future Development, Riga, 16 December 1999.

[130] Browning, C. 2001, p.27.

be identified in this emerging US policy: a Baltic component, a Russian component and a Nordic component. The main purpose of the first was to ensure that the Baltic states would ultimately become members of Nato. The main reason why the US launched the NEI and Charter of Partnership was to counter the possibility that the Baltic States might be squeezed out of the Euro-Atlantic integration process. US policy towards North-Eastern Europe has to be analysed in accordance with the overall US vision of a Europe whole and free, and US worries that this vision could be endangered if the Baltic issue were mishandled.

The main aim of the Russian component was closely related to the objectives of the Baltic component. Its principal object was, first, to make Russia's long term integration into Europe possible, and secondly to reduce Russia's opposition to Baltic Nato membership. Since the end of the Cold War the US has regarded Russia as a regional European power. Russia's eventual integration into the regional institutions had therefore become a matter of importance to the US.

Finally, the Nordic component had the twin objectives of giving US policy towards North-Eastern Europe a regional focus, and to ensure that the Nordic Region was not neglected in the European integration process. It was no surprise therefore that the US found that the EU's Northern Dimension complemented its own policy towards the Nordic States and the NEI in particular. The link between NEI and the Northern Dimension thus had the effect of fulfilling more amply the objectives of the Nordic component of US policy towards North-Eastern Europe.

The US, the EU and the Turkey-Cyprus Link

Christian Franck
**Professor at the Institut d'Etudes Européennes,
Université Catholique de Louvain
Secretary General of TEPSA, Belgium**

Since the early days of the Cold War, the US established strong ties with Turkey which were to play a key role in Nato's South-Eastern containment of the Soviet Union. Twice, in 1964 and in 1974, the US-Turkey relationship was put under strain by the Cyprus crises of those years. But in the post Cold War period relations blossomed and the Clinton Administration openly expressed its support for Turkish accession to the European Union. For the EC/EU, the special relationship with Turkey stems from the Ankara Association agreement concluded in 1963. In the sixties, the EC took great care to treat Ankara on the same footing as Athens. In the seventies, association with Turkey became part of the EC's overall Mediterranean approach. The military coup in Ankara in 1980 arrested the institutional development and the financial co-operation provisions of the association regime. In the nineties, the main question became the Turkish application for membership of the EU. In December 1999, the European Council finally placed Turkey among the candidates, opening the way for an eventual Accession Partnership. While Turkish accession represents a major geopolitical interest for Washington, for the Union it raises an existential question: by including Turkey, and possibly Ukraine as well as the West Balkan states, could the Union be exceeding its capacity to govern itself? The prospect of Turkey participating in a European *res publica* is challenging this concern about the governance of the Union.

While the Turkish accession question is likely to remain open for perhaps a decade, its linkage with the accession of Cyprus will serve as a permanent and sensitive reminder. The most realistic approach may be that Turkey allows the Greek part of Cyprus to enter the EU whilst refraining from annexing the Turkish Northern Cyprus Republic, even at the cost of refusing to contribute to a final settlement in Cyprus until its own accession to the EU has been secured.

The US and Turkey

The origins of the close American-Turkish relationship go back to the early days of the Cold War. Between the two World Wars, Ankara had sought to enhance its co-operation with Washington to counterbalance the UK's influence in the area, but American isolationism frustrated this attempt. Once the Cold War split the anti-Hitler coalition and gave way to East-West confrontation, Turkey's location became geopolitically crucial. Turkey had a long border with the Soviet Republics of Georgia, Armenia and Azerbaijan and with Socialist Bulgaria. It controlled the navigation through the straits of the Bosphorus and the Dardanelles. Like Greece, Turkey became part of the containment strategy of the Truman doctrine. Ankara benefited from Marshall Plan aid and US military assistance. Together with Greece, Turkey acceded to Nato in 1952. Turkish troops participated in the Korean war. Ankara became a member of the Baghdad Pact together with the UK, Iran, Iraq and Pakistan in order to contain Soviet influence in the Middle East and the Persian Gulf.

Supported by American economic and military assistance, participating in Western organisations like OECD and the Council of Europe, Turkey's commitment to the Western camp was consonant with the modernist ideology of the Kemalist regime. Thereafter, however, the intimate partnership with Washington was to be somewhat soured by the two Cyprus crises.

The Cyprus crises of 1964 and 1974

A first cause of Turkish misgiving was the US decision in 1963 to withdraw its Jupiter missiles deployed on Turkish territory. Their removal was a consequence of the Soviet-US deal which concluded the Cuban missile crisis in 1962. The fact that Washington failed to consult its ally gave rise in Ankara to the uncomfortable feeling that Turkey's security was excessively dependent on the US. The subsequent Cyprus crises in 1964 and 1974 would put the Washington-Ankara relationship under further strain, though without bringing it to breaking point.

It is useful to recall that the 1959 Zurich Agreement between the Greek and Turkish foreign ministers had shaped the constitutional framework of the Republic of Cyprus when it ceased to be a British colony and became an independent state in August 1960. While the Turkish Cypriot community at the time represented 18.3 per cent of the population, it received 30 per cent of the senior positions in the public administration, and 40 per cent in the army to be created. As the Head of the State, a Greek president jointly with a Turkish vice-president was to decide on nominations and the promulgation of laws. Two further Treaties were to reinforce the Constitution. Through the Treaty of Guarantee, Greece, Turkey and Great Britain secured the independence and territorial integrity of the island; whilst the Treaty of Alliance bound together Cyprus, Greece and Turkey. Article 182 of the Constitution further stipulated that the provisions of the Zurich Agreement could not be amended.

For the Greek Cypriots, the Zurich Agreement was a source of considerable frustration. They wanted attachment to Greece, the famous *Enosis*. They also considered the Turkish representation excessive. The 1963-64 crisis was triggered by the call to amend the Constitution and to reopen the question of *Enosis*. Inter-communal fighting broke out and provoked the withdrawal of the Turkish community ministers and civil servants and the formation of enclaves regrouping the Turkish Cypriot population. The then UN Secretary General U Thant mediated and a UN Force (UNFICYP) was despatched at the end of March 1964 to separate the parties. But the conflict could not be stopped. Greece obtained permission from Washington to send 5,000 soldiers in order to command the Greek Cypriot militia. Clearly, Turkey wanted then also to intervene militarily but was restrained from doing so by a letter of 5 June sent by president Lyndon Johnson to Prime Minister Ismet Inönü. This letter warned the Turkish authorities that they were not entitled to use US supplied weapons outside Nato operations and that Turkey could not rely on Nato assistance should its intervention trigger a Soviet response in support of the Greeks.

President Johnson's letter led to a considerable cooling of relations between Washington and Ankara. It made Turkey aware that it would have to do more by its own efforts to secure its interests. In consequence Ankara rekindled its relations with Moscow and refused to send troops to Vietnam.

President Johnson not only impeded Turkey from intervening in Cyprus; he also launched a mediation led by the former US Secretary of State Dean Acheson. The Acheson plan was genuine in the sense that it broke with the Zurich Agreement structure and decoupled Turkey's strategic concerns from protection of the Turkish minority. His plan offered Enosis to the Greek Cypriots, while two cantons would come under civil Turkish Cypriot administration. The rest of the Turkish Cypriot community would enjoy the same protection as the Turkish minorities in Greece. As a counterpart, Turkey would be offered the Karpas peninsula (5 per cent of Cypriot territory) and an Aegean island to be ceded by Greece. But neither the Cypriot president Makarios nor the Ankara government agreed and the Acheson plan was abandoned.

The 1974 Cyprus crisis was to inflict further, and probably more severe damage on the US-Turkey relationship. By 1967 the Colonels had come to power in Athens. They were hostile to President Makarios, whom they suspected of having become reluctant to implement Enosis. Thus in 1974 they backed a coup led by a former chief of the Greek Cypriot militia, Nicos Sampson. The 25 July saw Archbishop Makarios overthrown and Sampson proclaimed as Cyprus president. Approval of the coup by the Republican administration has been alleged, as it was clear that Washington feared the non-aligned policy espoused by Makarios. However, the coup and the reinforced prospect of Enosis triggered the Turkish military invasion of Northern Cyprus. By provoking the flight of Greek Cypriots from the North, the Turkish occupation effectively partitioned the island. A cease-fire entered into force in mid-August along the Attila line on the 35th parallel. On 2 November, the UN General Assembly adopted Resolution 373 calling for the withdrawal of foreign forces and for the cessation of external interference. But the Turkish army remained in Northern

Cyprus, stationing some 30 000 soldiers there. Ethnic cleansing inevitably took place in both parts of the island. Whilst for the international community legal authority still rested with the Greek Cypriot government in Nicosia, the Northern part (33 per cent of the territory and 18 per cent of the population) was in fact ruled as a Turkish federated state of Cyprus which would proclaim itself in 1983 as the Turkish Republic of Northern Cyprus (RTNC). Ankara would remain alone in recognising the RTNC as a state.

Judging that the Turkish military intervention in Cyprus had violated the rule that US supplied weapons be used only for Nato missions, the US Congress decided to put an embargo on further supplies to Ankara which was to last from February 1975 to September 1978. Influenced by the strong Greek lobby, Congress believed that an embargo would compel Ankara to withdraw its troops from Cyprus. But the manuoveure failed. The Turkish army remained in Northern Cyprus and US-Turkey relations were soured. After the Johnson letter of 1964, the US sanctions in 1975 reinforced the Turkish impression that American and other Western leaders were more inclined to favour the Greek side. But Greece was also disappointed that Washington had failed to prevent Ankara's invasion of Northern Cyprus and withdrew from the Nato military structure. Washington experienced then how difficult and delicate it was to maintain a balanced stance in the face of Turkish-Greek rivalry. The consequence of the 1974 Cyprus crisis was that Greece distanced itself from Nato, while the maintenance of US military and intelligence bases in Turkey was questioned by Ankara. In the light of the US embargo, the Turkish government embarked on a build-up of its military forces. Additional troops were mobilised for 'national purposes only,' meaning that they remained independent of the forces assigned to Nato. Turkish officers exerted control over the US air bases, except for Incirlik which remained directly under Nato command. Affected by its cooler relationship with Ankara, Washington began to strengthen its ties with Teheran.

The US embargo was lifted in September 1978. The following year, the overthrow of the Shah's regime in Iran and the Soviet invasion of Afghanistan gave strong signals to the US that privileged relations with Turkey needed to be restored. In January 1980, Washington and Ankara signed a new Defence and Economic Co-operation Agreement (DECA) which reopened the way for US military assistance. Turkey thus resumed its role as the Western alliance's South-Eastern fortress to guard the border of a broad area of geo-strategic instabilities.

This fortress function explains why US-Turkey relations did not suffer materially when the Army took power in Ankara to put an end to a decade of domestic political uncertainty. While the European Community reacted by suspending the institutional links under the Association Agreement and blocking its financial protocol, the US Administration attached greater priority to strategic considerations rather than those of democracy, human rights and the rule of law.

In September 1983, the generals released their grip on power and Turgut Özal became Prime minister before becoming Head of State. The Özal period proved to be a time of substantial reconciliation with the US as well as with the EC. The Turkish economy moved from state control to greater liberalisation. Trade and investment with the US increased. In April 1987, Ankara applied for accession to the European Communities. However, the Cyprus issue remained highly sensitive: in 1983, the Turkish Republic of Northern Cyprus had become self-proclaimed, but the UN Security Council denied its legal existence. From then on, Cyprus was to have a profound effect on relations with the EC, if less so with Washington. The Turkish military occupation of Northern Cyprus will remain a stubborn obstacle in Turkey's move towards EU accession. The United States, however, is unlikely to do more than actively support mediation by the UN Secretary General in order to achieve a constitutional settlement between the two communities.

Post Cold War ties

In 1995, the then Assistant Secretary of State for Europe, Richard Holbrooke, declared to the Turkish journalist Yasemin Congar that 'Turkey is the new front line state for the West, and in that sense, it has taken the role of Germany during the Cold War.'[131] Such a view illustrated how greatly Turkey's geo-strategic importance for Washington had grown. It had surpassed the

---

[131] Quoted by Congar, Y. 2000, 'A strong alliance yet to outgrow more geopolitics,' *Insight Turkey (Quarterly research and information journal on Turkey)*, Vol.E, No.8, p.85.

peripheral role as Nato's South-Eastern fortress on the Soviet border. It was now called upon to play a multifunctional role in the wider challenges extending from the Middle East to the Balkans, through the Gulf area, Central Asia and the Southern Caucasus. The decade of the 1990s has probably seen the swiftest blossoming of US-Turkish relations since the early fifties. According to the former US Ambassador in Ankara, Morton Abramowitz, the Gulf war 'marked the beginning of the renaissance in a somewhat battered Turkish-American relationship.'[132] Overcoming domestic reluctance to antagonise its powerful Arab neighbour, Turkish President Özal decided to make a strong contribution to the anti-Saddam Hussein coalition. He authorised the US heavy B-52s taking off from Spain to fly over Turkey on their bombing missions to Iraq. He also permitted the use of Turkey's Nato air base by US aircraft to strike at Northern Iraq. By moving its troops to the Iraqi border, Ankara exerted a military pressure on the ground which obliged Saddam Hussein to keep troops there and prevented them from being sent to Kuwait. If President Özal turned down the US request for a Turkish battalion to participate in the coalition forces assembled in Saudi Arabia, he accepted blocking of the pipelines channelling Iraqi oil to the Mediterranean.

Although the Gulf war was the most significant event for the Washington-Ankara geo-strategic partnership in the 1990s, it was not its only example. In the Balkans, Turkey played an important moderating role during the Bosnia and Kosovo crises. It supported US and OSCE endeavours to end the civil wars and restore stability, whilst resisting any temptation to fuel Bosnian or Albanian Muslim militancy. In Central Asia, Turkey is helping to contain Iranian influence by ensuring that the Roman-Turk alphabet would prevail over the Farsi alphabet in former Soviet republics like Uzbekistan, Turkmenistan and Kazakhstan. Ankara also acts as a counterbalance to Russian power politics in this area as well as in the Southern Caucasus. A Turkey-Azerbaijan axis is crucial to challenge the Russian outlet of Novorossisk in the Northern Black Sea, by offering the Baku oil producers a pipeline to take their oil to the Turkish Mediterranean terminal of Ceyhan. In the margins of the OSCE summit in Istanbul in November 1999, the Presidents of

---

[132] Abramovitz, M. 2000, 'American policy making on Turkey,' in *Insight Turkey*, Vol.E, No.8, p.5.

Turkmenistan, Azerbaijan, Kazakhstan, Georgia and Turkey signed an agreement setting out the terms for the Baku-Ceyhan pipeline project. President Clinton attended this ceremony, demonstrating that the US backs the project even if major US oil companies are still casting some doubt on its profitability.[133]

Turkey is also playing a significant role in attracting Azerbaijan and Georgia towards more Western orientations and distancing themselves from Moscow's influence. Only Armenia remains closely attached to the alliance with Russia. Sensitive as they are, Turkish-Armenian relations would improve if a solution could be found to the Nagorny-Karabakh stalemate. Ankara supports a plan of US origin which proposes an exchange of the Latchine corridor joining Armenia to Nagorny-Karabakh with that of Meghri, in Southern Armenia, which would connect the enclave Azeri Nakhitchevan to the main part of Azerbaijani territory.

In the Middle East, which was under Ottoman rule up to World War I, Turkey has also aligned itself with US policies. Ankara has recognised the State of Israel from its beginnings in 1948 and maintained a strict balance during the Arab-Israeli conflicts. In February 1996, it signed a military co-operation agreement with Israel, which might also be seen as a counter to the pro-Arab commitment of Greece, but whose useful side-effect has been to gain greater sympathy for Turkey from the powerful Jewish lobby in the US Congress. In the area of civilian co-operation, Turkey has taken regional initiatives for the management of water resources which involve Syria, Iraq, Jordan and Israel. Another example of civilian co-operation is the Black Sea Economic Co-operation Pact signed in Istanbul in June 1992 which groups the countries surrounding the Black Sea as well as Greece and Albania.

From the Balkans to the Middle East, there is a wide arc or crescent where Turkish and US political and strategic interests strongly converge. Turkey is playing a front line role in balancing Russia, containing Iran and

---

[133] On this issue, see 'Kazakhstan pledge boosts pipeline's viability', *The Financial Times*, 19 November 1990; and 'L'Asie centrale intéresse de nouveau les pétroliers,' and 'La bataille des oléoducs entre la Russie et les six Républiques soviétiques,' *Economic Supplement*, Le Monde, 3 April 2001.

isolating Iraq, all in accord with the main US geo-strategic goals for the broad area where Europe and Asia join. That Turkey is serving US interests in that area also justifies the US taking care of Turkish interests in the Eastern Mediterranean, as well as of Turkey's domestic problems with its Kurdish minority.

Since the 1975 US embargo which soured its relations with Ankara, Washington has refrained from leaning towards either side in the Greek-Turkish rivalry over Cyprus, or over delimitation of territorial waters and the continental shelf in the Aegean. The US plays the role of 'Big Brother,' hurrying to douse fires where they flare up and patiently working as mediator to bring the two sides closer to a solution. It was US pressure that stopped Greeks and Turks escalating towards war in June 1996 when Turkish troops invaded the small Aegean island of Kardak/Imia where Greek sovereignty is disputed by Ankara. In Cyprus, the Clinton administration constantly pressed the two Cypriot communities to negotiate under mediation of the UN Secretary General. Negotiations for a political settlement dealing with the four core issues of territory, property, security and constitution resumed in December 1999. New rounds of these so called 'proximity talks' in 2000 have, however, remained without success. For Washington, the new dynamic towards a settlement is the prospect of Cyprus' accession to the EU. Up to the mid 1990s, the ties between the EU and Turkey, and with the Cyprus Republic still legally represented by the Greek Cypriot government, were deemed complementary but not central to US Eastern Mediterranean policy. When the EU's Luxembourg Summit of 1997 opened the way for (Greek) Cyprus' accession even without a preliminary constitutional settlement, Washington became anxious that such an accession would trigger a Turkish extremist reaction which could lead to annexation of the Turkish Republic of Northern Cyprus. Cypriot and Turkish accessions to the EU had become linked and thus acquired high priority in the US Mediterranean strategy. Both will depend on the evolution of Greek-Turkish relations which Washington has strongly nurtured since its own rapprochement with Turkey.

As far as Turkish domestic politics are concerned, Washington has usually shown comprehension towards Ankara's handling of Kurdish claims. The US is less active than the EU in improving Turkish human rights and minority protection standards. It openly supports Ankara's fight against PKK rebellion and terrorism. The role played by the CIA in PKK leader Oçalan's capture in Nairobi is well known. On the other hand, the coming to power in 1996 of the coalition led by the leader of the Islamist Refah Party, N. Erbakan, raised US concerns that Turkey could be diverted from its constitutional attachment to secular democracy. The ban of the Refah issued in 1997 under pressure from the Turkish generals was less than strongly opposed by Washington.

The subject of Armenian genocide by the Ottoman Empire in the years 1915-1923 remains a sensitive issue for Turkish public opinion, and the government continues to reject the accusation. Yet the UN Human Rights Committee in 1985, the European Parliament in 1987, the Russian Douma in 1995 and the Italian Parliament in 2000 have all passed resolutions which recognised the Armenian genocide by the Turks. In France, the Senate in November 2000 and the National Assembly in January 2001 voted a law to the same effect. In Washington, President Clinton deemed that a House of Representatives resolution on Armenian genocide could be damaging to the Turkish-US partnership, whose geopolitical implications were of prime importance. He addressed a letter to the speaker of the House, Dennis Hastert, warning that resolution 596 calling for the recognition of the genocide suffered by Armenians in Anatolia in the early twentieth century would negatively affect the interests of the US in maintaining its vital relationship with Ankara. It was also feared that the resolution could trigger new Islamist terrorist attacks against US forces in the Middle East and it was quietly dropped.

US-Turkish relations improved throughout the 1990s and President Clinton's visit in November 1999 was to crown the new partnership. Addressing the Turkish Grand National Assembly in Ankara on 15 November, the US President declared that, 'the coming century will be shaped in good measure by the way in which Turkey itself defines its future and its role today and tomorrow, for Turkey is a country at the crossroads of Europe, the Middle East and Central Asia.' He then gave clear testimony that the US was backing Turkey's accession to the EU: 'the future can be shaped for the better if Turkey becomes fully a part of Europe as a stable, democratic-secular nation.' He also called for the European allies to have 'a real vision' and recognise that 'Turkey is where Europe and the Muslim world can meet in peace and harmony.'

The US and Turkish accession to the EU

The Clinton speech in Ankara confirmed roundly that the US supports Turkey's accession to the EU. In the sixties Washington and the EC countries shared the view that Greece and Turkey, both Nato members, were to be treated on the same footing. The Turkish Association agreement of 1963 therefore followed swiftly that concluded with Greece in 1961. Greek accession in 1981, however, made things more complex. As an insider, Greece shared responsibility for shaping EC/EU policy towards Turkey and could help to thwart more positive approaches many EC/EU members wished to make towards Ankara. In the nineties, the prospect of Cyprus accession began to worry the Clinton administration in case differential treatment by the EU of the Turkish and Cypriot applications, received in 1987 and 1990 respectively, were to lead to a crisis which could substantially damage the EU-Turkey relationship and divert Turkey from its Western orientation.

In March 1995, the EU Council struck a bargain that the Customs Union with Turkey would enter into force in 1996 and that accession negotiations with Cyprus should start six months after the conclusion of the 1996 Intergovernmental Conference. It was only this linkage with Cyprus accession which ensured that Greece would refrain from vetoing the Customs Union agreement. The US favoured the Customs Union and lobbied, with Israel, that the European Parliament should lift its reluctance to assent. The socialist MEP Pauline Green confirmed that these countries had addressed 'wise words' to the Assembly and the EP's assent was finally given in December 1995 by 343 votes to 149 and 36 abstentions.[134]

The conclusion of the Luxembourg summit in December 1997 not to include Turkey among the candidates for accession was clearly judged as a mistake by Washington. 'We think,' stated Under Secretary Richard Holbrooke, 'that the invitation to Cyprus was correct and the treatment of Turkey was a mistake, and we hope that the EU and Turkey will work together

---

[134] Krauss, S. 2000, 'The European Parliament in EU External Relations: The Customs Union with Turkey,' *European Foreign Affairs Review*, Vol.5, Issue 2, Summer, p.234.

actively to improve the situation for Turkey.'[135] Washington began to press EU leaders to revise the Luxembourg decision. As mentioned above, President Clinton's Ankara speech in November 1999 clearly expressed the wish that Turkey should be admitted to the EU. High level contacts between the White House and EU leaders were held on the eve of the Helsinki European Council in December 1999 which finally included Turkey among the thirteen candidates, although it deferred the prospect of opening the actual negotiations.

In October 1998, Holbrooke's successor, Under Secretary of State Strobe Talbott, reiterated the American view on Turkish accession:

> 'As a very interested non-member and non-applicant, the US has urged the EU to find ways to bring Turkey more fully into the process of enlargement. We have done so – and we will persist in doing so – for reasons that have as much to do with our hopes for Europe as with our hopes for Turkey. We do not believe that European unity and integration will be fully successful if a key European country is set uniquely alone and apart.'[136]

In the post-Cold War period, Turkey has regained and even increased the geopolitical importance it had for the US in the fifties. There is no other Nato ally which could play such a multifunctional strategic role in the arc encompassing the Balkans, the Southern Caucasus and the Black Sea, Central Asia and the Middle East. This contribution to US geopolitical aims demands that Washington play its part by supporting the Turkish ruling elite's goal to join the EU. But the question has also to be raised whether this support is not more than a mere pay-back but central to the US vision of what the European Union should be and do. In other words, there is a supposition that a Europe without Turkey would be failing to fulfil the geo-strategic tasks which Washington has assigned to it in the post-Cold War Atlantic Alliance. In 1992, General Colin Powell, at that time still Chairman of the Joint Chiefs-of-Staff, argued that the reason for keeping alive the Atlantic Alliance and

---

[135] The United States Mission to the European Union, 6 June 1998 – Last update, *Holbrooke departure remarks*, 5 April 1998, in Cyprus,' [Homepage of the United States Mission to the European Union], [Online], Available: http://www.useu.be/archive/cypru461.html [13 March 2002].

[136] The United States Mission to the European Union, 6 June 1998 – Last update, *Deputy Secretary of State Talbott on US-Turkish Relations*, 14 October 1998,' [Homepage of the United States Mission to the European Union], [Online], Available: http://www.useu.be/archive/talbo1014.html [13 March 2002].

guaranteeing America's engagement in Europe was that forces on the European side were no longer for exclusive use in Europe but that 'across the Atlantic' incorporated also the Middle East and South-West Asia. That implied that US forces in Europe would have an extra-European role.[137] James H. Wyllie reports in his writings that, 'in the contemporary world, Europe can act as a base for American transatlantic strategic interests and as a repository of dependable allies who will share the responsibility for the international security from which they also benefit.'[138] US advocacy of Turkey's accession to the EU needs to be placed within this geo-strategic design, with the European side of the alliance as a platform for American protection of its interests in the area where Europe and Asia meet, and which clearly includes the Middle East. If Turkey were left outside the European Union, its anchorage in the Western camp could be weakened and its ties with the US potentially loosened. The corollary would be a Europe handicapped in performing the tasks assigned to it under the USA's twenty-first century geo-strategy.

That the fundamental objective for supporting Turkey's accession to the EU lies in the US global strategy is confirmed in the geopolitical views expressed by Zbignew Brzezinski in *The Grand Chessboard*. According to the National Security Council's chief during the Carter Administration, global US supremacy rests on its preponderance throughout the entire Eurasian continent, and this constitutes the central basis for global US geo-strategy. In this context, Eurasia does not mean the grey zone where Europe and Asia join, but the whole twin-continental mass over which the US has to exert its control from the West (Nato in Europe) and from the South-East (Japan, South Korea). According to Brzezinski, 'Europe is America's essential geopolitical bridgehead on the Eurasian continent. Unlike America's links with Japan, the Atlantic Alliance entrenches American political influence and military power directly on the Eurasian mainland.'[139]

Since Europe constitutes this Eurasian bridgehead under US geo-strategy, Brzezinski argues that 'any expansion of the scope of Europe becomes

---

[137] Cf. Wyllie, J, H. 1997, *European Security in the New Political Environment*, Longman, London, p.88.

[138] Ibid., p.89.

[139] Brzezinski, Z. 1997, *The Grand Chessboard*, Basic Books, New York, p. 59.

automatically an expansion in the scope of direct US influence as well. Conversely, without close transatlantic ties, America's primacy in Eurasia promptly fades away.'[140] This kind of theorem illuminates the logic both of widening Nato to the new CEE countries and of enlarging the EU through Turkish membership: '... the essential point regarding Nato expansion is that it is a process integrally connected with Europe's own expansion.'[141] Turkey, for its part, is considered by Brzezinski as 'a geopolitical pivot.' This refers to the category of 'states whose importance is derived not from their power and motivation but rather from their sensitive location... The identification of the post-Cold War key Eurasian political pivots, and then protecting them, is thus also a crucial aspect of America's global geo-strategy.'[142] Among Ukraine, Azerbaijan, Iran, South Korea and Turkey cited by Brzezinski as the Eurasian geopolitical pivots, 'Turkey (with South Korea on the Eastern side) is obviously the most available pawn on the grand American chessboard. Ankara stabilises the Black Sea region, controls access from and to the Mediterranean Sea, balances Russia in the Caucasus and serves as a Southern anchor for Nato.'[143] Turkey's geopolitical role is therefore strongly connected with the concept of Europe as the Eurasian bridgehead. That means that Turkish accession to the EU would maximise the geopolitical function of an enlarged EU in the same way that it would complete the Western anchorage of Turkey. But if the EU were to close its doors to Ankara, and Turkey's Europeanisation grind to a halt, the capacity of the US to control the large zone of turbulence in Turkey's neighbourhood would be significantly reduced.

US-Turkey and EU-Turkey: A comparative approach

Since the early days of the Cold War, the main rationale for a close US-Turkey relationship has been geo-strategic. Ankara was to play the role of a South-Eastern fortress in Nato's containment of the Soviet Union. As a 'geopolitical pivot' in the grand US Eurasian strategy, Turkey remained mainly a geo-

[140] Ibid.
[141] Ibid., p.79.
[142] Ibid., p.41.
[143] Ibid., p.47.

strategic partner during that period. Turkey's relationship with the EC/EU, however, turned out to be different from that which Kemalist Turkey had always wanted, that is a close connection with the building process of the European Union itself. As early as 1959, the Turkish government laid claim to association with the EC under the Article 238 regime, arguing that Turkey was a component of the Western world and fully shared the EC's political and economic principles. According to the 1959 Turkish ministerial Committee, 'Turkey would not be able to remain outside a common market which created an economic union and was capable of one day becoming a political union.'[144] Walter Hallstein, the then President of the EEC Commission, echoed that view in 1963 by declaring, 'Turkey is part of Europe: today that means that she has established an institutional relationship with the European Community. As for the Community itself, that relationship is imbued with the concept of evolution.'[145] The institutional relationship created was that of the Ankara Association Agreement, signed in September 1963 to enter into force in December 1964. The EC-Turkey Association provided for the establishment of a Customs Union which would commence after a preparatory phase of five years and a transition period of twelve. Article 28 stipulates that, '...when the operation of the agreement makes it possible to envisage acceptance by Turkey of the full obligations deriving from the Treaty establishing the Community, the contracting parties shall examine the possibility of the accession of Turkey to membership of the Community.' In September 1970, an additional protocol to the 1963 agreement was signed in Brussels. It governed the transitional period for completion of the Customs Union, providing for a progressive tariff disarmament, economic convergence and progressive free movement of workers. The protocol entered into force in January 1973, but the transitional period was to last until January 1996.

Turkey's EC relations naturally reflected its economic importance. By the eighties, about 50 per cent of its trade was with the EC (against less than 10 per cent with the US). There were also clear political intentions. For

[144] Quoted in Vaner, S., Akagül, D., Kaleagasi, B. 1995, *La Turquie en mouvement*, Complexe, Brussels, p.105.
[145] Quoted in Billion, D. 1997, *La politique extérieure de la Turquie, une longue quête d'identité*, L'Harmattan, Paris, p.19.

Ankara, the Association expresses the pro-Western and secular orientation of the Kemalist regime and its ruling elite, whilst maintaining a strict parallelism with the Greece-EC relationship. For the EC, the Turkish Association forms part of its overall Mediterranean policy launched in 1972. The associations with Malta and Cyprus, signed respectively in 1970 and 1972, and the Co-operation agreements entered since 1975 with the Maghreb and the Mashrak countries, are also part of this total policy. The role that Turkey plays on the South-Eastern flank of Nato was not an explicit motive for sustaining durable and progressive EC relations with Ankara, but EC members never lost sight of it.

The Cyprus crises of 1964 and 1974 had little impact on the association with Turkey, but the Johnson letter of 1964 and the US weapons embargo in 1975 were to do significantly more harm to US relations with Ankara. The Ankara Agreement entered into force following the 1963-64 crisis. The 1974 crisis, however, and the occupation by the Turkish army of Northern Cyprus, initiated a relationship with the EC States through the channel of the new European Political Co-operation mechanism. EPC declarations stressed the necessity to preserve Cyprus' independence and territorial integrity from external interference. But the Cyprus Association Council meeting, due in July 1974, was postponed.[146] Compared with the US weapons embargo on Turkey, EC reaction towards the 1974 crisis was to give it a stronger position than Washington's when the military coup of September 1980 occurred in Ankara, to be followed by the fall of the Shah's regime in Iran and the Soviet military invasion of Afghanistan. The EC suspended the institutional arrangements of the Association agreement from 1982 to 1986, as well as the financial co-operation protocol. But the Turgut Özal government rebuilt its bridges with the EC in the global framework of a reinforced pro-Western foreign policy. In the meantime, Greek accession to the EC in 1981 had broken the parallelism with Greece. In due course, a letter sent in April 1987 by Prime Minister Özal to the then President of the Council, Belgian Foreign Minister L. Tindemans, requested full membership for Turkey. The opinion of the Commission on the Turkish application, issued in December 1989,

---

[146] See Drevet, J. F. 2000, *Chypre en Europe*, L'Harmattan, Paris, p.249.

pointed out that economic development gaps and political obstacles, including relations with Greece and the Cyprus problem, precluded a positive answer on Ankara's candidacy. According to J.F. Drevet, the Commission's opinion provoked neither surprise nor a sour reception in Ankara. EU membership was not yet the major objective for the Turkish political elite. But ever since then, the Turkish government has regarded the Cyprus question as its major bargaining counter for ultimately obtaining its own accession.[147]

In March 1995, the EU acknowledged the linkage with completion of the EC-Turkey Customs Union by agreeing that negotiations for Cyprus' accession should be opened after the 1996 IGC. The Luxembourg European Council decision in December 1997 to launch the negotiating process with Cyprus and five other applicants, while leaving Turkey off the full list of candidates, soured relations between Brussels and Ankara. However, these improved substantially after the Helsinki European Council in December 1999 which firmly placed Turkey among the candidates even if actual negotiations were unlikely to start at an early date. But the EU-Turkey relationship still continued to have its ups and downs. Fresh tensions with Ankara were raised when the Commission's proposal to the Council on guidelines for the Accession Partnership with Turkey included among the short term political criteria that Turkey should support the UN Secretary General's efforts to reach a global solution in Cyprus. The Turkish government argued that the Cyprus case lay beyond the Copenhagen criteria. Yet the EU Council's adoption of the framework regulation for the Accession Partnership in February 2001, and Turkey's endorsement in March of the *acquis communautaire* as part of its National Programme, demonstrate that the process of working towards Turkey's accession continues.

Conclusions

Turkish membership of the EU represents one of Washington's main geo-strategic goals, aimed at maximising the bridgehead function that Europe is to play in the US Eurasian geo-strategy, completing at the same time the process of anchoring Turkey within the Western camp. For the EU, Turkey's

---

[147] Ibid., pp.254-255.

accession raises above all an existential question: that of governing a Union comprising between thirty and forty Member States. If Turkey is accepted, there will be no more grounds for refusing Ukraine or Moldova, still less the countries of the Western Balkans.

That forms the argument of the French MEP Alain Lamassoure. The main objection to Turkish membership is not religious and does not concern the Muslim beliefs which prevail in a State with an expressly secular constitution. The real fear for him is that Turkey's accession would open the way to an over-extension of the Union's borders and make it to all intents and purposes ungovernable.

The opposite contention is that there is no reason to exclude peoples who are even partly European from participating in a European project which is founded on the values of human rights, the rule of law and the maintenance of an enduring peace.

In that perspective the admission of Turkey to a *European res publica* as an insider is seen as a higher political priority even than the dramatic challenge of how a EU grouping around thirty-five states might be governed. Turkish accession is, however, likely to require a horizon of up to twenty years to enable Turkey to comply fully with the Copenhagen criteria. In the meantime, the problem of Cyprus' accession remains to be overcome.

Even if Turkey were to threaten annexation of Northern Cyprus in the event of a Cypriot accession restricted to the island's Greek part, it seems unlikely that Ankara would take any excessive action which could damage its own chances for accession for a long period, if not indefinitely. But European hopes that Ankara would contribute to a constitutional settlement to facilitate Cyprus' accession could prove illusory. As Christopher Hill has stressed, 'Turkey holds all the cards over Northern Cyprus itself, and has little incentive to change the status quo.'[148] On the contrary, it may be expected that Ankara will hold on to the Cyprus card as the final lever for its own accession. 'If Greek Cyprus is allowed [to enter] despite the lack of a settlement with the

---

[148] Hill, C. 2000, *The Geo-Political Implications of Enlargement*, EUI Working Paper RSC No 2000/30, European University Institute, Firenze, p.20.

North, Turkey will become hostile unless bought off with its own accession.'[149] Considering that the EC lived for thirty-two years with a protocol on Inter-German Trade, could the EU live for a decade or more with an Inter-Cyprus regime adjusted to the Cyprus accession? That would seem to be a not unrealistic assumption.

In Luxembourg in 1995 the EU speculated that Cyprus' accession could stimulate its two components to reach a political settlement. It would perhaps be rash to bank on this. Nevertheless, if the EU remains determined to grant it membership in or around 2004, it is possible that Ankara might still cause Mr Denktash to soften his rigid position.

---

[149] Ibid., p.10.

The Mediterranean, Middle East and North Africa

Roberto Aliboni
Director of Studies
Istituto Affari Internazionali

This chapter considers the interplay between EU enlargement and EU-US relations with regard to the Mediterranean and the wider area of the Middle East and North Africa (MENA). To conduct this analysis, the first section is devoted to the main factors influencing current EU policies towards its Southern approaches. The second section considers the effects of enlargement on the EU's Southern policies. The third section draws some conclusions about the interplay between enlargement and transatlantic relations with respect to Southern policies and issues. A fourth section advances some recommendations.

Factors influencing the EU's southern policies

Many factors shape current EU policies towards the Mediterranean and MENA areas. The following sections consider three of the more significant: (i) the perceptions of the most relevant regional and extra-regional actors relating to the EU as an actor in the area concerned; (ii) the development of EU institutions; and (iii) the internal EU balance of power.

The EU in Arab and Israeli perceptions

How legitimate are the EU's Southern policies in the eyes of its most relevant counterparts in the areas concerned? In other words, what is the Union expected to do and, conversely, what is it expected to refrain from doing by other relevant international and regional actors in the Mediterranean and MENA area? The question is complicated by the fact that the EU's international role, beyond that of its member states, is ambivalent and for the time being quite different from that which Westphalian-like states normally play in the international arena. At the same time, the EU is in many respects similar to traditional international actors and is so regarded by other states.

One may begin by considering three actors, the Arab countries, Israel, and the United States. The Arab vision of the EU has passed through two apparently similar but in fact different stages. The first dates back roughly to the 1970s, when the Arabs put forward the idea of the Euro-Arab Dialogue in Copenhagen and the then European Community accepted the idea. At this stage, the Arabs believed in the positive and convenient dynamics of Western European political integration and looked upon the Euro-Arab Dialogue as reinforcing that integration, resulting in a fundamental shift in the balance of power between Europe, the United States and the MENA areas [Allen; Khader].

This Arab vision miscalculated the strength of transatlantic solidarity and European strategic dependence on the United States. In consequence, the Euro-Arab Dialogue failed. In the second and current stage, the Arabs' perception of the EU has become finely attuned to reality. They are now able to make a clear distinction between the EU and its member states and are well aware of the slow dynamics of political integration as opposed to the EU's strong economic power [Salem; Said Aly].

The basic concept of promoting the EU to counter or contain the United States remains. Illusions about the EU becoming a more or less fully-fledged Westphalian international actor, bringing about a novel global balance of power, have been abandoned. The end of the Cold War might have made Europe more firm and independent of the United States. But, in contrast, it has revitalised old nation states and failed to strengthen the process of supranational political integration. At the same time, it has strengthened the United States, leaving it as the only global superpower. In this new context, the Arabs clearly perceive that the EU (including its member states) is politically weak and depends on its alliance with the United States for an international role and other benefits.

Though a minor political actor internationally, the EU retains the advantage of a preferential relationship with the United States. Thus, compared with the earlier stage of the Euro-Arab Dialogue, the EU is now expected to play a more limited but still helpful role. It can be used selectively to help influence and moderate the United States with respect to Arab political and security interests. Furthermore, after almost two decades of economic decay, the Arabs understand quite well the significance of the EU's economic strength and geographical proximity to support their economies, their future growth, and the social and political stability such growth would bring.

Current Arab perceptions of the EU's role are decidedly more realistic than in the past. They have gained a more sober and accurate appreciation of that role as it concerns their own interests. Whilst willing to accept and support such EU policies as fit the role it can realistically play in the economic and social realm, they resist policies that in their view go beyond that role, as in the field of security. Developments over the last ten years, with the MEPP (Middle East Peace Process) and later the EMP (Euro-Mediterranean Partnership), attest to a revised and downgraded Arab vision of the EU's legitimate role towards Southern areas.

Within the MEPP, the Arabs welcome European initiatives geared to the support of Arab actors, especially the Palestinians, which facilitate and unblock negotiations. However, they are wary lest these initiatives overlap with tasks that, in their view, the EU (and its member states) are unable to accomplish, such as security functions and actual mediation between the parties involved. In other words, they do not wish to see the EU play a political and security role not matched by its perceived political status and institutional capabilities.

The Arab perception of EU legitimacy has been given an even more vivid profile in the EMP. In the 1995 Barcelona Declaration, the EU wished to include a first chapter aiming at the establishment of a kind of Euro-Mediterranean co-operative security area, similar in content and operation to a mini-OSCE. In the event, far from contemplating such an area, over the subsequent five years the partners negotiated a Euro-Med Charter for Peace and Stability which, on the one hand, postponed indefinitely the mini-OSCE the Europeans had had in mind and, on the other, asserted a concept of shared security in the area predicated on civilian and economic factors, while ruling out military security and security co-operation. Even the civilian use of military assets in a co-operative security context is subjected to strong reservations and limitations.

The crisis that erupted in Israeli-Palestinian relations after the failure of the July 2000 Camp David II negotiations has prevented the Euro-Med Partners from adopting the Charter (or more accurately, has provided the Arabs with a pretext to avoid adopting a document they dislike). Recent developments should not obscure the significance of what has amounted to a renegotiation of the Barcelona Declaration in which the Arab perception of the EU as an economic power with a substantial civilian character has once again emerged very clearly. What is in line with the EU's role and capability – and thus legitimacy – as perceived by the Arabs is its welcome policy of co-operation in the economic, social and cultural realms. But the same is not true of military or military-related policies.

The Israeli perception is very similar. It differs from the Arab attitude only in that almost no one in the country is prepared to regard EU initiatives as helpful to the Middle East peace process. While the Arabs look at the Europeans as ineffective but friendly partners, more often than not Israelis look at them as unfriendly and unreliable.

Only a minority in Israel understands that, for the time being, Europe and the EU can nevertheless play a positive role in the economic, social and cultural fields – and it is these quarters that provide the most solid support for the EMP in Israel [Ahiram, Tovias; Heller]. The same minority believes that a successful EMP could provide a good learning process against the time when peace will prevail and the EU could attempt a more political role in the area. It must be said that the concept of a post-peace EU role in the MENA is also widely shared in the Arab world.

But Israel's mainstream opinion is not even interested in the EU's economic and social role and regards it with suspicion and hostility. This became very clear during the MENA economic summits process. Both the US and Israel resisted EU attempts there to lay the foundations of a strengthened European leadership and economic role in the region within the Regional Economic Development Working Group (REDWG).

All in all, however, Israeli governments support the EMP because it puts an end to European ideas of special Euro-Arab relations and acknowledges MENA as a single region rather than making distinctions between its peoples, as does the Euro-Arab Dialogue. Furthermore, there is fundamental Israeli interest in the creation of a regional or inter-regional framework for developing economic, social and human relations, which could help to overcome its isolation after the peace, if not in the interim [Alpher]. EU legitimacy in Israeli eyes thus lies in the same factors as for the Arabs. The latter look more openly and confidently than the Israelis to a possible European political role in the area. But both believe that, for the time being, the only legitimate role the EU can aspire to is that of an economic and civilian power. Both would oppose a EU enlargement that would expand market opportunities but dilute external economic policy decision-making. An enlargement resulting in a stronger federal EU would be opposed by Israel as it could entail European attempts to shift the balance of power. On the other hand, the same development would be interpreted positively by the Arabs (even if more cautiously than present rhetoric may suggest).

The United States

The American perception of the role that the EU should play in the MEPP [Perthes] is substantially similar to the Arab and Israeli ones, though distinctly more articulated than the latter.

The United States believes that the economic support and diplomatic flanking provided by the EU in the MEPP is important and, in many respects, indispensable. Yet it does not believe that the EU could play a role of political mediation acceptable to all the parties. Consequently it considers EU political initiatives as generally awkward. Like other parties to the MEPP, the United States tends to exclude the EU from the central political process, while welcoming its broad diplomatic and economic support.

Furthermore, the United States greatly appreciates EU economic relations with and assistance to the whole of the Mediterranean and MENA areas. It is not entirely convinced, however, that EU policies of inter-regional co-operation and integration are consistent with the purposes of globalisation. Despite the fact that the EMP is officially predicated on 'open regionalism' [Joffé; Kebabdjian], the Americans are intermittently assailed by doubts that what the Europeans are in fact setting up is a closed area of co-prosperity. The latest move prompted by these doubts is the Eizenstat initiative [Ounaïes], which tries to resume with the Maghreb countries (including Mauritania and Libya) the attempts that collapsed at the MENA economic summits. After all, it must not be overlooked that EU regional economic links with its Southern approaches have been an irritant to the United States since the very inception of the European Communities.

However, when it comes to the US vision of the EU's role in the wider European Southern approaches, the most relevant question is what the United States thinks about the EU or, more broadly speaking, the European security role in these areas. Does the US contemplate an EU and European military role in these areas, in particular with respect to non-Nato Article 5 missions, i.e. international crisis management? The response is positive, though contingent on that role being effective and consistent with the interests of the US and the Alliance.

In principle, this response is not confined to the Mediterranean and MENA areas in particular. True, the post-Cold War debate about a Western presence out-of-area began with the 1990-91 Gulf War, i.e. in the MENA area. Subsequently, though, interventions were to take place in sub-Saharan Africa and the Western Balkans. Crisis management has gradually acquired a global and strategic significance, so that the positive US response to the question whether the EU and Europe should play a role in it refers to international security rather than a specific area like the Mediterranean or MENA. It concerns the evolution of the transatlantic relationship in terms of international security policy.

Nato's Berlin decision to assume an international role of crisis management at the service of the international community, the St Malo British-

French agreement to create a EU common defence organisation, and the subsequent Nato decision at the 1999 Washington Atlantic Council welcoming European-led operations, have begun to provide some reassurance for US concerns about the EU's consistency and effectiveness in becoming involved with international security through crisis management interventions. Within the emerging Euro-Atlantic re-arrangement to deal jointly with international security challenges, in particular the need for crisis management, the United States now seems to consider the EU as a security actor and to look favourably upon such a development.

This development is taking place in a global perspective. Thus it includes the Mediterranean and MENA areas but is not limited to them. It has, however, been suggested that within future more extended and global scenarios, the present Euro-Atlantic out-of-area policy should apply first to the peripheries of Southern Europe, i.e. the Western Balkans with the Mediterranean and MENA areas, as a kind of 'near abroad' [Lesser 2000]. In fact, such a scenario corresponds closely with AFSOUTH competences.

However, what matters in this new transatlantic development is less the geopolitical perspective than the political and institutional arrangements, namely which organisation is responsible rather than which areas are involved. From the American point of view, the security role pertains primarily to Nato, though this may well include a European articulation. What is clear from the transatlantic security debate that has taken place over recent years, is that Nato will be commonly regarded as the Western security organisation of last resort even for non-Article 5 missions. Depending on which model of integration is to prevail in the EU in coming years, its articulation with respect to Nato could prove more or less extensively autonomous and effective. The EU will certainly have its own security role. What matters is that this role should be in tune with the Alliance's political framework. In this sense, from the Alliance's point of view it will no longer be politically relevant whether an intervention in the Mediterranean and/or elsewhere is led by Nato, the EU and Nato in a CJTF operation, or by the EU alone.

In conclusion, returning to the Mediterranean and MENA areas, it is important to note that there is a consistent stream of thought in the United

States confirming that EU and European interests in the Mediterranean are legitimate and that European efforts to organise North-South co-operation across the basin must be recognised and supported by Washington [Lesser 1996]. Such legitimacy, however, is contingent on an appropriate EU-Nato division of labour between economic, social, cultural and soft security co-operation on the one hand, and hard security co-operation on the other [Lesser 1998].

This vision confirms a considerable convergence between US and Arab-Israeli perceptions on a pre-eminently civilian and economic role for the EU, particularly in the Mediterranean and the EMP. The US also appears interested in a EU security role in relation to the Mediterranean, but only to the extent that it is consistent with Nato and its enlargement and underpins allied interests. Washington's support is strictly contingent on the existence of an operational connection between Nato and the EU in crisis management, and a division of labour in which the EU would be essentially concerned with economic and civilian tasks. US policy was well expressed by Secretary Albright's dictum of 'no duplication, no decoupling and no discrimination.'

Institutional weaknesses and inadequacies

The above analysis suggests that, in the eyes of both regional and extra-regional actors, EU legitimacy as an international actor in the Mediterranean is limited to its civilian and economic role. Having failed to expand its role into the field of security co-operation and the peaceful use of military assets through the Barcelona Declaration, the EU's legitimacy in MENA affairs and its Southern policies are severely constrained by the perceptions and objectives of the principal actors. It must be emphasised, however, that these perceptions are to a significant extent rooted in objective factors, namely the weakness and inadequacy of the Common Foreign and Security Policy (CFSP) on one hand, and the institutional unilateralism demonstrated by the EMP experience on the other.

Even if Southern actors were to wish the EU to play a more effective political and security role, it would be hard for the EU to respond because the CFSP is weak and its member states have proved unwilling to reinforce it, either in Maastricht or significantly thereafter in Amsterdam and Nice. All in all, if the EU does not 'emerge from the sidelines' in the framework of the MEPP [Peters], it is because it has no adequate instrument for doing so, not even its CFSP. It is true that the United States puts strong pressure on the EU to refrain from 'interfering,' but it is also true that the EU, as it stands today, would hardly be able to 'interfere' if it wanted to. The EU Special Envoy to the MEPP clearly makes a helpful contribution from a diplomatic point of view, but the political background is too limited to invest him with a realistic ability to 'interfere.'

A good example of the inherent political limitations of the EU's political role in the MEPP emerged during the April 1996 crisis between Israel and Lebanon [Murphy]. While the EU troika was on a mission to the region, France quite independently took the initiative that led to the establishment of the monitoring committee on cease-fire violations, which proved one of the rare and effective instruments of conflict prevention in the region. On the one hand, the troika would not have been able to make its decisions as quickly as the French Foreign Minister. On the other, the regional actors in the crisis had confidence in France as a Middle Eastern actor, which was absent in the case of the EU. For such a feeling to emerge, France and the other member states would have to invest the EU with a very different kind of CFSP.

By the same token, even if the Euro-Med Partners had been willing to agree the first chapter of the Barcelona Declaration, foreshadowing further agreements on CBMs, CSBMs, disarmament, adequate defence and zones free of weapons of mass destruction – a considerable agenda of security co-operation – the EU would have been hard put to it to develop and manage the required arrangements with the institutional structures available to it.

More often than not, the Southern actors express doubts over the EU's role and aspirations by citing these institutional and political inadequacies. Pending improvements in its present institutional framework, the EU can hardly fault them. The truth is very simple: in order for the EU to become the legitimate actor which its Southern counterparts are presently reluctant to recognise, it needs a much stronger and more coherent institutional basis and a much higher level of common political will. As things stand today, the

Southern actors' minimal perceptions of the EU's role are justified by any objective view of the EU's institutional shortcomings.

The EU's institutional structure is not only weak but also looks inadequate for implementing policies as complex as the EMP initiative [Edwards; Philippart; Monar; de Guttry]. The multidimensional or holistic character of the EMP challenges the EU's centaur-like institutional structure more intensely than do specific policies. For example, WTO members negotiate with a one-voice EU, as represented by the Commission. In the EMP, where all three of the Union's pillars are involved, non-EU members are faced by either the Commission or EU governments, according to the subject, as well as by different decision-making processes. So far the experience of both the Euro-Med Committee for the Barcelona Process – the body in which EMP decisions are made – and the Senior Officials Committee – the EMP intergovernmental body dealing with political and security issues – has been frustrating. Once the EU has made its decisions, all that the non-EU partners can do is to accept or oppose them. If the EMP were to move on to deal with social and soft security issues like illegal and legal migration, international crime, terrorism and drug trafficking, the state of institutional imprecision within the third pillar would create the same – if not greater – difficulties as experienced so far with political, security and economic matters.

Improvements may be expected in the near future from the new troika, intended to ensure more effective co-ordination between the Commission and the Council. In addition, the adoption of a Common Strategy for the Mediterranean at the Santa Maria de Feira European Council should facilitate EU decision-making by allowing for majority voting on most issues except for Title VI and defence matters.

However, the difficulties in co-ordinating the EU's and EMP's decision-making processes cannot be fully or easily overcome, since they are inherently linked to the coherence of the EU institutions. For the time being, that coherence is far from satisfactory and will be put under further pressure by enlargement. The decisions taken by the European Council in Nice have not served to improve the situation.

EU neighbours and intra-EU cohesion

The Mediterranean policy has always been a component of the Community's cohesion, a trade-off by France and Southern European countries of their support for the external interests of Germany and other Northern European countries and Northern support for fostering stability in the Mediterranean, including other possible external Southern European interests [Aliboni 1992; Bonvicini].

In general terms, the distribution of EU resources to any external partner is affected by the balancing of two kinds of intra-EU considerations: allocations to less developed EU members, generally through the structural funds, and the general pattern of allocations to external partners.

During the last decade, the intra-EU political balance was strongly affected by the 'Drang nach Osten,' the preoccupation with Eastern Europe which followed the end of the Cold War. The process that brought about the renewal of the EU's Mediterranean policy in the shape of the EMP can be regarded as a redressing of the EU's South-East balance, by way of a fresh contest between the new interest in Central and Eastern European Countries (CEEC), predominantly on the part of Germany and other EU Northern-Central countries, and Mediterranean interests linked mostly to Southern European concerns. The Essen European Council restored the intra-EU balance by instituting the MEDA fund and allotting the Mediterranean area a substantial amount of EU resources. Today, this pattern of cohesion is once again affected by enlargement as well as by developments in the Balkans.

While the effects of enlargement will be discussed later, it must be noted here that EU involvement in the Balkans is already affecting its external pattern of resource distribution, since this area has altered the ranking of the EU's external interests. Thus on 14 November 2000 (the day before the EMP Ministerial Conference in Marseilles) the European Council, which had set aside 10 billion euro for external financial support in 2000-06, allocated 5.35 billion to the 240 million inhabitants of the Mediterranean and 4.65 billion to the 25 million inhabitants of the Balkans.

Enlargement and the EU's southern policies

The above has examined the most relevant factors shaping current EU Southern policies. This section will consider the likely impact of enlargement on these elements, so as to reach some conclusions also on its impact on transatlantic relations with regard to Europe's Southern approaches. To that end, two aspects will be discussed: (i) the shift in the EU's internal balance due to enlargement and its impact on the EU's Southern partners; and (ii) the impact of the EU's own perceptions and institutional developments on its Southern policies and the perceptions of its regional partners.

Enlargement and intra-EU politics

The second wave of candidates with which the EU is currently negotiating is made up of twelve countries: four CEEC countries (Czech Republic, Hungary, Poland and Slovakia); the three Baltic states (Estonia, Latvia and Lithuania), three Balkan countries (Bulgaria, Slovenia and Romania) and two Mediterranean countries (Cyprus and Malta). Turkey was recognised as a candidate by the 1999 European Council in Helsinki, but no ad hoc negotiations have been initiated. Other countries in the Western Balkans have as yet no candidate status (however, FYROM has been associated to the EU; Croatia is negotiating its association; and Albania has a commercial agreement). It is too early to talk about their inclusion in the EU. However, subject to a positive evolution, there would be no reason to exclude them from future enlargements – on the contrary, there would be good reasons for them to be included.

This agenda entails an extraordinary increase in the resources to be distributed to the EU's present and future less developed members. There is little doubt that community policies of solidarity and cohesion will in future have to be less ambitious and generous than previously. Even so, the amounts will still be considerable and could easily bring about a fall or moratorium in the resources devoted to external common policies.

Any such restriction in resources would result in a reshuffling of external priorities, complicate the balance among external geopolitical objectives, and make EU cohesion more difficult to attain. Inclusion of the CEEC and Baltic countries would redirect interest towards Russia and the CIS countries. This would in turn reduce the flow of EU resources towards the Mediterranean.

These shifts and their size will be influenced also by other factors. One of these concerns the need for EU cohesion with respect to immigration and soft security issues. These are an increasing feature of the EU's Southern approaches, but the problems are set to affect the EU in its entirety. It would be wrong to see them as only a Southern European hazard. Though mostly carried out in and by Southern EU countries, the control of Southern approaches is a common interest and concern whose costs will sooner or later have to be shared. For EU cohesion, this would require yet more common resources to deal with common concerns for Mediterranean stability. In summary, while resources assigned to the Mediterranean would diminish as a consequence of relative changes in resource and geopolitical priorities, such a decrease would to some extent be contained by the need to fund common policies on immigration and soft security issues.

Developments in the Balkans, however, can affect the relative amount of resources flowing to the Southern shore of the Mediterranean more than the factors just mentioned. In effect, the question is to what extent France and the Southern European countries (and EU members in general) will continue to give the Mediterranean the same security priority as in the past. The efforts of France, Italy, Spain, Greece (and Turkey) in relation to the Balkans have grown considerably in recent years. The traditional Southern Mediterranean focus of countries like France, Italy and Spain has become significantly modified. Also, many of the risks from the South, like illegal immigration and drug trafficking, which were explicitly contemplated by the Barcelona Declaration, now come not from Mediterranean countries alone, but to a large – or even larger extent – from the Balkans. What has emerged in the last few years is an East-South arc comprising the Balkans and the Mediterranean within which, in many respects, the latter now appears less pressing than the former.

While proximity interests characterise Northern EU policies and national security concerns in relation to Russia and western CIS countries, it must be noted that these areas have become high and growing foreign policy priorities also for France and Italy. Russia, Ukraine and Belarus must be regarded as common and important concerns and priorities for all EU members, independently of their geographical location. This realisation is also contributing to changes in EU geopolitical trends.

The conclusion could be that in the coming years the enlarged EU will have good reason to reassess the priorities for its external approaches. In principle, the cohesion of the enlarged EU will tend to divert resources from external to internal and from Southern to Eastern and South-Eastern tasks. That tendency will, however, be constrained by the necessity to meet new common interests in combating growing transnational risks and issues of soft security originating in the East as well as the South. Whilst resources for the South would diminish, the growing need for soft security measures would lessen the fall. The most significant changes would thus concern geopolitical orientations (from South to East and South-East) and the consolidation of an East-South security agenda predicated on soft rather than hard security tasks.

EU self-perceptions and institutional evolution

The EU's weak institutional evolution and its negative effects on EU political and institutional relations with its international partners, in particular the regional and extra-regional Southern actors, have already been considered in the first section of this chapter. This point must now be reviewed again in the perspective of enlargement. The question is whether enlargement will strengthen or weaken the EU's institutional basis and what impact it will have on the EU's Southern policies. Discussion of this question must consider the factors affecting the EU's institutional evolution, namely the interplay of different self-perceptions of identities and roles of the EU as an international actor which influence and shape EU foreign and security policies, including policies towards MENA areas.

Four basic European identity strategies have emerged so far in the framework of the process of European integration. The first is to achieve the status of a European global power, able to compete in a Westphalian-like international environment. This is the long-standing aim of France's European policy, which is directed at establishing a European global power under its own hegemony and making it an instrument for its national purposes. By the same token, in European federalist thinking there has always been a wing visualising a European federation as a global power geared to assuring Europe full independence in relation to other global actors. Though France opposes federalism as much as federalists oppose nation-states, the global power the two different schools aspire to is very similar in character: a federation or confederation (or just coalition) which at the end of the day would be a new Westphalian entity, greater and more powerful than present European states and characterised by the aim of asserting its interests against other international actors. This identity strategy could be related to the building up of a 'Westphalian global power' Europe (which, according to circumstances, would benefit individual members or the group as such).

A second strategy is concerned with national power, where national power is not translated to the nation-like interests of a European super-state or coalition. This finality defines the power of the individual nation-states that belong to the EU. Great Britain has been the initiator of this strategy, broadly guided by pragmatism and expediency. Today, however, this strategy reflects the wider European trend towards re-nationalisation, brought about by the end of the Cold War. Re-nationalisation has not brought about a renewed assertive nationalism, but has broadly reinforced an appreciation of and a search for national identities, particularisms and interests.

Like the Austro-Hungarian Empire's nationalities before the First World War [Waldenberg], today's EU member states strive for their national identities to be preserved, without asking for the Union to be dissolved. Within this diffuse national nostalgia, there are countries which uphold an open and incremental vision of the EU's role, and countries with a reductive vision, applying a sort of 'good-enough' rule of thumb to its role, in the sense that all the EU is supposed to do is to be 'good enough' with respect to any case in question. Under this strategy, member states refer to common institutions the tasks that would be less effectively managed in their narrower national framework, but while fully retaining the basic attributes and instruments of their identity and sovereignty. In this strategy, Europe can be seen as a 'national-subsidiary power.'

A third identity strategy refers to Europe as a non-competitive global power. Today, the idea of a democratic community, based on more or less stringent common institutions dedicated to the promotion of democratic and peaceful values internationally as well as to prosperity, is strong and widely accepted among Europeans. The finality can be regarded as that of building a 'co-operative global power' Europe. Can it be done? The liberal response is that generalised conflict is remote today; thus this is the right moment to introduce strategies to reinforce co-operative security policies so as to make international relations inherently less prone to conflict. The realist response is that a non-competitive global power can be set up only if it is contingent on the existence of another power that guarantees its overall security.

In the 1960s, the most coherent Europeanist and federalist schools of thought predicated the establishment of the European community or federation on a close security partnership with the United States. The delegation of Europe's existential security to the Atlantic Community enabled European states to avoid Westphalian constraints and costs and, in contrast, to concentrate on developing their democratic polities and prosperity. Today, with the Cold War ended, this delegation is far more problematic. The way in which the Europeans are trying to attenuate such constraints on the EU as a non-competitive global power is by redirecting Nato towards tasks of security co-operation, and more generally by reinforcing collective and co-operative security frameworks.

Finally, the fourth strategy is pursued by those who are profoundly convinced of the EU's co-operative task as a union of democracies in a Kantian sense. At the same time, they are also convinced that in order to implement its mission, the EU must have a consistent degree of autonomy or sovereignty. The supporters of this identity strategy have an incremental institutional notion of the EU and believe that a global EU actor would definitely have to compete and assert its interests, without however acting as a traditional Westphalian state. This identity may be defined as 'co-operative partnership.'

Needless to say, each EU member pursues more than one strategy at times, though in the end one of them is usually predominant. For example, Austria and Finland support an EU co-operative identity, but they also practise a 'national power' approach (Finland being more open to an incremental EU vision than Austria). For this reason, to gain a better insight into this multifaceted reality one has to consider, in addition to the identity strategies, the roles which the EU can play internationally. The roles that concern our argument are global ones (though in a more detailed discussion of the question, a regionally-dedicated EU role could well also be taken into consideration). These roles characterise the EU as an economic, civilian and peace power, not forgetting to count the benevolent projection of EU economic power.

As explained, such roles do not pertain to individual strategies, but cut across them, so that the same role can be played within the framework of different strategies. Currently, the supporters of the different strategies set out above converge in pursuing two kinds of EU global roles: peace power and civilian power Europe. All members agree that the EU has to contribute, within the framework of international legality, to managing international crises by equipping itself with the capabilities needed to pursue the range of so-called Petersburg tasks. In this framework, the 1999 European Council in Helsinki decided to provide the Union with a military and non-military crisis management capability. Thus the EU pursues, according to need, both its traditional role of civilian power and the more recently added role of peace power.

Supporters of the 'good enough' model, thanks to that model's pragmatic inspiration, are ready to accept even grand openings, if the latter are seen as convenient for national priorities. This was the case with the British initiative that led to the Saint-Malo process and the CESDP (Common European Security and Defence Policy). Other EU members, pursuing other strategies, regard these tasks from different perspectives. In the CESDP, realist globalists bet on the political and military power now being developed for peaceful purposes, and on the global role they make available to the EU and/or its states. New-realist globalists, on the other hand, bet on the cultural and political transformation that the exercise of a civilian and peaceful power will bring about within the EU, and liken this to the erstwhile CSCE process. Those more interested in a global civilian and peace role for the EU will pay greater attention to the legal and political legitimacy of operations, whereas global *Realpolitiker* will regard them as an opportunity to create and assert power to play a global Westphalian-type role.

The weakening or strengthening of EU institutions will depend on which strategies will tend to prevail. Those looking for global power would in general foster institutional developments and try to strengthen the Union in relation to the states. This rule of thumb would be subject to important exceptions, however, for those pursuing a French type global power Europe or those emphasising co-operative roles. Ultimately, the latter are both moved by an instrumental vision of the EU's global dimension and, when forced to balance their interests, they will prefer either strengthened hegemony or strengthened international co-operation over a strengthened Union.

Thus an institutionally weak Union is convenient for many supporters of a co-operative global power Europe, in particular the so-called neutral states. While the EU framework would make available more resources for peace-supporting operations and render them more practical, weak institutions would prevent these operations from promoting their military as distinct from their civilian and peace significance, and from turning the EU into a superpower. Of course, institutional weaknesses may make peace support operations as difficult and ineffective as to be hardly convincing. Still, the effect of preventing a Westphalian super-state from emerging would prevail.

On the other hand, an institutionally weak Union would certainly not favour strategies intended to make co-operative partnership possible. Indeed, if the CFSP were to remain unable to provide the necessary guidelines and objectives for decisions on crisis intervention, EU-led operations would continue to be very marginal and practically subservient to Nato decisions and requests. The Nato 'first refusal' right requested by the Americans with respect to such decisions has obviously been dramatised by France but, if accepted, would be a blow to any concept of co-operative partnership.

Expectations of institutional deepening were disappointed at the Nice European Council. There are strong countervailing forces against the re-nationalisation trend, led by Germany and supported by Italy and other countries, which may modify it and set in motion enlargement without detriment to EU institutions, or perhaps even allow for their strengthening.

One has also to take into account, however, the influence of the new members. For them, EU membership is largely an instrument for realising national political and security interests and their related needs. They are entering the game at a time when the overall European political framework is strongly influenced by trends towards re-nationalisation and have no reason to be more 'Europeanist' or 'federalist' than old members. Furthermore, any kind of institutional strengthening is bound to limit their influence in the Union even before they have been allowed to have any. All in all, enlargement will set in motion powerful forces against any institutional strengthening of the Union.

If in enlarging the Union, present members accept its institutional weakening, the EU's political handicap in dealing with Mediterranean and MENA partners will be exacerbated. Its ability to deal with complex regional institutions like the EMP will also remain disappointing or even dwindle. On the other hand, the contrary could be the case if enlargement were to bring about a more politically and institutionally compact Europe, with strong common decision-making in foreign policy, security and defence.

Would regional Southern partners be disappointed by an institutionally weak and politically more fragmented EU? Actually, a politically stronger EU would be a concern, at least for Israel. A politically weak EU would concern the Arabs, but only up to a point. The Arab perception of the EU as an international actor is declining and they do not expect decisive inputs from it. What would concern the Arabs, and to some extent the Israelis as well, is a decline in the EU's role as a civilian and economic power as a consequence of enlargement. However, while we may expect an institutional and political decline, the EU's civilian, economic and peace roles have a good chance of remaining and even of being upgraded. Since these roles, as global as they may be, would be played by a weak power, such an evolution would be welcomed by Israel and – in the end – by Arab countries as well. These comments introduce the question of what impact enlargement would have on EU-US relations with respect to Southern areas.

The EU's southern approaches and EU-US relations: The impact of enlargement

Contrary to expectations, the end of the Cold War has brought about a trend towards the reinforcement of transatlantic relations. This reinforcement rests on two pillars: the enlargement of Nato to include Central and Eastern European countries, and the addition of an important crisis management mission to its traditional defence mission. It is also due to the fact that developments in Nato have been shadowed by analogous processes in the EU: the enlargement of the latter, initiated early in the 1990s, and its recent decision to start the CESDP with a view to creating a European capability for crisis management. These twin processes are independent from one another but strictly inter-related and deliberately harmonised.

A further development in transatlantic relations consists of the defence missions that were designated as out-of-Nato-area missions during the Cold War. The New Strategic Concept (NSC), approved at the 1999 Atlantic Council in Washington, lists a set of 'vital' allied interests which would give rise to common action if they were affected, such as disruptions in supplies or 'uncontrolled' movements of people. However, this extension of the notion of common defence is still somewhat controversial. Where and to what extent the NSC will apply remains to be seen. What matters here is that, while the development of a civilian and military capability to manage crises and conduct peace support operations is a unifying factor which could lead towards EU-Nato co-operation, the development of an out-of-area capability could progress as a Nato task but has little chance of becoming part of the twin processes that link Nato and the EU currently.

In this broad perspective, the EU will continue to develop its co-operative civilian, economic and peace roles internationally, acting independently in the civilian and economic fields, but playing its peace role in co-operation with Nato and the United States. There would be autonomous EU-led operations, but no doubt the latter would be undertaken on the basis of a more or less detailed understanding within the transatlantic circle. The logical implication of this pattern of transatlantic relations would be a division of labour between an EU civilian and economic role, directed in particular towards neighbouring regions of the East-South arc that flanks the EU, and a common or concerted Nato-EU peace role in the same areas. The development of some kind of common perspective on security co-operation would not be excluded from EU relations with the Mediterranean (the EMP) as well as with Russia, Ukraine or the Balkans, but an EU peace role in its Southern approaches and elsewhere would be politically and – in the event – operationally linked to the transatlantic circle.

Against this larger and stronger background of transatlantic relations, EU geopolitical priorities would tend to change and, from the security angle, EU regional policies would tend to incorporate a more important global component. As it is, post-Cold War developments have already brought about a common, reinforced EU-US interest towards areas in the European East whose strategic perspective has definitely overshadowed the Mediterranean and MENA areas. These latter areas, of course, still hold great importance, but there is no doubt that both EU and US efforts towards the East have become more important (and productive) than those towards the South. Even at a time of campaigns against terrorism in which the Middle East is a significant element, strategic risks and stakes continue to be more important in the East than in the South. Accordingly, Western endeavours at regional governance concern the East commensurately more than the South.

This scenario can be set alongside both strong and weak EU institutional developments, with variations reflecting which EU identities would tend to prevail. In any event, the outcome of EU enlargement, in parallel with Nato enlargement, would tend to favour the kind of transatlantic division of labour and security co-operation that already seems to be envisaged. Most new EU members have participated in the peacekeeping programmes of the Partnership for Peace and OSCE, so that they would integrate easily and willingly with the emerging EU and Nato transatlantic co-operation in international crisis management. Transatlantic co-operation would indeed be very important for them because Nato Article 5 defence missions are perceived as crucial to their national security. For the same reason, they would be opposed or reluctant to develop a EU defence and military capability decoupled from Nato and the Atlantic Alliance. Because of their national security perspective, the new members would hardly conceive of an EU in competition, let alone in dispute, with the United States, and even less would they conceive of such important contradictions arising between their memberships of the EU and of Nato.

Besides favouring security co-operation within the transatlantic circle, enlargement would also support the idea of a Nato-EU or transatlantic division of labour with respect to the countries South of the EU, i.e. the concept of the EU's Southern policy focusing on civilian and economic tasks. This is not to say that some kind of EU security role towards these and other areas would be opposed; but it is to say that the new members would oppose an EU security role decoupled from Nato and are thus likely to prefer the idea of concentrating EU Southern policies in fields other than security. The fact that this would contribute to limiting resource transfers to the South is nevertheless in line with the general downsizing of the South vis-à-vis the East in the West's overall strategic and policy framework.

These attitudes would bring the new members close to the group of neutrals who, for different reasons, are also interested in upholding a clear distinction between crisis management and defence, between the EU and Nato. The new members would also side with those willing to develop Europe as a factor in supporting national power. Overall, they would contribute to encouraging the strengthening of transatlantic relations in the framework of looser EU political integration and the performance of global roles by the EU in the framework of a looser European identity.

In conclusion, enlargement will bring to the EU trends and countries that do not prefer an increase in the priority of the Mediterranean and MENA areas in relation to other EU geopolitical realities – rather the contrary. Furthermore, to the extent that enlargement may result in an institutionally weakened EU, the political and security presence of the EU in the Southern areas, already put in question by other regional and extra-regional actors, is likely to become more difficult to sustain than it is today. There would therefore be a EU tendency to emphasise its civilian and economic roles towards its Southern approaches. This is not to say that the EU's political and security role would disappear in these areas. They would be developed, however, in the framework of the emerging Nato-EU and US-EU co-operation in crisis management. The EU would play a role, but one shared with Atlantic allies and played out in a global rather than a regional setting. By including a number of new countries that, more often than not, are very close to Atlantic and American interests and also involved in Nato enlargement, EU enlargement would consolidate the EU tendency to exercise its security role within the transatlantic circle. As a result, the Mediterranean policy of the enlarged EU, though less important than other external policies, would on the one hand project specific civil and economic responsibilities and on the other share security tasks with the United States. This result would not be in tune with reinforced European independence, but would be consonant with its ability to play global roles. It would also be very much in tune with US perspectives and would therefore contribute to reinforcing transatlantic relations.

Recommendations

In relation to the regions South of the EU, enlargement will tend to render transatlantic relations more convergent, bringing EU objectives and policies closer to, and making them more consistent with those of the United States. Policy responses to this evolution by EU governments and the Commission may range all the way from opposition to acceptance. However, most of the new and existing EU members will tend to accept. The Commission cannot be expected to act as the lone champion of a federalist course of action; but it will fundamentally remain the custodian of an independent identity for the Union. Rather than either accepting or opposing EU convergence towards the US, what the Commission can be expected to do is to pursue a policy of containing and fine-tuning such convergence with a view to strengthening the Union and preserving its identity and independence. This strategy would attempt to ensure both the EU's autonomy and an efficient transatlantic relationship. Led by the Commission, it would no doubt have some influence on overall EU policy and have the support of several member states.

If the Commission and the EU were willing and able to retain this stance with respect to the EU's Southern approaches, the following recommendations would be appropriate:

- the EU framework for conducting relations with the Mediterranean and MENA states should be retained and strengthened, even if its diminishing importance for EU members may call for some restructuring and downsizing;

- for it to be strengthened, the EMP should become more comprehensive, so as to include Libya, Iraq and Iran. It should also become more flexible, so as to incorporate workable sub-regional articulations. The free trade area envisaged under the Barcelona Declaration should be enlarged. At the same time, the EU should select sub-regions, like the Maghreb, the Middle East or the Gulf, so that instruments, timing and sequences can be adapted to sub-regional differences and aspirations;

- the EU should develop this enlarged regional and sub-regional structure by reinforcing its civilian and economic role and fostering North-South co-operation in these fields. This is the form in which co-operation is welcomed and requested by the EU's Southern regional partners, as well as by most existing and new members of the Union and the United States;

- the expansion of community as distinct from governmental roles in the third pillar of the Union is an essential prerequisite for reinforcing the EU's civilian role. In particular, the key to a successful EU Southern policy is an effective immigration policy. But this will depend on the EU's will and ability to harmonise national immigration policies and establish the required body of community policies to deal with immigration as a single entity;

- a greater capacity of the Commission to deliver its resources with enhanced planning and more rapid intervention is another essential factor in attaining the performance expected from the Union by Southern areas and improving its partners' perceptions of its role;

- improved co-ordination between the Commission and the Council will be crucial. In the transatlantic as well as the enlargement perspective, this appears particularly important when it comes to the institutional development of the CESDP. EU-led crisis management operations will not necessarily concern the Southern regions; they will in any event be part of a complex transatlantic decision-making and intervention process. Yet they could affect the Southern regions as well and be decided and implemented by the EU as such. With its relationship with Nato, the Union has the advantage of being able to deploy both civilian/economic and military instruments. Thus the Union must be organisationally and institutionally prepared either to carry out complex and well co-ordinated interventions, or to play a specific and important role in combined operations by providing civilian and economic inputs. The strengthening and effectiveness of the EU's organisational structure remains a crucial task, even within the looser constitutional framework that enlargement may be expected to bring about;

• while the non-duplication rule tends to exclude the EU from managing even elementary forms of security co-operation such as training and information, the development of an EU military command structure with its headquarters staff and the remnants of WEU (the Torrejón satellite centre and the Institute for Security Studies) will create more opportunities for enlarging EU-Nato combined capabilities. These opportunities must be taken by the EU and expanded, for they could be the concrete basis for developing a European Security and Defence Identity as distinct from the transatlantic identity. For example, Southern liaison officers could be integrated into the staff of Euromarfor, something which Nato cannot do. These policies would also pave the way for the EU to manage some confidence-building measures. In turn, this could permit co-ordination between the Commission and the Council or member governments and give it a role in using military instruments for civilian purposes, or combining civilian and military instruments for such purposes;

• despite perceptions to the contrary, the EU has played an essential political role in the MENA regions, in particular in the Middle East peace process, both by supporting US policy and by making up for its deficiencies and correcting its unilateralism. At the same time, certain differences between the EU and the US have served to prevent the Arabs from feeling isolated and contributed to consolidating allied governments. The EU's distinctiveness and role in the MENA region represents a largely underestimated transatlantic asset. It may, however, become submerged by the convergence of the EU with the US, which will be nurtured by trends towards enlargement and re-nationalisation. One example of the negative perceptions which EU-US convergence may create in the MENA region is the EU-Nato combined effort for crisis management. This is perceived as a very negative development by Arab countries. The EU and the Commission should try uphold their identity in relation to Nato and the US, in particular by establishing and reinforcing a EU political dialogue with the regions concerned, and by developing at least a minimal security co-operation distinct from that with Nato.

The EU as a Global Actor: Concepts and Realities

Wolfgang Wessels

Jean Monnet Professor, Forschungsinstitut für
Politische Wissenschaft und Europäische Fragen
Chairperson of TEPSA

In consolidating the European Union as the anchor for Europe, the enlargement process will be of crucial importance both for the present EU and for the applicant countries. What is at stake is more than formal membership in another organisation. It is a marriage affecting the lives of all those involved: economically by creating a large free trade area and a market to increase Europe's international competitiveness; politically and in the security field, by ensuring greater stability and preventing new conflicts; and culturally, by reuniting the continent.

But enlargement will affect not only the present and future members; it will also bring about a new Europe with a role to play on the international scene. After enlargement, the Union will have a diversity of new neighbours, each with specific problems, with whom appropriate relationships will have to be built. The Union will also be called upon to assist in dealing with regional problems beyond its direct neighbourhood: the Middle East Peace Process, ethnic wars and poverty in Africa, and many others. In addition, there are the latest global challenges: international terrorism and crime, drug trafficking, mass migration, the environment, nuclear safety, transmittable diseases.

The aim of this chapter is to analyse whether the future enlarged Union will be better equipped to be a global actor.

The EU and the international system: Concepts and realities

Assumptions: The EU as a global actor

The European Union is the product of the new world order, as well as being an actor within it. The global upheavals since 1989 have exercised their effects also on the Europe of the European Community. The Treaty of Maastricht, negotiated in 1990/91, was in its inception and central characteristics significantly shaped by the changing constellations within the international and European system. In this treaty the EU partly confirmed and partly reformulated its goals, instruments and procedures for acting in the international arena. In the Amsterdam revision,[150] effective since 1999, the member states as 'Masters of the Treaty'[151] consolidated their experience during the crises of the nineties into the regulations of the Common Foreign and Security Policy, the so-called second pillar of the treaty.[152]

The claim that the EU is a global actor is more controversial. Even the connection of the European Union with the term 'global player' causes doubts about both the appropriateness and the desirability of the concept. However, more than it ever did in its earlier existence, the European Union of the nineties has expressed in word and deed its desire to shape Europe's regional environment and influence the global political system. This interest in building or guaranteeing a specific order beyond its own borders is enduring: additional articles to the EU treaty have given the principles of democracy and rule of law a constitutional dimension. Even after the adoption of the general provisions of the treaty, the EU's search for a meaningful role for itself has continued – see for example the relevant decisions of the Cologne Council with regard to the development of a common defence policy.[153] The

---

[150] Treaty on the European Union at http//:www.europa.eu.int/eur-lex/en/treaties/dat/eu_cons_treaty/en.pdf.

[151] Judgement of the Federal Constitutional Court from 1993 about the constitutional appeal against the Treaty of Maastricht (1993), Judgement of October 12 1993, in: Andrew Oppenheimer (ed.), The Relationship between European Community Law and National Law: The Cases, Cambridge.

[152] Elfriede Regelsberger/ Mathias Jopp, Gemeinsame Außen- und Sicherheitspolitik', in: integration 4/1997, p.255-263; Elfriede Regelsberger/ Mathias Jopp, ,Die Stärkung der Handlungsfähigkeit in der Gemeinsamen Außen - und Sicherheitspolitik', in: Mathias Jopp/ Andreas Maurer/ Otto Schmuck (ed.), Die Europäische Union nach Amsterdam. Analysen und Stellungnahmen zum neuen EU-Vertrag, Bonn 1998, p.155-170.

[153] The European Council: Presidency Conclusions at http://www.europa.eu.int/council/off/conclu/june99/june99_en.htm.

engagement in Kosovo also demonstrated a specific formula to deal with challenges in its near neighbourhood.

Despite numerous and varied initiatives in this direction, there remain some fundamental questions. While the EU is understood as a 'power with a mission,' its role in the international system is far from well defined.[154]

Theses: Six role attributions

The confusion regarding Europe's role is reflected in the variety of divergent and even contradictory models and views.[155] If the term 'global actor' is understood to refer to a state that is endowed with the traditional attributes of a large power or even a superpower,[156] then the EU should be excluded from being counted as such within the new world order. If the rhetorical question is asked how many tanks and nuclear weapons are available to the EU, then the EU is a 'zero power:' the ability and willingness of its member states to integrate the existing potential into a hierarchically structured decision-making system is still subject to doubt.

Apart from Europe's irrelevance to the international political system by these measurements, there are also other objections. For neo-realists[157] and politicians like de Gaulle and Thatcher, who understand the nation state as the only legitimate actor in the international system capable of action, a supranational (West) European power with pretensions to autonomy simply does not exist and should not be allowed to arise. In this perspective, attempts

---

[154] Curt Gasteyger, An Ambiguous Power. The European Union in a Changing World, Gütersloh 1996, p.138.

[155] Heinrich Schneider, ‚Ein Wandel europapolitischer Grundverständnisse? Grundsatzüberlegungen, Erklärungsansätze und Konsequenzen für die politische Bildungsarbeit‛, in: Mathias Jopp/Andreas Maurer/Heinrich Schneider (ed.), Europapolitische Grundverständnisse im Wandel. Analysen und Konsequenzen für die politische Bildung, Bonn 1998, p.19-147.

[156] Bull, H. *The Anarchical Society, A Study of Order in World Politics*, London, 1977; Schwarz, S. H. 'Der Faktor Macht im heutigen Staatensystem', in: ibid., p.61-72; Christian Hacke, Weltmacht wider Willen, *Die Außenpolitik der Bundesrepublik Deutschland*, Stuttgart 1988; Werner Link, Die Neuordnung der Weltpolitik. Grundprobleme globaler Politik an der Schwelle zum 21. Jahrhundert, München 1998.

[157] Rittberger, V. Internationale Organisationen, Politik und Geschichte, Opladen 1994, p. 75f; Reinhard Meyers, Begriff und Probleme des Friedens, Opladen 1994, p.124-136.

to develop a supranational power are doomed to failure and considered detrimental to rational policy-making based on the pursuit of national interests.[158] Since the end of the Cold War, with German reunification and the lack of an external threat, re-nationalisation of the 'vital interests' of the larger EU members is expected to become more pronounced, even to the extent of implying that Germany might acquire nuclear weapons.[159] Europe is important only insofar as 'national power' remains protected. The Maastricht Treaty, which in its second pillar of a Common Foreign and Security Policy provides for the 'establishment of a common defence policy' (Art. B, Art. J4 TEU in the version of Maastricht) must then be viewed as an outdated reflex to a past condition. The conditions of the 'new world order' encourage the renaissance of the nation state in contrast to former ambiguous European rhetoric. The provisions of the Amsterdam Treaty (Art. 2 and Art. 14 EU), which introduced only limited change, have also to be seen in this light.

From the perspective of leftist peace studies, the concept of the EU as a global power raises concerns of a conflict-prone hegemony. In this view the EU is becoming a 'capitalist superpower,'[160] a bureaucratic monster that closes itself off from neighbours and developing countries as a 'fortress Europe' and attempts to dominate them through a deliberate policy of 'divide et impera.' The provisions of the EU Treaty on development policy, for example Art. 177-181 EU, are interpreted as strengthening Europe's neo-colonial dominance. Similar abuses of power are cited in the thesis of the 'trading power.'[161]

This mistrust and disapproval of the EU from quite diverse backgrounds stands in stark contrast to several schools of thought that stress the positive role of the European Union. In an analysis of the international system based on

---

[158] Major, J. 'Raise Your Eyes, There is a Land Beyond,' in: *The Economist*, 25 September 1993.

[159] Mearsheimer, J. J. 'Back to the Future. Instability in Europe After Cold War,' in: *International Security*, 1/1990, p.5-56.

[160] Galtung, J. *Kapitalistische Großmacht Europa oder die Gemeinschaft der Konzerne?*, Reinbek 1973.

[161] Rosecrance, R. N. 1986, *The rise of the trading state. Commerce and conquest in the modern world*, New York .

realism, the thesis of a 'global power'[162] concludes that the European states will be able to play a role in the global competition of great and superpowers only if they act in common. From this perspective the end of the East-West conflict and 'protection' by the US has only increased the necessity to strengthen common European efforts to play a role in the international system. Following neo-realist notions of 'balance of power,' the EU would constitute an agent of 'co-operative balancing,'[163] that is a counterweight to the US as the only superpower. From similar assumptions, different conclusions are reached: the national power thesis and the global power thesis, reflecting, with some slight exaggeration, the differences between British and French key strategies concerning the EU.[164]

The global power thesis leaves open two questions: whether the decision making centre of the EU should be effectively and legitimately organised in a federal or in an intergovernmental manner, and within which circle of European states such a function should be located. Discussion is centred on either a European Union with more than twenty member states or a 'core Europe' with three to seven states willing and capable of concerted international action.[165]

The 'civilian power thesis'[166] links the subject of Europe as a global power with a strategy according to which the EU would contribute to the

---

[162] See among others Kennedy, P. *1990 The rise and fall of the great powers. Economic change and military conflict from 1500 to 2000*, London; Kennedy, P. *1993, Preparing for the twenty-first century*, New York; Kissinger, H. 1995, *Diplomacy*, New York.

[163] Link, W. 'Die europäische Neuordnung und das Machtgleichgewicht,' in: Thomas Jäger/ Melanie Piepenschneider (ed.), Europa 2020. Szenarien politischer Entwicklung, Opladen 1997, p.9-32; Werner Link, Die Neuordnung der Weltpolitik. Grundprobleme globaler Politik an der Schwelle zum 21. Jahrhundert, München 1998.

[164] Wessels, W. 'Zentralmacht, Zivilmacht, Ohnmacht? Zur deutschen Außen- und Europapolitik nach 1989,' in: Weilemann, P. R., Küsters, J. K., Buchstab, G. (eds.), Macht und Zeitkritik. Festschrift für Hans-Peter Schwarz zum 65. Geburtstag, Paderborn u.a. 1999, p.389-406, hier: p.394-397.

[165] Schäuble/Lamers-Papier: CDU/CSU-Fraktion des Deutschen Bundestages, Überlegungen zur europäischen Politik, Bonn, 1.9.1994; Äußerungen Edouard Balladurs in: Le Monde, 30. 11.1994; Gisela Müller-Brandeck-Bocquet, 'Flexible Integration – Eine Chance für die europäische Umweltpolitik,' in: integration 4/1997, p.292-305; Wessels, W. 'Der Amsterdamer Vertrag – Durch Stückwerksreformen zu einer effizienteren, erweiterten und föderalen Union?,' in: integration 3/1997, p.117-135.

[166] Still a classic François Duchêne, 'Die Rolle Europas im Weltsystem: Von der regionalen zur planetarischen Interdependenz,' in: Max Kohnstamm/ Wolfgang Hager (ed.), Zivilmacht Europa-Supermacht oder Partner?, Frankfurt a. M. 1973, p.19-26; for the term also Hanns W. Maull, 'Zivilmacht Bundesrepublik Deutschland. Vierzehn Thesen für eine neue deutsche Außenpolitik,' in: Europa-Archiv, Bd. 10, 1992, p.269-278.

establishment of universal values and the avoidance of conflicts by non-military means of a socio-economic nature and through regulation and law-making.[167] The incomplete status of the EU from the perspective of the global power thesis is therefore not a weakness but a positive precondition for a different kind of international politics. The European Union as a peaceful community of former arch enemies is the model and factor for a new regional and global order. Its *mission civilatrice*[168] is superior to the confrontational behaviour of traditional great powers.

It is unclear how this school of thought views the potential role of the EU in military conflicts. The end of superpower bipolarity also implies that the EU has to be more finely attuned to the local conflicts in its immediate neighbourhood. In the face of this necessity the notion of a 'civil power' is complemented and elaborated by the thesis of the 'peace power Europe.'[169] According to this thesis the European Union – in conjunction with the US as 'partner in leadership' – is supposed to defend the international order established by the global community and the OSCE Europe through sanctions of an initially diplomatic and economic nature, but if necessary also with military means. The EU might be the 'deputy sheriff' of the US as 'global policeman,' acting solely, however, on the basis of authorisation by the relevant and legitimate international organisations.

Definitions of actorness

The variety of contributions to the debate shows that the political as well as the theoretical significance of the initial assumptions and theses needs to be elaborated. For this purpose the term of an 'international actor' will be defined as a political unit which –

---

[167] For the definition of Civilian Power see also Kirste, K., Maull, H. W. 'Zivilmacht und Rollentheorie,' in: *Zeitschrift für Internationale Beziehungen*, 2/1996, S 283-312, here: pp.303-305.

[168] Maull, H. W. 'Europa als Weltmacht? Perspektiven für die gemeinsame Außen - und Sicherheitspolitik,' in: Jäger, T., Piepenschneider, M. (ed.), Europa 2020. Szenarien politischer Entwicklung, Opladen 1997, p.81-95, p.94.

[169] Kirste, K., Maull, H. W. 'Zivilmacht und Rollentheorie,' in: *Zeitschrift für Internationale Beziehungen*, 2/1996, p.283-312, here: p.289.

- develops goals for a normative order of the regional and international system and defines its own role and identity in the international system;[170]

- disposes over the necessary instruments and resources to implement its policy internationally; and

- employs these on the basis of efficient and legitimate procedures.

The capability of the EU to act as an international actor is thus dependent on the clarity of its goals and the subjective and objective conditions of their implementation.

Reality: Observations from the nineties

The Treaty on European Union: Provisions for an international actor

The principal concepts of Europe[171] which dominated the debate on the European integration process after World War II – apart from their immediate objectives – were steeped in a democratic ideal creating the preconditions for a peaceful community. The European Coal and Steel Community (1952) and the European Economic Community (1958) were designed not solely to deal with a range of common functional problems but through these measures to create a peaceful union of democratic states. This basic understanding has become constitutionally anchored in the Amsterdam Treaty: 'the Union is founded on the principles of liberty, democracy, respect for human rights and fundamental freedoms, and the rule of law, principles which are common to the Member States.' (Art. 6 TEU). Procedures for the implementation of these principles within the Union were established for the first time (Art. 7 TEU).

The effect of this original concept of integration on the regional and international role of the EU is evident: the EU embraces a certain set of values, which are – even if not always consistently – the basis of its international role.

---

[170] Wessels, W. 'The EC and the New European Architecture, The European Union as Trustee for a (Pan-) European Weal,' in: Telò, M. (ed.), *Vers une Nouvelle Europe? Towards a New Europe,* Brüssel 1992, p.35-48,p.41ff.; Schneider, H. 'Vom KSZE-Prozeß zum gesamteuropäischen Kooperationssystem: Die europäische Architektur und ihr Architekturdilemma,' in: *Integration,* 4/1990, p.150-164.

[171] Schneider, H. 'Ein Wandel europapolitischer Grundverständnisse? Grundsatzüberlegungen, Erklärungsansätze und Konsequenzen für die politische Bildungsarbeit,' in: Jopp, M., Maurer, A., Schneider, H. (ed.), *Europapolitische Grundverständnisse im Wandel,* Bonn 1998, p.19-148; Jachtenfuchs, M. Ideen und Interessen: *Weltbilder als Kategorien der politischen Analyse,* Mannheim 1993; Jachtenfuchs, M. 'Ideen und internationale Beziehungen,' in: *Zeitschrift für Internationale Beziehungen,* 2/1995, p.417ff.

Accordingly, the member states of the CFSP aim to use the EU not only 'to safeguard the common values' but also 'to develop and consolidate democracy and the rule of law, and respect for human rights and fundamental freedoms' (Art. 11 (1) TEU).

These norms are of special importance within a regional strategy towards the European neighbourhood as formulated in the accession criteria of Copenhagen, 'membership requires that the candidate country has achieved stability of institutions guaranteeing democracy, the rule of law, human rights, and respect for and protection of minorities; furthermore the existence of a functioning market economy as well as the capacity to cope with competitive pressures and market forces within the Union.'[172]

When entering close contractual relations in the form of association agreements, the EU places high expectations on the democratic credentials of its treaty partners. The Europe agreements with the Central and East European Countries (CEE) require,

> 'Reaffirming their commitment to pluralist democracy based on the rule of law, human rights and fundamental freedoms, a multiparty system involving free and democratic elections, to the principles of a market economy and to social justice....'[173]

Equally, in so-called third generation co-operation agreements with states in other continents, human rights provisions have become a part of the EU's treaty doctrine. From these texts it becomes clear that the concept of an international order is not limited to a political and constitutional dimension but extends to 'good governance' in a wider sense.

The concept of creating an international order also bears on several articles of the EC Treaty (the first Pillar). Thus the common trade policy includes among other objectives, 'the harmonious development of world trade, the progressive abolition of restrictions on international trade and the lowering

---

[172] http//:www.europa.eu.int/comm/dg1/enlarge/agenda2000_en/strong/21.htm.

[173] Europe-Agreement with Hungary, Preamble, at: http://www.europa.eu.int/eurlex/en/lif/dat/1993/en_293A1231_13.html.

of customs barriers' (Art. 131 TEC); whilst in its co-operation and development policy the Community supports, 'the sustainable economic and social development of the developing countries, the smooth and gradual integration of the developing countries into the world economy' and a 'campaign against poverty' within those countries (Art. 177 (1) TEC). The EU contributes to the 'general objective of developing and consolidating democracy and the rule of law, and to that of respecting human rights and fundamental freedoms' (Art. 177 (2) TEC). In addition, the EC intends to promote certain measures internationally, for example in its environmental policy (Art. 174 (2) TEC), and to demonstrate its willingness to co-operate with other states and international organisations, as in its policy on research and development (Art. 164 TEC).

Significant effects on the role of the EU in the international system derive also from co-operation in the areas of Justice and Home Affairs which, according to the Amsterdam Treaty, are regulated partly by the provisions of the Treaty on European Union (Title IV Art. 61 – 69 TEC) and partly by the provisions of the Third Pillar on police and judicial co-operation. The EU treaty also roundly declares in Art. 2 TEU the intention 'to assert its identity on the international scene.' These and other formulations demonstrate an explicit understanding by member states of the Union's claim to an autonomous role in the realisation of its objectives in the international realm, though without replacing the international role of its members.

The catalogue of the Treaty on European Union thus contains provisions that include large areas where the EU itself aims to be an actor in international politics. On the basis of two constitutional changes in the EU, the member states as architects of the treaty have repeatedly voiced their intention of pursuing these goals and provided the procedures and resources to implement them.

Instruments and resources: The EU's effectiveness

The EU has developed a range of instruments for its international actor role which exhibit a great variety of judicial, economic and diplomatic means.[174]

---

[174] Lippert, B. 'Politik gegenüber Mittel- und Osteuropa sowie den GUS-Staaten,' in: Weidenfeld, W., Wessels, W. (ed.), *Jahrbuch der europäischen Integration* 1993/94, Bonn 1994, p.253-259; Monar, J. 'Außenwirtschaftsbeziehungen,' in: ibid., p.227-236; Regelsberger, E. 'Gemeinsame Außen- und Sicherheitspolitik,' in: ibid., p.237-246.

These activities can be systematically classified with the initials MEAD: Access to Markets, Euro-subventions, diplomatic Action and Dialogue.

With a global import percentage of over 18 per cent (excluding trade within the EU member states),[175] the European single market is the second largest market of the world. Employing a wide range of instruments, the EC regulates access to its market autonomously or to an ever larger extent in the framework of international treaties, especially through the World Trade Organisation. The arsenal of instruments includes common external customs duties, anti-dumping and anti-subsidy measures, import quotas for sensitive products such as textiles, and norms for goods and services, that can turn into non-tariff trade barriers.[176]

Strong tensions are especially evident in the EU's bilateral trade relations with the US, its largest trading partner. Disputes have ranged from the 'chicken war' in the sixties, TV quotas for Hollywood productions in the eighties, to bananas and hormone treated meat in the nineties. The effects of the EU's Common Agricultural Policy have been particularly controversial. In contrast to media-led exaggerations, however, the normality with which economic and trade relations function is widely underestimated.

Due to the EU's growing trade deficit with Japan, bilateral relations here are of increasing importance. Both sides still claim that the other upholds non-WTO-compatible trade barriers. The demand of third countries for fair, or if possible privileged, access to the internal market has prompted the EC to react with a large network of trade agreements. In the early nineties the European Economic Area was established together with the EFTA states. As three of the EFTA states subsequently joined the EU, it became of merely transitory significance. The EC has concluded special association treaties with the so-called Lomé states in Africa, the Caribbean and the Pacific region, with nearly all Mediterranean states ranging from Turkey to Morocco (with the exception of Libya) and, since 1989, with the Central and East European countries (CEEC).

---

[175] WTO statistics at www.wto.org/wto/statis/i0be.xls.

[176] Monar, J. 'Außenwirtschaftsbeziehungen,' in: Weidenfeld, W., Wessels, W. *Jahrbuch der Europäischen Integration* 1997/98, Bonn 1998, p.223-231.

These agreements comprise a reduction of tariffs – at least for industrial products – and controlled access for agricultural products. Free trade agreements are also planned with the Mediterranean states of the Barcelona process[177] and the Latin American MERCOSUR states.[178] Since the beginning of the sixties, trade preferences have substantially changed. Turkey for example has lost its former privileged status relative to other trading partners. Market access is often made dependent on the state of democracy, good governance and respect for human rights.[179] The current debate on social and environmental dumping shows the far-reaching dimensions of a global trade policy. An extensively used instrument of EU external relations is financial assistance.

In 1998, close on 6 billion euros (DM 12 billion) were approved for external policy areas.[180] That constitutes about 7 per cent of the total EU budget, while in comparison the German budget allocates about 3 per cent (DM 14 billion) in external assistance.[181] These resources were primarily distributed to countries in the immediate geographic vicinity. Initiatives for the promotion of democracy and respect for human rights also received special support.

Diplomatic action also forms a regularly employed instrument of the Union. Apart from declarations – regularly made for example by the European Council – the Amsterdam Treaty (Art. 12 TEU) provides for 'common strategies,' 'common positions' and 'joint actions.' Since the Maastricht Treaty came into effect in 1993, EU member states have reached 63 common positions and taken 74 joint actions in response to international developments.

Repeated formulations of EU concepts of order in the international system have become expressions of the guiding doctrines of European foreign

---

[177] Behrendt, S. 'Nahost und Mittelmeerpolitik,' in: Weidenfeld, W., Wessels, W. *Jahrbuch der Europäischen Integration* 1997/98, Bonn 1998, p.253.

[178] Diedrichs, U. 'Die Lateinamerikapolitik der Europäischen Union,' in: Weidenfeld, W., Wessels, W. *Jahrbuch der Europäischen Integration* 1998/99, Bonn 1999, p.289-294.

[179] Generalsekretariat des Rates der Europäischen Gemeinschaften, Neununddreissigster Überblick über die Tätigkeit des Rates (Bericht desGeneralsekretärs), 1. Januar – 31. Dezember 1991, Luxemburg 1993, p.149.

[180] Guth, E. 'Haushaltspolititk,' in: Weidenfeld, W., Wessels, W. *Jahrbuch der Europäischen Integration* 1997/98, Bonn 1998, p.155-162, p.160.

[181] Report of the German Ministry of Finance at: www.bundesfinanzministerium.de/finwiber/berichte/fpl2003.pdf.

Means Available for the EU's External Policy Activities

External Policy Areas	Total available means 1998 million ECU (Commitments)	per cent of budget for external policy areas
Food aid and supporting measures	579.038	9.71
Humanitarian aid	539.600	9.05
Co-operation with developing countries in Asia	396.150	6.64
Co-operation with developing countries in Latin America	274.500	4.60
Co-operation with developing countries in Southern Africa and South Africa	137.500	2.31
Co-operation with developing countries in the Mediterranean Region and the Near and Middle East	1142.00	19.15
Co-operation with the Central and Eastern European Countries	1126.340	18.89
Other supporting measures for the Central and Eastern European Countries and the newly independent states	83.115	1.39
European Bank for Reconstruction and Development	33.750	0.57
Co-operation with the former Yugoslavia	264.000	4.43
Co-operation with the newly independent states and Mongolia	465.250	7.80
Other co-operative measures	410.211	6.88
European Initiative for the promotion of democracy and the protection of human rights	92.400	1.55
International Fisheries agreements	292.700	4.91
External aspects of certain policies of the EC	88.130	1.48
Common Foreign and Security Policy	38.000	0.64
TOTAL	5962.684	100

Source: General Report on the Activities of the European Union 1998, Luxembourg 1999.

policy. The real impact of these declarations and actions on the specific situation, that is their effectiveness, needs to be examined case by case.

The EU is involved in peace processes such as in the Middle East, and to a large extent finances concrete projects; 'common actions' in support of democratic elections, e.g. in South Africa, are well established. The EU has also initiated 'stability pacts' to build peace and democracy in Central and Eastern Europe. A first 'common strategy' was adopted by the European Council in 1999 in order to shape the 'partnership with Russia.'[182] In international organisations, such as the General Assembly of the United Nations and the Organisation for Security and Co-operation in Europe,

---

[182] Common Strategy of the European Union for Russia from 4th June 1999, SN 150/ 99, Appendix II.

European Political Cooperation/Common Foreign and Security Policy

	1970	1972	1973	1986	1987	1990	1994	1997	1998	1999	2000	2001	Total
a) declarations	-	2	10	54	63	115	110	123	141	123	184	186	1111
b) common positions[1]	-		-	-		-	8	13	22	35	33	20	131
c) joint actions[2]	-		-	-		-	14	15	20	20	21	19	109
d) common strategies[3]	-		-	-		-	-	-	-	2	1	-	3
e) decisions[4]	-	-	-	-	-	-	-	-	-	-	5	6	11
f) conclusion of international agreements[5]	-	-	-	-	-	-	-	-	-	-	-	2	2
g) enhanced co-operation[6]	-											-	-

1 introduced in Maastricht (Art. 15 TEU A.V.)
2 introduced in Maastricht (Art. 14 TEU A.V.)
3 introduced in Maastricht (Art. 13 TEU A.V.)
4 on CFSP institutional aspects
5 according to Art. 24 TEU
6 introduced in Nice Treaty 2001 (Art. 27 a-3 TEU N.V.)

Source: Own calculations based upon the bulletins of the EC/EU and Annual Reports of the Activities of the EC/EU
Legislative acts according to http://ue.eu.int/pesc/

member states' diplomats aim to integrate national positions into a single voice, albeit with varying success.

A prolific variety of activities can be observed under the heading of 'dialogue.' In 1996 the EU had diplomatic relations with 187 third countries.[183] It has developed a particularly high degree of diplomatic innovation in the form of regular consultation with third countries or groups of countries (group-to-group dialogue).[184] The German Presidency of the Council in the first half of 1999 held 16 meetings with representatives of individual countries or foreign ministers of other regional groupings.[185] Such contacts encompass a wide range of levels. There is a fixed schedule of high-level presidential summits where the presidents of the European Council and

---

[183] Fallik, A. (ed.), *The European Public Affairs Directory*, Brüssel 1996, p.247ff.

[184] Edwards, J., Regelsberger, E. *Europe's Global Links. The European Community and Interregional Cooperation*, London 1990; Monar, J. 'Political Dialogue with Third Countries and Regional Political Groupings: The Fifteen as an Attractive Interlocutor,' in: Regelsberger, E., Schoutheete de Tervarent, P., Wessels, W. (ed.), *Foreign Policy of the European Union: From EPC to CFSP and Beyond*, London 1996, p.263-274.

[185] Agenda of the Presidencies of the Council of Ministers at: http://www.eu-praesidentschaft.de/01/frameset.htm.

the European Commission meet with heads of state such as the presidents of Russia or the US; and regular meetings of foreign ministers, as well as routine briefings of civil servants from like-minded states following European Council sessions. The ASEM summit with the states of South East Asia, and the Rio Summit comprising all the Latin American countries, were special events that underline the EU's claim to a global role, but whose concrete effects are difficult to grasp.

The network of global consultations of the EU is dense and diverse in form and direction. Increasingly some grave shortcomings have become apparent. The frequency of meetings exceeds the time available to EU heads of state and foreign ministers. The dialogue partners then compare the lofty declarations with the low level of participation, the short duration and the trivial speeches by EU representatives. These discrepancies are a striking demonstration of the 'capability-expectations gap.'[186]

A catalogue of EU activities using the MEAD formula shows up several gaps compared with those of traditional international actors. Some new instruments were added during the nineties, for example Art. 111 EC which regulates the external relations of the Economic and Monetary Union. An external cultural policy was initiated under the Maastricht Treaty (Art. 128 (3) TEC), but its significance is limited in comparison with national efforts.

Especially in the military field, the EU lacks the instruments of other global actors. However, the EU consciously sees many of the above activities as an integral part of the security policy of a civilian power. Traditional military instruments are not available to the EU, as the experience with former Yugoslavia has repeatedly underlined. As a result of this experience, the member states have formulated a 'common security policy' to allow the EU to formulate a coherent response. According to the Amsterdam Treaty (Art. 17 (1) TEU) Western European Union (WEU) 'is an integral part of the development of the Union.' Thus the long-term goal of progressively framing a common defence policy 'which might lead to a common defence' (Art. 17 (1) TEU) is

---

[186] Hill, C. 'The Capability Expectations Gap or Conceptualising Europe's International Role,' in: *Journal of Common Market Studies*, September 1993, p.305.

accommodated by using an existing institution which consisted of 10 of the 15 EU member states.

Under the Amsterdam Treaty, the EU also integrated the so-called 'Petersberg Tasks' into the CFSP; thus 'humanitarian and rescue tasks, peacekeeping tasks and tasks of combat forces in crisis management, including peacemaking' (Art. 17 (2) TEU) now form part of the EU's security policy. Experience with such territorial interventions has yet to be gained.

For its international role the Union has employed a wide variety of instruments, whose effectiveness needs to be examined specifically in respect of individual regions and policy areas. However, it is possible to formulate a general working hypothesis: the EU is most effective where the partner states are dependent on its aid and assistance; and it can exercise a particularly strong influence over those European states wishing to join the Union.

Institutions and procedures: The EU's efficiency and legitimacy

Apart from the EU's effectiveness, the efficiency and legitimacy of its procedures need also to be discussed. Under the EU Treaty – and especially its almost completely reworded and supplemented Amsterdam version – member states have at their disposal a diversity of institutions and a complex range of procedures for their common activities.

The EU Treaty seeks to establish the coherence of the EU's activities, which are based on different treaty foundations. The EU intends to ensure within 'a single institutional framework,' 'the consistency of its external activities as a whole in the context of its external relations, security, economic and development policies.' (Art. 3 TEU). In the institutional hierarchy, 'the European Council shall provide the Union with the necessary impetus' (Art. 4 TEU) and 'shall define the principles of and general guidelines for the common foreign and security policy, including for matters with defence implications' (Art. 13 (1) TEU). According to the Amsterdam Treaty this body is also to decide on the 'Common Strategies' (Art. 13 (2) TEU). Since the inception of the European Council in the seventies, the heads of state and government have regularly made declarations on international events –

frequently based on proposals of the foreign ministers – and have thus significantly shaped European positions and doctrines.

There are grave institutional and procedural differences between the different pillars of the Treaty on European Union, some of which were already present in the EC Treaty. Under the EC Treaty the Council could only decide to act on the basis of a Commission proposal. The Commission now also leads negotiations with non-member countries based on directives mandated by the Council and supported by special committees of high national officials (Art. 300 (1) TEU). This committee (Art. 133 TEU trade policy) has also been called the 'mother-in-law committee' due to its control function. The Council can generally decide with qualified majority on trade issues but, due to the political implications, rarely does so.

The European Parliament (EP) plays a special role. While its opinion is not necessary for conventional trade agreements under Art. 133 TEC, association agreements according to Art. 310 TEC require EP approval. Without a relative majority of Members of Parliament, this kind of treaty cannot therefore enter into force. In some instances during the nineties the EP gave its approval only after further negotiation. The EP's role is even more significant in relation to accession agreements, where an absolute majority is required (Art. 49 TEU). The European Court of Justice has also influenced agreements with non-member states through its interpretations under Art. 300 (6) TEU. In contrast to the EC Treaty which is based on a combination of supranational elements and comprehensive participation of national governments and administrations, the procedures of the CFSP are intergovernmental. This difference is particularly evident in the absence of jurisdiction of the European Court of Justice (ECJ), which can only check the appropriateness of procedures in terms of the EC Treaty (Art. 46 TEU). The half-yearly rotating presidency, which is endowed with the principal functions of internal procedures and external representation (Art. 18 TEU), is characteristic of this form of co-operation. After the negative experiences of the crises in former Yugoslavia, the presidency is now supported by a High Representative of the Common Foreign and Security Policy (Art. 18 (3) and Art. 26 TEU), who in turn is aided by the policy planning and early warning unit (Declaration (6) TEU).

Majority voting in the CFSP is possible only after a unanimous decision on a Common Strategy and the implementation of a Joint Action or Common Position. Each member state furthermore has the right to veto such a decision, which often leads to a long and complicated process based on a modified version of the 'Luxembourg compromise' (Art. 23 (2) TEU). The European Parliament 'shall be kept regularly informed [and] may ask questions of the Council or make recommendations' (Art. 21 TEU). The Commission 'shall be fully associated with the work carried out in the common foreign and security policy field' (Art. 27 TEU). The actual scope for EP influence is small, despite repeated efforts and some partial successes; but diplomats usually decline to be questioned, using the need for confidentiality and speed as a cover. The role of the Commission is also limited. On the administrative level, the political committee, consisting of the political directors of national foreign ministries, advises the Council of Ministers; but the Committee of Permanent Representatives also has a preparatory role, whilst a special department of the Council secretariat deals with administration.

After long years of experience with co-operation, diplomats of the EU member states have developed useful practices to arrive at common positions in different arenas. But throughout many attempts at crisis management, the EU's single voice has remained indistinct and the single hand weak: Europe still has no spokesman and no phone number.

Of particular difficulty are the procedures for those agreements which, as 'mixed treaties,' concern both pillars of the EU treaty. Most of the important treaties with third states – such as the Europe agreements with the CEE countries – encompass both rules within the exclusive jurisdiction of the EC, and rules of the Second Pillar, and possibly regulations, within national competencies. These constellations lead to such a complex division of procedures between Council Presidency and Commission that the EU's international partners are easily confused. The procedural fusion[187] of national and Community instruments is not accidental, but it clearly testifies to the

---

[187] Wessels, W. 'Staat und (westeuropäische) Integration. Die Fusionsthese,' in: Kreile, M. (ed.), *Die Integration Europas*, PVS-Sonderheft 23, Opladen 1992, p.36-61., Wessels, W. 'An Ever Closer Fusion? A Dynamic Macropolitical View on Integration Processes,' in: *Journal of Common Market Studies*, Vol.35, 2 June 1997, p.267-299.

struggle between two different strategies for a Common European Foreign and Security Policy. Controversy over the legitimacy of the European Union as an international actor is still one of the main limitations on its ability to make a contribution on the international stage.

Conclusion – The EU as a regional or global actor?

Testing the theses

The image of the European Union as an international actor that developed from its contribution to the new world order of the nineties is ambiguous and open to several interpretations. The EU's objectives have been repeatedly formulated and reflect quite clearly its intention to be a forceful actor in its own neighbourhood and in the international system. The effectiveness of its instruments, however, varies substantially. In some sectors of traditional trade policy the EU has become a 'global power' that articulates certain principles and interests strongly and comprehensively. Especially in negotiations within the GATT and the WTO, and in the UN environmental conferences, the EU has stood out as a 'global player.' In the area of traditional diplomacy, the EU has become a 'global talker' capable of dealing with international problems only through declarations and dialogue.

At the same time, EU member states continue to act individually and autonomously – in line with the power of the resurrected nation state – alongside and in addition to common or community activities. The contact groups for the Balkan crises marked a significant trend towards a *directoire* of larger states.[188] An assessment of the power of the European Union also remains ambiguous. Violations against the norms of the international system have been punished with sanctions of varying degree – for example Argentina during the Falkland conflicts and Iraq after its invasion of Kuwait. Diplomatic and economic measures were also taken in order to coerce states – such as South Africa, Poland, Romania, Slovakia and now Zimbabwe – to maintain the proclaimed norms of the international order in their internal affairs.

---

[188] Wessels, W., Jantz, B. 'Flexibilisierung: Die Europäische Union vor einer neuen Grundsatzdebatte? Grundmodelle unter der Lupe,' in: Hrbek, R. (ed.), *Die Reform der Europäischen Union*, Baden-Baden, 1997.

Military crises – such as the armed conflicts in the former Yugoslavia – can, however, be influenced only to a limited degree by economic and diplomatic measures.

To neighbouring countries which are dependent on the EU or have great expectations of future membership, the EU might appear as a 'capitalist great power' that is concerned only with its own short term sectoral interests and, in contrast to its proclaimed ideals of free trade, protects its own sensitive trade from competition. Part of this impression of a regional hegemony is due to the fact that the complex procedures of the EU are difficult to influence from outside. The EU might easily evoke the image of an economic dinosaur suffering from the weight of its own structure. Other partners in the international system, such as the Asian states, might perceive the proclaimed ideas of order as empty self-serving rhetoric which cannot be put into practice in the global context for lack of suitable instruments. The image comes to mind of an ageing paper tiger with an imperial heritage, who still thinks in terms of global power without being able to act according to its own high expectations. This would then validate the 'zero power thesis.'

Other European and non-European assessments view the EU's efforts more positively, at least its ability to implement its ideas of international order in its own region and to ensure the internal democratisation of the partner states. The membership conditions demanded by the EU have a permanent effect on the internal structures of the European accession candidates. These effects could be clearly observed with the Iberian states in the seventies and the CEE countries in the nineties.

The added value of community and common activities is high when compared with the alternative of a sovereign foreign and commercial policy practised by each member state. A trend towards 'civilian power' can thus be discerned, while efforts towards an efficient and effective 'peace power' have remained underdeveloped. This approach has been strengthened with the integration of the Petersberg Tasks into the Amsterdam treaty and pursued more intensively since Kosovo.

Gradual decline or Renaissance?

Different scenarios for the future shape of the EU's international role may be expected or desired. The corridor for constitutional changes in the union treaties is narrow. Based on the experiences of the Maastricht treaty and the limited revisions of Amsterdam, no fundamental reforms leading to a more efficient, effective and legitimate foreign and security policy are to be expected. Thus, despite well-meaning intentions and efforts, a qualitative change towards a 'global power' role or a regional 'peace power' seems unlikely.

Nevertheless, a European contribution towards the establishment and stabilising of regional and global order will still be demanded by many actors within Europe and outside. The inclusion of some CEE countries will not block all further initiatives. Developments towards a 'civilian' and perhaps also a 'peace power' could well be supported by these states. CEE countries' expectations from accession encompass not least the hope of a more powerful regional role for the EU. Further enlargement and deepening of the common foreign and security policy is also demanded by member states from within, so as to shape a peaceful order in two particularly unstable neighbouring areas. Most EU states attach a vital importance to constructive relations with Russia, including the entire security structure of Eastern Europe, and a policy promoting peace and security in the non-European Mediterranean states.

EU expectations of participating in the global concert of great powers will remain. That claim could, however, lead to a self-serving complacency which, rather than leading to a renaissance of Europe's international role, may subsist for a while on the fading glory of its historical role and its decline as a global power.

The resources available to the EU are becoming increasingly less effective in the international system while its internal inefficiencies serve to weaken its credibility. Neither the fixation of some member states on their historical power roles, nor fears of a neo-colonial hegemony can be realistic. Equally, with such a diminution of power resources, hopes of a role as a global or civilian power can become utopian. The controversial debate on the different concepts of Europe's role in the international system would then quickly lose relevance. However, implementation of those parts of the Amsterdam Treaty dealing with foreign and security policy, as well as the decisions of the 1999 Cologne European Council, could still become the real test of the EU's ability to assume a power role within the international system.

Scenarios for the Future

Hans Labohm
Senior Visiting Fellow

Alfred Van Staden
Director
Clingendael
(Netherlands Institute for International Relations)
The Hague

There are several reasons why enlargement of the European Union with the countries of Central and Eastern Europe (and Malta and Cyprus) holds the potential for a positive impact on future relations between Europe and the United States.

First, successive US administrations have very much favoured EU enlargement. The overall objective of European governments to overcome old dividing lines coincides with the official American goal of building 'a Europe whole and free' announced immediately after the collapse of Soviet rule in Central and Eastern Europe. EU enlargement is also a main component of American ideas on burden sharing between the two sides of the Atlantic. American leaders have recognised the vital importance of economic integration and assistance as instruments for the creation of stability in the Eastern part of Europe, in parallel with the enlargement of Nato. To them, the price required of the Europeans for building a security community with their former adversaries is fair, having regard to America's disproportionate contribution to Nato's military capabilities and to the low level of European defence spending.

Secondly, fears of trade diversion seem unfounded. On solid grounds, EU enlargement is estimated to have minimal effects on trade with non-member regions in general and with the United States in particular. True, some sectors of the American economy will be affected. Thus, for example, US exports of grains, bovine animals, bovine meat products and dairy products to the EU are expected to decline. But these limited negative effects will be abundantly compensated by the opportunities an enlarging EU is likely to offer American companies for expanding their operations within a growing European market. Even today, the total stock of two-way investment is little short of $ 1 trillion, almost equally divided between American investment in the EU and that of European companies in the US. About three million Europeans are already employed by American subsidiaries.

Thirdly, as a result of enlargement the EU will command greatly enhanced economic and demographic resources. This should enable the Union to become a stronger actor on the world stage, capable of sharing with the US greater responsibilities for providing international public goods, amongst them peace and security in specific regions, openness of the world economy, and monetary stability. At the same time the Union could further increase its contribution to combating international challenges such as transnational terrorism (a top priority since the events of 11 September 2001) and environmental degradation.

Whether the potential of enlargement for strengthening EU-US relations will actually be realised is by no means a foregone conclusion. Apart from the nature of American reactions, two factors are of critical importance: (i) the speed and scope of the enlargement process itself, and (ii) the ability of European governments to adapt the EU's institutions to the challenges and problems arising from increased size and greater diversity. Although the EU's 2000 Nice summit removed the final internal institutional obstacles to the candidates' membership of the Union, it does not necessarily mean that the accession of all interested countries will happen soon. Precisely in this respect, there seems to be some conflict of interest between the US and the EU. In order to ease pressures on Washington to accept new members in Nato, the US is urging more rapid enlargement of the EU, embracing as many candidate countries as possible. In contrast, Germany, France and other EU members, from varying motives, prefer a gradual enlargement stretching over a relatively long period of time, with only a few candidates being admitted within the next four years or so. Stalling the enlargement process will cause misgivings in Washington about Europe's implied half-heartedness; but in Europe's view enlarging the EU too quickly carries the risk of over-stretch. In fact, premature enlargement may adversely affect Europe's decision-making capacities, including those in the field of external relations.

The scenarios

One could envisage the following four scenarios within a continuum ranging from a 'weak Europe' to a 'strong Europe.'

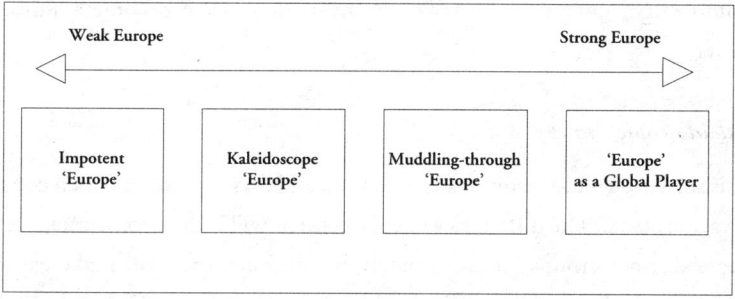

Impotent Europe

An inward looking Union would reveal itself as an impotent actor on the international stage. This image of the future is based on worries of a 'nightmare' scenario of an over-stretch and overload of the enlarged Union, making it unable to cope with the welter of problems connected with the premature accession of too many candidate countries. The 'dinosaur effect' will make the EU larger but less effective. The Union then fails to restructure its institutions so as to preserve their political and administrative effectiveness. The traditional 'community method' of arriving at policies on a proposal from the Commission and agreement through the Council of Ministers and Parliament will definitely lose out to 'intergovernmental' decision-making. As a result, the Union is not able to generate solutions to cope with the tensions emanating from increased heterogeneity of membership. Thus, for example, it will be forced to impose long transitional periods for the free movement of people. And it also fails to redirect the flow of structural funds from the Southern European members to the new member states. The common agricultural policy is renationalised. Domestic protectionist pressures threaten the internal market. Though the EU will try to move outward into more hazardous zones (for instance, the Balkans), the Union is likely to face more problems than now in being a forceful actor in its immediate regional neighbourhood, let alone in being capable of global engagement. Furthermore, demonstrations of discord among EMU members about the direction of European monetary policy undermines public confidence in the value of the euro, thus making the EU a less rather than more equal partner of the US also in the global financial system. Because of its unwieldy policy-making procedures and its reluctance to accept subordination to Washington, the Union might not just be a weak ally but perhaps even become a 'nuisance power.'

Kaleidoscopic Europe

This scenario would result in a fragmented and divided Union which consists of various tiers. The difficulties of enlargement will induce some members to create distinct groups, and ultimately institutions, that will make external representation even more difficult. Henry Kissinger's question, 'whom do I call in a crisis when I need someone to speak for Europe?' remains unanswered. The number of telephones will increase both within sectors (European Commission, ECB, Eurogroup) and among sectors. European co-ordination on matters of security remains both limited and uneven. A larger EU will create several coalition groups, among them a directorate of larger countries on security and defence matters. This directorate will be resented by smaller member states that feel marginalised, thus airing complaints about 'taxation without representation.' The enlarged Union might be a wilful though a weak partner; at any rate, it will be a complex entity to deal with. The US may be tempted to exploit the confusion by applying a *divide et impera* policy.

Muddling-through Europe

In this scenario the EU's present role of a semi-dependent, semi-autonomous actor in relation to the USA, and therefore in international affairs, would basically continue. The Union would make incremental adjustments to its institutions along the lines of the modest decisions of the Nice summit. The hybrid system of community and intergovernmental decision-making would persist. The adaptations are sufficient to prevent paralysis in the Union's functioning but not radical enough to give it the institutional strength or managerial capacity necessary to fulfil its international ambitions. The gap between the rhetoric of expectations and achievements does not narrow; it makes itself particularly felt in the domain of military affairs. Thus the Union cannot move beyond the scope of conducting traditional peacekeeping and very limited enforcement operations in or close to Europe. It is not able to participate in global crisis management. On the other hand, in forums like WTO and the IMF, the EU's institutional weaknesses can still be offset by its enhanced economic and financial weight. In the non-military arena, the Union remains a force to be reckoned with.

Europe as a Global Player

In this scenario the EU features as a fully-fledged, powerful global actor: widening and deepening will have led to a mutually reinforcing dynamic towards a strong Union capable of external action. As a response to the institutional challenge posed by enlargement, a quasi-federal core develops among members of Economic and Monetary Union. The Commission reasserts its authority; its President will be elected directly by the European people. A 'Mr Euro' represents the Union at international monetary talks. There will be beneficial spill-over effects from monetary union into other policy fields, particularly budgetary, fiscal and structural economic policies. By virtue of its success, in time the inner core attracts most other member states. The Union is propelled towards a strong leadership role within its own neighbourhood. Largely by virtue of rationalisation and integration of national defence structures, it redresses the lack of equilibrium in its military relationship with the US. Thus, in addition to being a strong commercial and industrial power, the EU succeeds in building impressive military force-projection capabilities, enabling the Union to join the US in acting as an effective crisis manager on the world stage.

In this scenario, in accordance with the main thrust of (neo-)realist thinking,[189] the EU might wish to define itself as a *counterweight* to the US, challenging America's hegemonic position and seeking an independent role for itself in world politics. Alternatively, Europe might wish to see itself as a *counterpart* or an equal partner of the US. As such it would place its increased resources, both economic and military, at the service of the common objectives of the transatlantic community.

Implications for the US-EU relationship

What are the likely implications of these different scenarios for the quality of the future EU-US relationship? The first scenario, the EU as an impotent actor, could hold some superficial attraction for American politicians of the right sympathetic to the idea of American hegemony in the world and supportive of unilateralist tendencies in American foreign policy. A Union which is preoccupied with its own problems and whose internal governance is paralysed by the burdens of enlargement cannot be a challenger to America's wider interests in the world in either the military or economic and financial domain. The primacy of the US in strategic affairs and the supremacy of the dollar will go uncontested. A weakened EU creates opportunities for Washington to strengthen political control over Europe. But in all likelihood, rather than regarding Europe's inability to put its house in order as an opportunity to tighten the reins of power over European allies, for most 'mainstream' American political leaders this impotence would be a cause for exasperation. They can be expected to blame European governments for failing to assume responsibility for the stabilisation of Europe as a whole and shifting ever greater burdens onto the US. They will most certainly ask why American taxpayers' money should support American troops in Europe if the Europeans are not ready to help themselves. The first scenario must therefore be considered a recipe for increasing American disengagement from a feckless Europe. Clearly, its impact on the evolution of EU-US relations would be negative.

---

[189] See, for instance, Layne, C. 'The Unipolar Illusion: Why New Great Powers Will Arise,' *International Security*, 17 (4), Spring 1993, pp.5-51.

From a US point of view the second scenario, a 'Kaleidoscopic Europe,' might offer some appeal. American leadership will remain unchallenged, whilst in the military field the major European powers will continue to side with the US in securing peace and stability, especially in Europe's 'near abroad.' But this scenario also implies continued fragmentation, which runs counter to the original idea underlying European integration as expressed in the preamble to the Treaty of Rome: 'determined to lay the foundations of an ever closer union among the peoples of Europe...' and consistently supported by the US.

Almost by definition the 'Muddling-through Europe' scenario will have neither a positive nor a negative effect on the development of the transatlantic relationship. As in the past, this relationship will be characterised by many instances of intensive co-operation between the EU and the US but also by sporadic crises of varying intensity. The latter may arise from different causes, ranging from familiar trade disputes or monetary rivalries to disagreements about strategic issues such as national missile defence. A major feature of this scenario is that the fundamental imbalance between the EU's economic strength and military weakness is only marginally redressed. The discrepancy between Europe's status in the two most significant dimensions of international power – military and economic – remains an important cause of friction and frustration. Given its military preponderance, the US is unwilling to yield its position of political leadership and its right to impose its will where necessary. On the other hand, the Europeans will increase their demands for a political voice commensurate with the EU's economic and financial clout. The US remains militarily engaged in Europe but probably at a reduced level.

Only under the final scenario of the EU as a fully-fledged, powerful global actor, can the potential of EU enlargement for strengthening the Atlantic relationship be realised. However, this scenario, too, could entail serious risks. If an increasingly global Europe were to define itself as a counterweight to US power and leadership while seeking to play a balancing role in a new multipolar world system, there would be no prospect of an evolution of the Atlantic partnership based on equality. A rebalancing of roles and responsibilities between Europe and the US must take place at the heart of the Alliance. The aim must be 'not less America, but more Europe.' Enlargement may be taken as a positive development in this direction, because it will weaken tendencies to establish defence structures outside Nato. Countries like Poland are not interested in pursuing policies that risk incurring US resentment. The EU's new member states will want to focus their security interests primarily on close co-operation with Washington.

Policy recommendations

In the light of this analysis it goes almost without saying that Europe should aim at the realisation of the final scenario. As the heartland of Western society and values – democracy, the market economy, human rights and protection of minorities – both the US and Europe have the vocation to foster the further development and diffusion of their beliefs so as to promote 'the greatest happiness for the greatest number of people.' The Western claim that the values underlying these concepts are universal has become progressively accepted by a growing number of countries over the last ten to twenty years. It is important to uphold these claims with increased vigour against the revival of religious intolerance and fundamentalist obscurantism which are among the root causes of terrorism. But, although many emerging countries have formally adopted democracy, their political practices still carry the imprint of one-time autocratic regimes. And in the economic field, the transition to the market economy still needs consolidation and deepening before it will succeed in fulfilling its promises. It is very likely that these developments will not follow a straight-line path. Progress may alternate with occasional set-backs. All this bestows a particular responsibility on the Western heartland as a role model, a source of inspiration and a defender of last resort.

This line of reasoning challenges the (neo-)realist proposition that a fully-fledged and powerful Europe will inevitably develop into a counterweight Europe. Yet such a development is even less likely if one looks at the longer-term perspective. The transatlantic community represents 12 per cent of the world's population, but its share of world production is approximately 46 per cent. However, if current trends continue, the corresponding figures for 2050 will be drastically reduced. Closer transatlantic ties are needed to compensate for this decline.

In the security dimension of transatlantic relations, the structural reform of Nato from an American 'holding' to a truly equal partnership would require the American administration to accept greater European political influence in exchange for larger European military inputs. It is by no means certain that the Bush administration, not above suspicion of unilateralist proclivities, will consider the sharing of leadership with Europeans ('partnership in leadership') essential for the long-term survival of the Atlantic Alliance. Regardless of short-term American reactions, European governments have no alternative but to show by their deeds that their ambition is not to weaken the Alliance but to strengthen it. They must show that greater European unity and improved European force capabilities are in America's strategic interest, too. Apart from material and non-material costs, Washington should not fail to understand that healthy collaboration with Europe remains the prime antidote to the 'loneliness of superpowerdom,' to borrow Samuel Huntington's phrase.[190] More generally, one might ask whether the movement towards an equal partnership would not require a new comprehensive Transatlantic Treaty. Such a question would immediately trigger another: Why does one need to revalidate a marriage certificate if the marriage is going well? Transatlantic relations have been formalised in a multitude of treaties, most importantly those pertaining to Nato, IMF, OECD and the WTO. In any event, it is obvious that the *de facto* co-operation is close, not only between governments but also business-to-business and people-to-people. This should not mean that all is well and that there is no room for further improvement. The economic field in particular offers opportunities for strengthening co-operation. Here the most important dimensions of a new transatlantic partnership would be closer ties in the field of trade and investment, as well as in monetary co-operation. So far, however, attempts to progress in these directions have been bedevilled by numerous differences and technical obstacles.

In order to promote trade and investment, the US and Europe have a special responsibility to act as the vanguard of further liberalisation within the WTO framework. Free trade and investment are still subject to the famous

---

[190] Huntington, S. P. 'The Lonely Superpower,' *Foreign Affairs*, 78 (2), March/April 1999, p.48.

'bicycle theory' – you have to pedal constantly just to avoid falling off. A renewed effort is called for to prepare the ground for launching the Millennium Round.

In monetary matters it should be recognised that the introduction of the euro is the most significant event in the international monetary system since the end of Bretton Woods. It is set to make a major impact on global economic and financial relations. Although the EU represents 6 per cent of the world's population, it accounts for more than 20 per cent of total world GDP and about a quarter of world trade. The euro will be an international currency to match this economic weight. It may be expected that the euro will eventually take its place alongside the dollar as a major reserve currency.

The introduction of the euro has also altered the international monetary constellation. It has given Europe more monetary power. Yet more power also implies greater responsibility. We have entered a new monetary era and a new monetary relationship. A new relationship requires a fundamental reflection on its rules and the way in which they will have to be exercised. New relationships should also be accompanied by new institutional arrangements. The EU and the US have been major driving forces behind trade liberalisation. Together they could play a similarly positive role in the monetary field.

Currency stability is a boon to trade and to a better international division of labour. That was one of the principal inspirations behind the Bretton Woods system of fixed but adjustable currencies, and now the European single currency. In principle, the same applies to the dollar/euro relationship. But today the exchange rate is subject to benign neglect, effectively left to the market to determine. At the moment there may be no real alternative; but before long it will be desirable for the monetary authorities of the US and the EU to seek closer co-operation aimed at achieving greater stability between their two currencies. In a first stage, they could aim at common analysis of monetary developments. They could also intensify their co-operation to be ready to play a positive role in financial crises such as those that beset Asia, Mexico, Brazil and more recently Argentina. However, such a role should be supportive of IMF interventions and on no account constitute a substitute for them.

Looking to a more distant future, one might draw a parallel with the pre-history of EMU, and particularly the Werner Plan of 1970 which was its precursor. Named after the Prime Minister of Luxembourg at the time, it was to have been realised in 1980. A variety of factors made the plan come to nothing. But now, thirty years later than originally planned, EMU is a fact. Against this background, it is not completely inconceivable that, another thirty years hence, one may succeed in establishing a transatlantic currency union.

For the moment, however, policy attention is focused on the enlargement of the EU. The adoption of the full *acquis communautaire,* as a precondition to membership, is of paramount importance. Marx (Groucho ... not Karl) once said: 'I wouldn't want to belong to a club which would have me as a member.' And indeed, if enlargement means dilution of the disciplines embodied in the *acquis* and thereby also the decomposition of the common market and all other common structures, the price of enlargement will be too high. This applies not only to the Union, but also to the candidate countries. The latter's interests would not be served well if the EU were to become a pale imitation of what it is now. That would imply the partial demolition of the laborious integration efforts of decades. And it would equally undermine Europe's capacity to play a constructive role in global affairs.

As to the time frame for enlargement, one should not overlook the fact that, since the stagflation of the seventies, it has taken the Union already more than twenty years to shake off the shackles of 'Eurosclerosis.' Europe has come a long way since then. In terms of growth it had recently even begun to challenge the US. In other fields, however, such as the flexibility of labour markets and technological innovation, it still lags considerably behind. But the efforts which Western Europe had to make in order to catch up are dwarfed by those required of Central and Eastern Europe, which have to overcome the legacy of centrally planned economies with all their endemic inefficiencies. Such a transition cannot be achieved overnight; it must be implemented with the utmost care. Precipitate transformation might cause serious setbacks, not only to the transformation process itself, but also because of an adverse impact on public opinion, which could undermine the political support for enlargement in those countries.

Nevertheless, the EU should be sensitive to US perceptions over tpace of enlargement. The art of politics is not based purely on objective facts and events. Perceptions play an important role in themselves, if only because they may give rise to behaviour and decisions that can create new objective facts and events adverse to the common goal. Real partnership requires close and continuous political and economic dialogue so as to prevent the emergence of misconceptions and their potentially damaging effects.

Appendices

Much of the European Union's ability to follow the most dynamic of these scenarios will depend on internal factors. Time and again the contributors to this volume have stressed the vital need for deep reforms of the EU's institutions. Of equal significance are the EU's budget instruments, the essential lubricant of the whole integration – and now enlargement – process. Here, too, reforms are crucial, on both the income and expenditure sides. Instruments such as the Common Agricultural Policy impose an incubus on budgetary soundness, enlargement and transatlantic relations. The combination of 'deepening and widening' should have made the Union ready to receive new members. But has it?

The following two technical papers have been placed at Appendix as they do not bear directly on the principal subject of this book but are nevertheless indispensable to an understanding of the problems confronting the EU. The political debate on the future of the Union and its enlargement is usually uninstructed by what goes on in the engine room. Yet it is here that the real battles still need to be fought, and a settlement reached before the EU can safely welcome its new members – and they know with greater precision what is in store for them.

Laurent Van Depoele provides a critique of the Nice Treaty and concludes that the present limited reforms will not lead to a successful enlargement, though the next reform process is already scheduled for 2004. Meanwhile enhanced co-operation offers a tool for a limited degree of EU-US co-operation in the international field.

Kalman Deszeri gives a detailed analysis of the EU's budgetary structure and the changing emphasis of its external actions. Substantial funds are already flowing into the candidate countries and will no doubt continue after accession. Yet here, too, the prognosis for the EU's own growth into an international political role to match its economic might is gloomy. Much will depend on the extent to which member states are ready to place more effort and funding behind the Union's foreign and security policy rather than their own.

Appendix A

The Political and Institutional Dimension

Laurent Van Depoele
Professor, Université Catholique de Louvain
Vice President, Groupe d'Etudes Politiques Européennes

The need for institutional reform

The basic choices for the EU's future were stated in 1995 by the then Commissioner in charge of enlargement, Hans van den Broek, who recognised that the outcome of the enlargement process would critically affect the role of the EU as a political actor:

> 'Either the Union will be enlarged as a genuinely integrated structure...
> speaking with one voice in world affairs; or a wider Union will become a kind of
> United Nations of Europe, with little internal coherence and consequently little
> external clout in world affairs; [an]... organisation... unable to compete on an
> equal basis with the United States, Japan and the world's other major powers.'[191]

In his contribution, Professor Serfaty points out correctly that 'there can be no meaningful enlargement without effective institutional reform.' The key question therefore is to know whether the institutional reforms laid

---

[191] Hans van den Broek, 'The Challenge of Enlargement,' speech to the East-West Institute, Brussels, 1 December 1995, cited by Feldman, L. G.: 'The EU's Enlargement Project and US-EU co-operation in Central and Eastern Europe,' in : Burwell, F. G. and Daalder, I. H. *The US and Europe in the Global Arena*, NY, 1999, p.45.

down in the Treaty of Nice can qualify as 'effective' for enlargement and as a contribution towards making Europe into a true political actor.

Generally speaking, the Nice Treaty placed the candidate countries on the map of the EU institutions; and consequently its ratification means that the 'formal conditions for enlargement are met.'[192] A certain acceleration of the enlargement process is implicit in indicating that those candidates whose accession treaties are signed before 1 January 2004 will be able to participate in the 2004 elections of the European Parliament. The fact that Nice has raised the prospect of accessions earlier than previous optimistic forecasts does not constitute a binding commitment but rather a pronounced political aspiration. The timetable could slip again unless progress in the negotiations is accelerated accordingly.

For the Council, a new system of weighted votes is introduced which will make it still more difficult to reach decisions after enlargement than it is today. Power games seem to have blocked the introduction of the 'double simple majority' system, whereby each decision would have had to command a majority of votes, on the basis of one vote per state; and a second majority of countries comprising over 50 per cent of the EU's total population. This more comprehensible system would have gone some way to creating the desirable transparency needed in order to 'bring Europe closer to the people.'

Qualified majority voting (QMV) requires three different majorities. First, as from 1 January 2005 a qualified majority decision in the EU of the present 15 will need 169 votes out of 237 or 71.3 per cent; and after enlargement to 27 member states, 258 votes out of 345, or 74.7 per cent. Secondly, qualified majority decisions have to be approved by a majority of member states; and thirdly, at the request of a single member state, the Council is to verify if the population of the member states voting in favour represents 62 per cent of the EU total (the demographic safety net). The Portuguese Prime Minister Antonio Guterres termed the agreement 'an institutional coup d'état,' with the larger states gaining influence at the expense of the smaller ones. The highly complex system of re-weighting the votes of member states

---

[192] Minister Saryusz-Wolski, 5th ECSA-World Conference, Brussels, 15 December 2000.

does indeed shift power to the larger ones. The 71 per cent threshold for QMV, already high, is raised to 74.7 per cent and consequently lowers the threshold for blocking minorities. In addition, large countries are rewarded with a rule that enables them to query a decision, allowing it to go forward only if countries representing 62 per cent of the EU's population are in favour, or alternatively to block it if 38 per cent of the population is against it. This means that Germany plus two of the next largest states, the UK, France or Italy, could collectively veto a decision. This new system of QMV will not, however, come into force until all twelve accession candidates are incorporated into the EU. For this, the wait could be long. The mathematics of the Nice agreement are at best esoteric and, at worst, a significant encumbrance to transparent and simple decision-making in an enlarged Union.

The veto is maintained in respect of a number of major community policies, of equal importance for the candidate countries, such as taxation, co-ordination of social security rules and the environment, which increases the risk of blocking decisions and of political inconsistencies within the enlarged Union. It is also important to note that Spain succeeded in maintaining its right of veto over structural funds until after the adoption of the new financial perspectives for the period 2007-2013, under which the Union may be unable 'to channel the flow of structural funds from the southern European members to the new member states' (Van Staden & Labohm). After accession, veto powers will also be in the hands of the 'weak accession candidates' who may then become 'strong co-players' (Wessels).

As far as the Commission is concerned, it should be noted that the reformulation of article 217 increased the powers of the President who will inter alia allocate portfolios to the Commissioners and may demand their resignation. No single Member State can block the nomination of the President, since here too, MV will apply. As from 1 January 2005 and until 12 more members join the Union, there will be one Commissioner per Member State. A reduced Commission was also rejected informally by the candidate countries. Once the Union has 27 members, there will be fewer commissioners than the number of member states, but the precise number will have to be decided unanimously by the Council which will also have to decide on the 'equal rotation system.' This modification will apply only from the date of entry into office of the first Commission following the accession of the 27th member.

Without consulting the European Parliament, the number of its members was increased from 700 to 732. EP seats were used to compensate for lower weighted voting power in the Council. Two points are worth mentioning: Hungary has two seats less than Portugal although it has more inhabitants; and the Czech Republic has only 20 seats while Belgium with the same population has 22 seats. From a democratic point of view, however, some progress has been made, since the co-decision procedure is to be used to a greater extent.

Progress was made at the level of the Court of Justice and the Court of First Instance. This reform will enable the Community Courts to function and deliver verdicts within a reasonable period of time even after enlargement, when the number of questions of interpretation and explanations of Community Law are certain to increase.

Real progress was made at the level of 'enhanced co-operation.' It should be noted that this was not an Amsterdam remnant but had been formally placed on the agenda of the IGC at Feira in June 2000. Two major changes were made: after enlargement it will no longer be necessary to have a majority of Member States to start an enhanced co-operation and, secondly, no single member state will be able to block it.[193] This second modification does not, however, apply to the introduction of enhanced co-operation within the second pillar.

Trade, foreign policy, security and defence

The Nice reforms of EU trade policy and foreign and security policy are not greatly impressive. When they look at Western Europe, most CEEC see two integration processes: one is of an economic nature, the other political. The first is led by the EU, while the second operates through the Atlantic Alliance under USA guidance. Both the EU and the USA are, jointly and severally,

---

[193] See Louis, J. V. 5th ECSA-World Conference, Paper 'Maintenir le Momentum de l'Integration Européenne.'

extending the Euro-Atlantic structures of the EU and Nato to Central and Eastern Europe in order to safeguard long term peace, stability and welfare.

Progress was made in the field of international trade (new article 133) since, with a few exceptions, QMV will also be applied in the negotiations and conclusion of international trade agreements on goods, services and the commercial aspects of intellectual property (though not investments). For certain trade agreements, member states will, however, maintain exclusive competences or mixed competences, as in cultural, educational, social and health services. All these exceptions are certain to contribute to increased complexity in trade relations with third countries.

The CFSP, under the second pillar, remains intergovernmental, since the veto power is maintained. Although enhanced co-operation was in principle not applicable to the second pillar, Article 17 of the Amsterdam Treaty had not ruled out the development of closer co-operation between two or more member states on a bilateral level, within the framework of WEU and Nato, provided such co-operation did not run counter to or impede multilateral co-operation. Co-operation was also possible between two or more member states in the defence industry field. The Treaty of Nice now allows enhanced co-operation in the implementation of a joint action or a common position but excludes it in military or defence matters.

Another illustration of the intergovernmental nature of the second pillar is the fact that the High Representative for the CFSP also remains the Secretary General of the Council. He assists the Council in matters coming within the scope of the CFSP, in particular by contributing to the formulation, preparation and implementation of policy decisions and, at the request of the Presidency, by conducting political dialogue with third parties.

Lack of planning and analysis was generally seen as one of the main weaknesses of the original CFSP. Accordingly, a declaration attached to the Amsterdam Treaty established the Policy Planning and Early Warning Unit within the Council Secretariat, under the authority of the Secretary General/ High Representative. The Presidency may authorise the unit to present policy papers for the Council's deliberation. The Commission is closely involved in the tasks of the Presidency and, since Amsterdam, forms part of the Community

Troika together with the Presidency and the High Representative. Although fully associated with the work carried out in the CFSP, the Commission does not have the exclusive right of initiative as it does in the first pillar. A Political Committee – in the Nice Treaty referred to as the 'political and security committee' (PSC) – monitors the international situation in areas covered by the CFSP. It consists of member states' representatives with political-military expertise and benefits from the advice of a military committee. It makes recommendations and contributes to the definition of policies by delivering opinions to the Council at the latter's request or on its own initiative. Alongside, Coreper also plays its normal role in preparing the work of the Council.

Reform of the system in preparation for enlargement should have simplified the institutional framework of the CFSP and transferred the function of the High Representative from the Council to the European Commission.

The Amsterdam Treaty incorporated the WEU's Petersberg Tasks (humanitarian and rescue tasks, peace-keeping and crisis management, including peace-making) in exchange for a reaffirmation of the EU's commitment to Nato (Art. 17 §1). This text, unchanged in Nice, clearly indicates that Nato remains the principal framework for security and defence on the European continent.[194] Following the Anglo-French Declaration at Saint Malo in December 1998, the Cologne European Council's Declaration of June 1999 on strengthening the Common European Security and Defence Policy (CESDP) calls upon the EU to provide the multinational framework for a future 'autonomous' European military contribution to international security. The CESDP is intended to reinforce the CFSP.

The 'rapid reaction force' agreed at the European Council in Helsinki in December 1999, to be operational in 2003, 'should enable Europeans to keep order in their own house without American assistance.' With all 15 member states participating and the number of troops pledged exceeding the headline goal of 50-60,000 agreed at Helsinki, it seems to have gathered more support than Monetary Union.[195] The important question now is how the CESDP will

---

[194] See Dehousse, F., Galer, B. 'De Saint-Malo à Feira : les enjeux de la Renaissance du projet de défense européenne,' in : *Studia Diplomatica*, vol.LII, 1999, n°4.

[195] See Neuhold, H. Background paper for the Conference on the Belgian Presidency 2001.

affect relations with Nato and the USA. At their bilateral meeting in Washington on 6 February 2001, the US Secretary of State Colin Powell and British Foreign Secretary Robin Cook clearly stated that CESDP must not lead to an erosion of the Atlantic Alliance. Foreign Secretary Cook said both he and Secretary Powell had agreed that an increase in Europe's rapid reaction capability could strengthen Nato, 'and we are both determined that this new European capacity shall be firmly anchored in Nato.' Powell said the Bush administration had a very good understanding of what it was all about, and that if it is 'firmly embedded in Nato and we're not duplicating planning capabilities… then there's no reason to see this as destabilising Nato in any way.'[196] However, it cannot be denied that the EU is divided on this issue, which illustrates clearly the old dichotomy between those favouring a 'European Europe' led by France and others more interested in an 'Atlantic Europe' led by the UK.

The United States is watching with great interest how enlargement will affect Europe's role in the world and more specifically, the transatlantic relationship. At the EPC meeting in Brussels in June 2000, Ambassador Morningstar indicated that the US is 'vitally concerned about the strategic implications of enlargement but we also know that enlargement is a European issue. We want it to be successful and we hope it happens in a way that does not unnecessarily prejudice third countries, like the US and others.'[197] So far, the Bush administration has not changed that position.

To conclude, Nice was the result of a series of unsatisfactory compromises necessitated by the imperatives of Realpolitik and inherent in the IGC methodology which automatically leads to the lowest common denominator. A post-Nice reflection on Europe's future should base itself on a methodology different from the traditional IGC formula, and this should emerge from a wide-ranging public debate including the European Parliament, national parliaments and civil society. The present limited institutional reforms will not lead to a successful enlargement. The European Council in Nice must have been fully aware of this since they agreed the date for the next reform process in 2004.

---

[196] Press Release – US Department of State, February 6 2001.

[197] US Mission to the European Union, Brussels, July 6 2000.

Enlargement, even without any real deepening, will raise the EU's profile in international affairs and this should increase the need for better co-ordination between the EU and the US. That is probably why it was stated at the EU-US summit in Washington on 18 December 2000 that 'the US looks forward to working with a European Union playing its full role and assuming its full responsibilities on the international scene.'[198] The basic question, however, remains how an enlarged EU with complex procedures, ineffective institutions and a hybrid system of supranational and intergovernmental decision-making (Van Staden & Labohm) will be able to respond to these expectations. Because of the failure in Nice to carry through effective institutional reform, the answer is probably that the enlarged EU will look more like an 'impotent power' rather than a real political actor. The only grounds for optimism reside in the possibility of making effective use of enhanced co-operation, thanks to the element of flexibility introduced in the Nice Treaty.

---

[198] Highlights of the EU-US co-operation under the New Transatlantic Agenda, Washington, 18 December 2000.

Table A.1 Post-Enlargement Distribution of EP Seats and Council Votes - (figures as agreed in Nice)

Country	Population	Seats in European Parliament	Weighted Votes in EU Council	Seats in the Economic and Social Committee	Seats in the Committee of the Regions
Germany	82,008,455	99	29	24	24
United Kingdom	59,555,228	72	29	24	24
France	58,679,375	72	29	24	24
Italy	57,579,163	72	29	24	24
Spain	40,032,756	50	27	21	21
Poland	38,640,141	50	27	21	21
Romania	22,355,121	33	14	15	15
Netherlands	15,967,897	25	13	12	12
Greece	10,779,739	22	12	12	12
Czech Republic	10,279,995	20	12	12	12
Belgium	10,235,462	22	12	12	12
Hungary	10,086,040	20	12	12	12
Portugal	9,994,610	22	12	12	12
Sweden	8,862,504	18	10	12	12
Bulgaria	8,270,215	17	10	12	12
Austria	8,106,083	17	10	12	12
Slovenia	5,418,706	13	7	9	9
Denmark	5,363,897	13	7	9	9
Finland	5,182,982	13	7	9	9
Ireland	3,706,224	12	7	9	9
Lithuania	3,698,523	12	7	9	9
Latvia	2,424,150	8	4	7	7
Slovenia	1,792,603	7	4	7	7
Estonia	1,437,358	6	4	7	7
Cyprus	794,815	6	4	6	6
Luxembourg	434,772	6	4	6	6
Malta	382,246	5	3	5	5
TOTAL	482,069,050	732	345	344	344

Table A.2 - Major Indicators: US and EU Present and Enlarged

	United States of America	EU 15	EU 27	EU 27 + Turkey
Population	272,639,608	374,324,512	479,779,201	545,378,407
GDP	$8.511 trillion	$8.053 trillion	$8.747 trillion	$9.172 trillion
GDP per capita	$31,500	$20,927	$15,061	$14,759
Military Expenditure	$267.2 billion	$166.3 billion	$221.6 billion	$228.4 billion
Military Expenditure as per cent of GDP	3.4 per cent	1.84 per cent	1.97 per cent	2.06 per cent
Total Exports	$0.905 trillion	$2.032 trillion	$2.189 trillion	$2.233 trillion
Exports as per cent of world total	16.5 per cent	37.0 per cent	39.9 per cent	40.7 per cent
Total imports	$0.757 trillion	$2.028 trillion	$2.146 trillion	$2.174 trillion
Imports as per cent of world total	13.5 per cent	36 per cent	38.1 per cent	38.9 per cent

Source: Z. Brzezinski, *Living with a New Europe* in 'The National Interest,' Summer 2000, p.18.

Appendix B
Budgetary Matters and Policy Reforms

Kalman Deszeri
Senior Research Fellow
Magyar Tudományos Akadémia
Világgazdasági Kutatóintézet
(Institute for World Economics
of the Hungarian Academy of Sciences)

Since the end of World War II, close co-operation between Europe and America has been one of the basic elements of the international system. The political alliance did not, however, prevent all conflicts of interest either in political or economic matters. Several issues have led them to compete on the global stage. The introduction of EMU and the euro, and the forthcoming eastward enlargement of the EU will in the long term modify their respective roles in global political and economic affairs. In the short term, a number of ambiguous trends may also influence their relations.

Basically three scenarios may be drawn up for the future of transatlantic relations, determined by the relative political and economic strengths of the EU and of the US:[199] (i) a strong EU will eventually emerge after the consolidation of EMU and eastward enlargement; (ii) a weak inward-looking

---

[199] More detailed description of the scenarios is in the chapter of Staden A. V., Labohm, H.

EU will emerge because of the accumulated problems of EMU and enlargement; and (iii) the EU will divide itself into several subgroups.

One of the key factors determining the outcome and probability of each scenario is the budgetary position of the EU. This analysis will look at the main trends, policies and effects of enlargement on the EU budget. The main question is how much the budgetary effects of enlargement will influence the global role of the EU and its relations with the US. Another question is likewise important: what kind of policy reforms may be expected to be introduced? The following analysis aims to answer these questions in the context of the three posited scenarios.

EU budgetary expenditures related to external relations

The special budget instruments

The EU's expenditure has increased and diversified considerably over the whole course of European integration. Some headings and subsections of the budget are related specifically to foreign political and economic activities of the EU.

Subsection B7 of the general budget contains expenditure coming under heading 4 (external action) and the emergency aid reserve (part of heading 6). This subsection has covered a range of activities involving types of assistance and financial instruments. A distinction may be made among financial, technical and economic co-operation divided into geographical areas, and other co-operation measures of a horizontal nature and which normally apply to all non-member countries.

Financial, technical and economic co-operation measures are intended to help the development and economic restructuring of non-member countries. Among these are the countries of Central and Eastern Europe and the independent states of the former Soviet Union – whose total share has substantially increased since the early 1990s – as well as Mediterranean countries and states in Asia and Latin America.

Other co-operation measures include humanitarian and food aid, initiatives for democracy and the protection of human rights, rehabilitation, reconstruction, environment and health in developing countries, international fisheries agreements and, wherever necessary, emergency aid.

The EDF (European Development Fund) is another of the EU's financial instruments related to external actions, but which for various reasons is not included in the general budget. The EDF finances mainly economic development projects and development co-operation with over 70 developing African, Caribbean and Pacific (ACP) states. First three Yaoundé Conventions (1964-70) and then five Lomé Conventions, each for a period of five years, have provided the institutional framework for this activity. The total funds earmarked under the EDF-ACP Lomé Conventions have represented 40 – 50 per cent of the total amount of commitments allocated to the EU's external actions (Subsection B7 including the pre-accession strategy, Subsection B8 and the EDF). A wide range of financial aid is available under the EDF.[200]

Principal characteristics of expenditures related to external activities

The funds provided for the EU's external actions (Subsection B7 under Heading 4) have increased significantly over the decades. The nominal value of these funds multiplied more than tenfold (from euro 603.9 million to 6377.8 million) between 1980 and 2001 (Table B.1). The share of these funds in the general budget total almost doubled (from 3.81 per cent to 6.79 per cent), as did their share in the grand total of the EU's budget[201] (from 3.67 per cent to 6.6 per cent).

Meanwhile the nominal value of the amounts allocated to the EDF rose more than fivefold (from euro 481.9 million to 2553 million) and their share in the grand total of the EU's budget decreased only slightly between 1980 and 2001 (from 2.9 per cent to 2.6 per cent).

There has been one significant difference between the nominal values and budgetary shares of both expenditures. Whilst those for the EU's external

---

[200] Apart from subsidies for national and regional programmes and the allocation of venture capital there are five more specific instruments: STABEX, Sysmin, emergency aid, aid to refugees, interest subsidies.

[201] General budget total plus EDF, ECSC, Euratom make up the Grand total of the budget.

activity increased almost continuously, particularly since 1990, the values of successive EDFs have fluctuated although their budget shares have remained fairly stable. This means that the relative position of the ACP countries has deteriorated to the advantage of the countries covered by the 'external action' budget subsection.

Looking at the geographical areas covered by the external budget from the point of view of transatlantic relations, the following facts can be noted:

There has not been a budgetary item of any substance for EU-US relations. These have nevertheless been influenced indirectly by other budgetary items. The main determinant is the role which the EU plays in certain international affairs and whether this role is co-operative or conflicting with that of the US.

There are budget items for financing co-operation with countries in Asia and Latin America. The combined share of such projects in the budget has been stable or declining.

The nominal value and share of external activities with the Central and Eastern European countries and with the successor states to the former Soviet Union have been continuously increasing. Since 1998, the EU has pursued a pre-accession strategy to prepare the ground for a new wave or waves of enlargement consisting of 13 countries.[202]

The expenditure structure of the EU's external budget has increasingly turned towards the neighbouring Central and Eastern European countries. Other regions or countries in other continents have received gradually less attention over the last decade. The role of the EU in international non-European political and economic affairs does not seem to have increased substantially during that time. In the longer term this trend may change substantially. However, one has also to take into consideration the bilateral actions of the EU member states. The EU's community based actions need to be viewed in combination with these bilateral projects and activities.

---

[202] Central and Eastern European countries plus Turkey.

Table B.1 - Values and Shares of External Activity and EDF in the General Budget with Grand Totals

	External Activity (EUR m)	General Budget Total	EDF (EUR m)	Grand Total (EUR m)	A/B %	A/D %	C/D %	F/G %
	(A)	(B)	(C)	(D)	(E)	(F)	(G)	(H)
1966	0.9	125.2	108.3	393.7	0.72	0.23	27.5	27.74
1967	0.8	476.1	104.6	747.9	0.17	0.11	14.0	14.09
1968	1	1487.9	106.5	1626.8	0.07	0.06	6.5	6.61
1969	1	1904.8	115	2065.5	0.05	0.05	5.6	5.62
1970	1.4	3385.2	145.6	3576.4	0.04	0.04	4.1	4.11
1971	0.4	2207.1	154.4	2411.3	0.02	0.02	6.4	6.42
1972	71.8	3122.3	131.5	131.5	2.30	2.17	4.0	6.15
1973	63.3	4505.2	157.8	3304.8	1.41	1.35	3.4	4.70
1974	358.8	4826.4	172	4703.5	7.43	7.09	3.4	10.49
1975	250.9	5816.9	208.5	5056.4	4.31	4.11	3.4	7.53
1976	202.8	7562.8	248.6	6101.4	2.68	2.57	3.1	5.72
1977	194.1	8735.9	244.7	7895.6	2.22	2.14	2.7	4.83
1978	313.2	12041.8	401	9076.1	2.60	2.50	3.2	5.71
1979	443.7	14220.7	465.3	12510.1	3.12	3.00	3.1	6.15
1980	603.9	15875.3	481.9	14773.5	3.81	3.67	2.9	6.60
1981	738.4	17726	663.7	16454.8	4.17	3.99	3.6	7.57
1982	891.2	20469.6	647.2	18529.4	4.35	4.18	3.0	7.22
1983	901.3	24506	718.8	25432.5	3.68	3.54	2.8	6.37
1984	996.5	27081.4	703	28039.6	3.68	3.55	2.5	6.06
1985	963.8	27867.3	698	28833.2	3.46	3.34	2.4	5.76
1986	1057.3	34675.4	846.7	35820.2	3.05	2.95	2.4	5.32
1987	809.2	35088	837.9	36234.8	2.31	2.23	2.3	4.55
1988	768.1	41.021.7	1196.3	42495.2	1.87	1.81	2.8	4.62
1989	1044.3	40757.1	1297.1	42284.1	2.56	2.47	3.1	5.54
1990	1430.6	44062.9	1256.5	45608	3.25	3.14	2.8	5.89
1991	2209.6	53510.6	1191.3	55016.2	4.13	4.02	2.2	6.18
1992	2140.6	58490.2	1941.7	60844.1	3.66	3.52	3.2	6.71
1993	2857.5	64783.4	1353.6	66733.4	4.41	4.28	2.0	6.31
1994	3055.2	59273.1	1781.6	61478.7	5.15	4.97	2.9	7.87
1995	3406.2	66547.4	1563.7	68408.6	5.12	4.98	2.3	7.27
1996	3855	77032.2	1317.4	78604.9	5.00	4.90	1.7	6.58
1997	3822.6	79819.1	1213	81491.9	4.79	4.69	1.5	6.18
1998	4159.7	80878.1	1439.6	82502.6	5.14	5.04	1.7	6.79
1999	4729.5	83491.6	1275.4	84951.6	5.66	5.57	1.5	7.07
2000	5541.6	89440.6	2635	92253.6	6.20	6.01	2.6	8.86
2001	6377.8	93940.4	2553	96683.4	6.79	6.60	2.6	9.24

Source: EUROSTAT

Examining the scenarios for the future development of the EU's external activity, its international role and its transatlantic relations, one may expect a relatively weak and mainly inward-looking EU in the short to medium term. The main reasons will be the budgetary problems and financial burdens imposed by the eastward enlargement. In the longer term, the EU's financial condition will most probably allow it to pursue a more active role in global affairs, provided that the main problems have been resolved and the necessary adjustments to the new circumstances completed in the functioning of EMU and the enlarged EU. The political and economic effects of moderate increases in expenditures under the EU's external activities budget will, of course, be enhanced by the member countries' bilateral expenditures.

External activities and EDF in the current financial perspective (2000-2006)

In July 1997, the Commission issued a communication entitled 'Agenda 2000.' In March 1998, the Commission presented the new financial perspective for the period 2000-2006 relating to the EU's future priorities. Both documents included proposals for reform of community policies. The main components of Agenda 2000 were agreed by the European Council meeting held in Berlin in March 1999. The financial perspective was adopted by the Parliament in May 1999. It earmarked appropriations for EU accession of the Central and Eastern European countries without jeopardising the EU's current main priorities. In effect, that means that the issues deriving from the EU's global role, including transatlantic relations, were subordinated to the priority of enlargement. The financial perspective is a strict framework because the member states' contributions to the EU budget as a percentage of their GNP were also stabilised at their 1999 levels.

Allocation of financial resources for external relations

The new programming period has new priorities and modified instruments. Allocations of financial resources for external relations will continue to increase over the coming years (Table B.2). Both nominal and real values in the column 'external activity' will increase from euro 4627 million to 5040 million, but their share will decrease slightly, from 4.92 per cent to 4.67 per cent, between

2000 and 2006. Meanwhile the nominal as well as the real value of the amounts to be allocated for the accession countries will increase about sixfold,

Table B.2 - Financial Perspective 2000-2006: Values and Shares of Headings related to External Relations

Headings	2000	2001	2002	2003	2004	2005	2006
External action	4627	4755	5019	5025	5029	5035	5040
Pre-accession aid	3174	3240	3260	3260	3260	3259	3259
- Agriculture: SAPARD	529	540	540	540	540	540	540
- Structural Adjustment: ISPA	1058	1080	1080	1080	1080	1080	1080
- Phare	1587	1620	1620	1620	1620	1620	1620
- Mediterranean Strategy	-	-	20	20	20	19	19
Commitment total	**93952**	**97372**	**97696**	**97226**	**95680**	**95040**	**94551**
Payment for accession			4306	6979	6979	6979	6979
- Agriculture			1665	2112	2112	2112	2112
- other expenditure			2641	4867	4867	4867	4867
Appropriations for payment			**102281**	**105650**	**104828**	**105658**	**107989**

(values in euro million at 2000 prices)

Headings	2000	2001	2002	2003	2004	2005	2006
External action	4.92	4.88	4.91	4.76	4.8	4.77	4.67
Pre-accession aid	3.38	3.33	3.19	3.09	3.11	3.08	3.02
- Agriculture: SAPARD	0.56	0.55	0.53	0.51	0.52	0.51	0.5
- Structural Adjustment: ISPA	1.13	1.11	1.06	1.02	1.03	1.02	1.0
- Phare	1.69	1.66	1.58	1.53	1.55	1.53	1.5
Mediterranean Strategy	-	-	0.02	0.02	0.02	0.02	0.02
Commitment total	**100**	**100**					
Payment for accession			4.21	6.61	8.82	11.26	13.7
- Agriculture			1.63	2.0	2.43	2.88	3.28
- other expenditure			2.58	4.61	6.39	8.38	10.42
Appropriations for payment			**100**	**100**	**100**	**100**	**100**

(shares of headings as percentage of total value)
Source: EUROSTAT

from euro 3174 million to 18051 million. This increase will be reflected also by the growing combined share of these items in the total budget over the same period, which will show a fivefold rise from 3.38 per cent to 16.72 per cent.

The combined real values of the external activity and pre-accession aid will increase only moderately during the financial perspective. Thus their combined budget shares will decrease slightly, from 8.3 per cent to 7.7 per cent. However, the amount to be allocated for the new Central and Eastern European member countries after their accession will increase substantially over the course of the financial perspective. Its share of the budget will grow from 4.21 per cent in 2002 to 13.7 per cent in 2006. These are the maximum amounts in payment appropriations to cover expenditure resulting from new accessions over the period.

The 'external action' heading of the EU's budget covers the immediate needs for reconstruction (e.g. in the Western Balkans, Kosovo, East Timor, Turkey) and fisheries agreements (e.g. with Morocco) as well as more permanent financial support for the Central and Eastern European countries. The pre-accession strategy was identified in a new heading 7 in the financial perspective. In addition to the enhanced Phare programme, a new instrument for agriculture (SAPARD) and one for infrastructure and structural improvements (ISPA) were introduced. There is a strict rule, which was endorsed by the European Council in Berlin in 1999, that the annual ceiling for the three sub-headings should remain at a constant level throughout the period and should not be exceeded.

According to the same decision, an appropriate balance should continue to be struck in the geographical distribution of the EU's external commitments, taking account of the Union's policy commitments, political priorities and the countries with greatest need. At the same time, the level of commitments for the EU's external policies covered by heading 4 of the financial perspective should not be exceeded.

Table B.3 – Headings 4 and 7: External Actions and Pre-Accession Strategy

Purpose	Title/Chapter
External action (heading 4)	
European Development Fund	(Title B7-1)
Food aid and support operations	(Chapter B7-20)
Humanitarian aid	(Chapter B7-21)
Co-operation with Asian developing countries	(Chapter B7-30)
Co-operation with Latin American developing countries	(Chapter B7-31)
Co-operation with countries of Southern Africa and South Africa	(Chapter B7-32)
Co-operation with Mediterranean third countries and the Middle-East	(Chapter B7-40)
Co-operation with countries of Central and Eastern Europe	(Chapter B7-51)
EBRD	(Chapter (B7-52)
Co-operation with Newly Independent States and Mongolia	(Chapter (B7-53)
Exceptional assistance for Armenia, Georgia and Tajikistan	(Chapter (B7-54)
Co-operation with Balkan countries	(Title B7-6)
Other co-operation measures	(Title 7-7)
European initiative for democracy and the protection of human rights	(Chapter B7-80)
International fisheries agreements	(Chapters B7-81
External aspects of certain Community policies and support expenditure	to 87and B7 95)
Support expenditure for external policies	(Chapter B7-95)
CFSP	(Title B8-0)
Pre-accession strategy (heading 7)	
Agriculture (SAPARD)	(Chapter B7-01)
Pre-accession structural instrument (ISPA)	(Chapter B7-02)
Phare	(Chapter B7-03)

Principal Features of External Actions

The external policy of the EU's institutions is aimed at non-member countries across the world and has gained in importance in recent years. Development aid and humanitarian aid have both been stepped up, and support for the CEEC has increased significantly over the last decade. Allocations for external actions will increase moderately during the financial perspective, the more so as they serve several purposes.

The external action items of the EU's 2000 annual budget illustrate the main priorities (Table B.4). Since 1988, annual budgets have been drawn up in conformity with the financial perspective, which is a medium-term budgetary framework. The financial perspective laid down the annual expenditure limits.

In 2000, a total of nearly euro 5.5 billion, or 6.2 per cent of the general budget, was allocated to the external policy.

EU enlargement is one of the major budgetary issues. To prepare for new accessions, a sum of some euro 3.17 billion was earmarked for 2000. Compared with the amount of euro 1.37 billion which had been allocated for this purpose in 1999, it represented a very substantial increase, rising to 40 per cent of total external expenditure. In agriculture, the main aims of the SAPARD programme of euro 530 million in 2000 were to modernise holdings in the Central and Eastern European countries, to improve product quality and safety, to promote respect for the environment, and to diversify economic activity in rural areas. Through the ISPA structural instrument of over euro 1 billion in 2000, the EU is helping the Central and Eastern European countries to establish transport and environmental infrastructures compatible with those of the EU. The euro 1.5 billion in the 2000 Phare programme is funding the modernisation and adaptation to EU standards of the Central and Eastern European countries' economies and administrations.

First and foremost, the EU is a leading world player in the provision of humanitarian and food aid (B-20 and 21). In 2000, the EU's Humanitarian Office (ECHO) had euro 475 million at its disposal, and euro 465 million was spent on food aid. An emergency aid reserve of more than euro 200

Table B.4 - The 2000 Budget - External Actions (Subsection B)

	Value Euro m	per cent	Change
Actions defined by geographic areas			
B7-0 Pre-accession strategy	3166.7	39.7	++
B7-1 European Development Fund	-	-	
Co-operation with developing countries	905.7	11.3	
B7-30 Asia	446.3	5.6	+
B7-31 Latin America	335.9	4.2	+
B7-32 Southern Africa and South Africa	123.5	1.5	+
Mediterranean			
B7-40 Mediterranean third countries and the Middle-East	1142.9	14.3	+
Co-operation with countries of Central and Eastern Europe	907	11.3	
B7-52 Newly Independent States and Mongolia	450.4	5.6	+
B7-54 Balkan countries	456.6	5.7	+
Humanitarian and food aid	**936**	**11.7**	
B7-20 Food aid and support operations	436,4	5.8	++
B7-21 Humanitarian aid	472.6	5.9	++
General co-operation measures			
B7-51 EBRD	⌉ 65.8	0.8	+
B7-53 Exceptional assistance for Armenia, Georgia and Tajikistan	⌋		
B7-6 Other co-operation measures	336.9	4.7	-
B7-7 European initiative for democracy and the			
protection of human rights	95.4	1.2	-
B7-80 International fisheries agreements	276.1	276.1	+
B7-81 to B7-87 External aspects of certain Community policies	103.3	1.3	--
B7-95 Support expenditure for external policies			
B8-0 CFSP	47	0.6	+++
Subsection B7 – Total	7971.8	100	+
B7-9 Reserves	203		+++

Legend:
+ or - (change of 1-5 per cent)
++ or -- (change of 6-10 per cent)
+++ or --- (change of 15 per cent)
Source: EUROSTAT

million is also there to be drawn upon. This action reflects the EU's solidarity with regions in the grip of disasters.[203]

Non-member countries around the Mediterranean basin also received approximately euro 1.1 billion in 2000 to foster social and economic development and promote the Middle East peace process.

The newly independent states of the former Soviet Union received euro 450 million, primarily under the TACIS programme of technical assistance to aid economic recovery.

---

[203] Such as in 1998 the countries of Central America which were hit by Hurricane Mitch.

About the same amount was provided for the Balkan region, including euro 360 million for the reconstruction of Kosovo.

Economic and financial co-operation on the part of the EU to assist developing countries in Latin America and Asia in 2000 accounted for euro 336 million and 446 respectively. This aid covers a wide range of fields, including health and education.

The EU also funds general measures in support of democracy and human rights (euro 95 million in 2000), not forgetting measures to protect tropical forests and the environment.

The EU signed fisheries agreements with many countries, giving European vessels access to the fishing grounds of these countries. These agreements included total transfers of euro 276 million in 2000.

A part of the external action budget is spent on co-operation with industrialised non-member countries (such as Japan and the US) and on activities in association with international organisations.

The aid amounts for the Central and Eastern European countries are currently distributed among all the applicant countries. As some of them join the EU, the same amount will be divided among the others. This practice means that the budgets for the remaining applicant countries will increase, which will in turn help to boost their EU membership potential. For each year from 2002, the financial perspective 2000-2006 also makes provision for an amount, expressed as payment appropriations, to supplement allocations under the various headings in line with accessions.

The main trends in the EU's previous external policy will be continued in its budgetary policy during the present financial perspective. As in the 1990s, the EU's focus will be on the accession countries during the coming years, and its financial commitment to helping the accession process of these countries will be even more pronounced. However, in terms of financial assistance the EU's presence on the global stage will remain modest and it will not be able to pursue a very active global role. This situation is likely to lead to a more co-operative partnership with the US rather than to any prospect of confrontation.

Table B.5 - The Impact of successive EU Enlargements

Enlargement	Area (% increase)	Population (% increase)	Total GDP (% increase)	Average per capita GDP	per capita GDP (% of EC 6)
EC6 ≻ EC9	31	32	24	-6	94
EC9 ≻ EC10	9	4	2	-2	92
EC10 ≻ EC12	34	16	9	-8	85
EC12 ≻ EU15	17	6	8	1	86
EU15 ≻ EU20	17	16	3	-12	75
EU20 ≻ EU25	33	28	4	-19	69

Source: European Commission, Agenda 2000

Further reform of the EU budget's expenditure structure and system

There is no doubt that EU enlargement will have a profound impact on EU behaviour in its budget financing. The potentially high budgetary costs are a very important consequence of CEE accession to the EU, and differ substantially from previous enlargements. The applicant countries have relatively low incomes, which will reduce the average per capita GDP of the EU when they join.

The evolving situation after enlargement

Upon EU enlargement, the present net contributors will have to increase their budgetary outlays substantially, while net recipients will lose considerable benefits – some even losing to the extent of becoming net contributors. Under the new conditions the EU will need either a bigger budget or a reform of the present structure and size of budgetary expenditures. Were budgetary resources for transfers not to be increased to match the criteria applied by today's 15-member EU, enlargement would imply a lowering of the cohesion expectations of the enlarged EU. Of all potential political and economic problems to arise, this is the most fundamental one. This problem has internal, that is European aspects as well as global aspects capable of influencing transatlantic relations.

The budgetary situation of the post-enlargement EU can influence Europe's international role both directly and indirectly. Financial problems could reduce the power and influence of the EU in international affairs, whereas a consolidated financial position would strengthen the role of a reunited Europe. On this basis, several more alternative scenarios can be sketched out.

1. The pessimistic scenario

In this scenario the budgetary situation of the EU is overstretched and there will be many more demands for EU assistance than the financial resources available. There will be frictions between those EU member countries which have benefited so far from the structural and cohesion funds and the new Central and Eastern European members expecting greater financial support. The result of such an internal conflict may be to block or impede an active international policy and presence of the EU. The leadership of the EU and the member states will be immobilised by such overwhelming problems and dissensions.

2. The optimistic scenario

In this scenario the accession of five to ten Central and Eastern European countries will not cause any disturbing financial problems for the EU budget. The costs of transition and the economic catching up process with EU levels can be financed basically from three sources: first, from the domestic resources of the applicant countries (domestic savings); secondly, from international private and official sources (borrowing on international capital markets, IMF, World Bank); and thirdly, by transfers from the EU. The success of accession and the reunification of Europe can increase the international importance of the EU. Under such conditions, the world's confidence in the international role of the EU can be reinforced and the EU may become one of the few fully-fledged leading participants in world politics. This situation may allow the EU to fulfil enhanced political and economic missions in international relations.

3. The realistic scenario

Since continuation of the present budgetary policies is almost bound to lead to a crisis, reforms of the CAP and the Structural Funds will be necessary and unavoidable. The actual outcome of these scenarios will depend on various external and internal factors. Among the external ones, the most important are the WTO negotiations, and the influence of the US. The most potent internal factors are opposition to the high costs of the CAP, budget capping, and the distribution of structural funds.

Principal financial expenditures of the EU budget

The EU budget is dominated by expenditures on agriculture and structural policies. As has been obvious for more than a decade, both policies give rise to conflicts among member states on grounds of eligibility and distribution. Moreover, the Single European Act (SEA) of 1987 introduced a new article that codified social and economic cohesion as formal objectives of the EU. It accorded the EU budget a crucial role in the success of the integration process.

The structural funds and the CAP will be the main sources for the new member countries to finance their economic and social development after accession. Since, on the one hand, this support is crucial for the Central and Eastern European countries but, on the other, the benefits for the present recipients may be reduced, this issue has particular political importance. To satisfy all these needs the EU would have to have a greatly increased budget capable of yielding ever-increasing financial resources.

From the point of view of global issues and transatlantic relations, the two main financing sources of the EU's budget and their reform are of differing importance. Both financing sources can significantly influence the structure and balance of the EU's budget, but it is the CAP and its sustainability and reform which have important implications for international trade policy and transatlantic relations.

(a) Structural funds

The eastward enlargement of the EU will mean a widening of income disparities. Thus the need for economic and social cohesion as a vital contribution to the EU's stability will be even greater. The structural policies have always had redistribution as a tacit objective, aimed at reducing income disparities among the member states. For the last decade, structural funds have been increasingly concentrated in poorer regions and in poorer countries.

The accession of the Central and Eastern European countries raises problems for the overall level of structural fund expenditure and its distribution among the increased number of member states. Under current rules, all the CEEC would qualify for Objective 1 status and thus the highest level of regional aid. After their accession, the greatly increased number of regions and states vying for structural funds will have a profound influence on the EU budget.

(b) Agriculture - The CAP

Tighter budgetary controls were imposed on the CAP by the MacSharry reforms in 1992 and again in 1999. While these reforms could reduce fluctuations in expenditure levels, the agriculture budget has steadily increased due to the growing compensation payments in exchange for reductions in intervention prices.

One of the paradoxes of the EU is that the net contributor states complain about the size of the budget and the contribution required of them, whilst it is almost the same group of countries which stolidly opposes drastic reform of the CAP. This paradox reflects a set of complex interests. The present structure of the CAP favours disproportionately the larger farms and continental types of agricultural products, whose governments are precisely the net contributors to the budget. CAP reform and cuts in its budget would reduce their receipts from the EU budget and increase their net contributions.

This situation is becoming even more complicated through several other factors and interests. US agricultural production and exports are concentrated on a very similar set of commodities to those supported by the CAP. The future member countries of Central and Eastern Europe also have similar agricultural products which will make the negotiations between the EU and the applicant countries, and between the US and the enlarged EU, even more complex. Moreover, the net contributor EU members have active and politically well organised agricultural lobbies. The reduction of CAP subventions is a politically charged issue.

The likelihood of reform or substantial changes to the structural funds is different from that of the CAP. Compared with the CAP, the EU's structural policies are fairly coherent and effective. The main aim of the structural policies is to reduce interregional disparities and ensure a harmonious process of economic development in member states. They achieve this by supporting regional and national development, primarily by measures to increase efficiency. The multiplication of funds and distribution channels under the Single European Act has, however, also prompted increasingly serious disputes between net recipients and net contributors.

The details of CAP reform are more difficult to agree because there are stronger conflicting interests among the member states. The Commission's Agenda 2000 proposed reform of the CAP and of economic and social policy, and the establishment of a pre-accession strategy. It also dealt with the effects of enlargement on the financing of the EU. In March 1999, the Agriculture Council reached agreement by accepting a plan for an equitable and worthwhile reform of the CAP. The scope of this reform ensured that agriculture is multifunctional, sustainable, competitive and spread throughout Europe. The reform paid special attention to regions with specific problems, so as to make the CAP an instrument for maintaining the countryside, conserving nature and making a key contribution to the vitality of rural life. Moreover, the reform tried to respond to consumer concerns and demands in relation to food quality and safety, environmental protection and the safeguarding of animal welfare.

Within the framework of this reform, efforts have been made to curb the budget and exercise rigour in the management of the CAP. The efforts made, notably in terms of reducing support prices, represent an essential contribution by the European Union to stabilising the world's agricultural markets. The European Council considers that the decisions on reform of the CAP adopted within the framework of Agenda 2000 will constitute essential elements in defining the Commission's negotiating mandate for future multilateral trade negotiations within the WTO. These trade negotiations constitute one of the most sensitive issues in transatlantic relations.

Budgetary aspects

According to article 269 of the TEU, the budget is to be financed entirely from the EU's own resources.[204] With expenditure on agricultural and

---

[204] Own resources are: customs duties, agricultural levies, and 1 per cent of VAT.

structural policies constantly rising, meeting this requirement became increasingly difficult. During the 1990s, the EU's budget once more became an issue. To balance the budget, the EU had two alternatives: either the member states increased their budget contributions, or the structure and size of expenditures had to be reformed and reduced. The decision on budgetary policy was made in the course of the negotiations on the Delors II package. This package reduced the ceiling on expenditure from 1.37 per cent of GNP to 1.27 per cent. The best reform would, of course, have been to increase the efficiency of the agricultural policy by cutting costs.

There have been several proposals for reforming the budget. By the end of the 1990s substantial and looming budgetary problems had accumulated. Enlargement of the EU will aggravate these problems. To find solutions to them, the Commission presented initial proposals for a future financial framework after enlargement. However, some experts consider certain aspects of these proposals rather controversial.

The Commission's proposal set out in Agenda 2000 was aimed at preparing the EU for enlargement and at improving its negotiating position in the WTO talks. The latter was an important aspect for US trade policy. The Commission suggested continuing on the reform path taken in 1992, which implied substantial further cuts in support prices and partial compensation through direct payments to farmers. For the structural and cohesion funds, the Commission proposed to concentrate expenditure much more on smaller areas or regions and to reduce the number of policy objectives and initiatives.

At the start of the Agenda 2000 negotiations, several issues were raised, such as the excessive budgetary burden for net contributors, reforming the own resources system, and a generalised correction mechanism, which demonstrated that member states were not then prepared to accept the financial consequences of enlargement. During the subsequent negotiations, new proposals for budgetary rebates as well as other measures for reducing the budgetary burden were presented,[205] but no significant progress was achieved.

The budgetary problem of excessive net contributions dominated the debates and pushed aside the financial problems of enlargement. Yet the real issue is not the former but the latter. The former problems derive from the inefficiencies on the expenditure side of the budget, which cannot be changed because some net contributors reject the introduction of reforms. The dominant view during the debates was against agricultural reform. Even those few countries which called for radical reform of the CAP could not agree on the direction the reforms should take.

Due to these contradictory views the agreement on budgetary issues concluded at the Berlin summit in March 1999 could not be fully satisfactory. The outcome of the negotiations was to some extent similar in structure to the original Commission proposal, but in essence had little effect upon the prevailing systems of the CAP.

The agreement may be undermined by future developments because the calculations were based on two doubtful assumptions. The first was that the Central and Eastern European countries would not be eligible for direct payments under the CAP, which has already proved unrealistic. The second was that the initial group of Central and Eastern European countries would join the EU in 2004-5 and that, for the purposes of the financial framework, their transition period would last until 2006. The actual impact of enlargement on the EU budget may therefore turn out to be different. If enlargement were delayed, 2006 expenditures would be lower. This underlines the uncertainty of attempts to calculate the ultimate impact of enlargement on the budget.

---

[205] Núlnez Ferrer and Emerson (2000) discussed these proposals in detail:

a) reforming the budget own resources system by abolishing the VAT resource and keeping the others;

b) renegotiating the British budget rebate;

c) introducing a correction mechanism for excessive net contributor members;

d) co-financing direct payments to farmers;

e) phasing out Cohesion Funds for EMU member states;

f) reducing and limiting Structural Funds expenditures;

g) imposing a ceiling on agricultural expenditure for the period 2000-2006.

As reformed by the Berlin summit, the CAP seems to be less expensive than estimated in the original Agenda 2000, since reforms were effectively postponed. Most of the impact of delaying reform is on the agriculture budget expenditures, which still approximate the levels originally planned in the Commission's financial framework. That means that the real burdens of the CAP are shifted to the next generation, and they will clearly be aggravated by enlargement.

Conclusion

The emerging enlarged EU will occupy a different position on the global economic and political scene from the old. This applies equally to its transatlantic relations. The EU's eastward enlargement will influence its role and potential in global and transatlantic relations both directly and indirectly. Among the main factors are budget constraints, which will have a significant bearing on its global activities and commitment to global politics. Whilst the amounts allocated under the heading 'external activity' of the EU budget have increased steadily over past decades, recent trends show a much stronger focus of the EU's interests, financial support and development projects on the Central and Eastern European applicants.

The Commission's Agenda 2000, as well as the decision of the European Council in Berlin and the new financial perspective 2000-2006, have reinforced the orientation of external activities developed over the past decade. The Central and Eastern European countries will be accorded priority. In the context of enlargement, reform of the CAP and structural funds was debated vigorously, but internal conflicts of interest among the 15 EU member states over the direction the reforms have blocked any radical change in the prevailing system.

Among possible scenarios for the future development of the EU's external activity and international role, including its transatlantic relations, the most likely is a relatively weak and mainly inward-looking EU in the short and medium term. In the longer term, financial conditions will most probably allow the EU to pursue a more active role in global affairs, once the major problems of the functioning of an enlarged EU and EMU have been resolved and the necessary adaptations completed. The political and economic role of the EU in global and transatlantic affairs should not, however, be inferred exclusively from the size of the 'external activity' budget heading. The activities and combined financial expenditures of all EU member countries will also have to be counted as part of the total contribution. Over a 30-50 year timespan, the enlarged EU is clearly destined to play a more significant and powerful role in the global economic and political arena, including the transatlantic dimension, than it is capable of now or in the early aftermath of its enlargement.

List of Tables

Glossary

ACP – African, Caribbean and Pacific countries
AFSOUTH – Allied Forces Southern Europe
ASEM – South-East Asia summit meetings
BALTBAT – Baltic common peacekeeping Battalion
BALTDEFCOL – Baltic Defence College
BALTNET – Baltic Air Surveillance Network
BALTRON – Baltic regional Sea Squadron
BALTSEA – Baltic Security Assistance Group
BEAC – Barents Euro-Arctic Council
BITs – Bilateral Investment Treaties
CAP – Common Agricultural Policy
C[S]BMs – Continental [Strategic] Ballistic Missiles
CBSS – Council of the Baltic Sea States
CEE – Central and Eastern Europe
CEEC – Central and East European Countries
CESDP – Common European Security and Defence Policy
CFSP – Common Foreign and Security Policy
COREPER – Committee of Permanent Representatives to the EU
CSCE – Conference on Security and Co-operation in Europe (now OSCE)
DANBAT – Danish regional peacekeeping Battalion
EAPC – Euro-Atlantic Partnership Council
EBRD – European Bank for Reconstruction and Development
EC – European Communities (now EU)
ECB – European Central Bank
ECHO – European Communities' Humanitarian Office
ECJ – European Court of Justice
ECSC – European Coal and Steel Community
EDC – European Defence Community
EDF – European Development Fund
EFTA – European Free Trade Area
EMP – Euro-Mediterranean Partnership
EMU – Economic and Monetary Union
EP – European Parliament
EPC – European Policy Centre
ESDI – European Security and Defence Identity
ESDP – European Security and Defence Policy
EU – European Union
EURATOM – European Atomic Energy Community
EUROMARFOR – European Maritime Force
FYROM – Former Yugoslav Republic of Macedonia
G-24 – Group of 24 contributor countries to Balkan reconstruction

GATT – General Agreement on Tariffs and Trade
IFOR – Nato-led Implementation Force for Bosnia
IMF – International Monetary Fund
ISPA – Pre-accession instrument for Infrastructure and Structural Improvements
MEAD – Access to Markets, Euro-subventions, Diplomatic Action and Dialogue
MENA – Middle East and North Africa
MEPP – Middle East Peace Process
MERCOSUR – Latin American Common Market
MNMC – Mediterranean non-EU Member Countries
Nato – North Atlantic Treaty Organisation
NEI – Northern European Initiative
NORDBRIG – Nordic integrated peacekeeping Brigade
NSC – New Strategic Concept
NTA – New Transatlantic Agenda
OECD – Organisation for Economic Co-operation and Development
OSCE – Organisation for Security and Co-operation in Europe
PfP – Nato's Partnership for Peace
Phare – Economic assistance programme for Central and Eastern Europe
PSC – Political and Security Committee
QMV – Qualified Majority Voting
REDWG – Regional Economic Working Group
RTNC – Turkish Republic of Northern Cyprus
SAPARD – Pre-accession instrument for Agriculture
SECI – Southeast European Cooperative Inititative
SFOR – Nato-led Stabilisation Force for Bosnia
SLG – Senior Level Group
STABEX – Export Stabilisation Mechanism for ACP countries
SYSMIN – Mining industry support mechanism for ACP countries
TACIS – Technical Assistance to Newly Independent States
TAFTA – Transatlantic Free Trade Area
TEC – Treaty of the European Communities
TEP – Transatlantic Economic Partnership
TEU – Treaty of the European Union
UN – United Nations
UNFICYP – UN-Force in Cyprus
USTR – United States Trade Representative
WEU – Western European Union
WTO – World Trade Organisation

Bibliography

Chapter 6 – Mediterranean, Middle East and North Africa

Ahiram, E., Tovias, A. (eds.) 1995, *Whither EU-Israeli Relations? Common and Divergent Interests*, Peter Lang, Frankfurt a. Main.

Aliboni, R. 1992, 'Europe between East and South: Security and Development Cooperation,' *The International Spectator*, Vol. 27, No. 2, pp.5-15.

Allen, D. 1979, 'The Euro-Arab Dialogue,' *The Journal of Common Market Studies*, Vol. 16, No. 4, June, pp.323-342.

Alpher, J. 1998, 'The Political Role of the European Union in the Arab-Israeli Peace Process: An Israeli Perspective,' *The International Spectator*, Vol. 33, No. 4, October-December 1998, pp.77-86.

Bonvicini,G. 1992, 'The Mediterranean and Eastern Europe: Two Worlds in Competition?,' in Telo, M. 1992, *Vers une nouvelle Europe?*, l'Université de Bruxelles, Bruxellses, pp.169-76.

De Guttry, A. 1998, 'Possibili scenari di evoluzione istituzionale del Partenariato euro-mediterraneo,' in Attinà, F. et al. 1998, *L'Italia tra l'Europa e il Mediterraneo: il bivio che non c'è più*, Il Mulino for Arel, Bologna, pp.63-90.

Edwards, G., Philippart, E. 1997, 'The EU Mediterranean Policy: Virtue Unrewarded Or ...?,' *Cambridge Review of International Affairs*, Vol. 11, No 1, Summer/Fall, pp.185-207.

Joffé, G (ed.) 1998, 'Perspectives on Development: The Euro-Mediterranean Partnership,' *The Journal of North African Studies*, Vol. 3 (Special Edition), No. 2, Summer.

Heller, M. A. (ed.) 1999, *Europe & the Middle East. New Tracks to Peace?*, The Jaffee Center for Strategic Studies & Friedrich Ebert Stiftung, Herzliya.

Kebabdjian, G. 1995, 'Eléments d'une prospective Euro-Méditerranéenne,' in Bistolfi, R. 1995, *Euro-Méditerranée, une région à construire*, Publisud, Paris, pp.57-100.

Khader, B. 1992, *L'Europe et le monde arabe, Cousins, Voisins*, CERMAC, Paris.

Lesser, I. O. 1996, *Southern Europe and the Maghreb: US Interests and Policy Perspectives*, Rand, Santa Monica.

Lesser, I. O. 1998, *The Changing Mediterranean Security Environment: A Transatlantic Perspective*, in Joffé, G. (ed.), 1998, pp.212- 228.

Lesser, I. O. 2000, *Nato Looks South. New Challenges and New Strategies in the Mediterranean*, Rand, Santa Monica.

Monar, J. 1998, 'Institutional Constraints of the European Union's Mediterranean Policy,' *Mediterranean Politics*, Vol. 3, No. 2, pp.39-60.

Murphy, R. W. 1996, 'France, États-Unis: médiations croisées', in Kodmani-Darwish, B., Chartouni Dubarry, M. 1996, *Le Liban ou les dérives du processus de paix*, IFRI, Paris, pp.11-15.

Ounaïes, A. 2000, 'Le Partenariat US/Maghreb. Le Projet Eizenstat,' *Réalités*, actes du colloque international 'Europe-Maghreb: Bilan et Perspectives,' Tunis les 19 et 20 Avril 2000, Tunisia, pp.89-92.

Perthes, V. 2000, 'The Advantages of Complementarity: US and European Policies toward the Middle East Peace Process,' *The International Spectator*, Vol. 35, No. 2, pp.41-56.

Peters, J. 1999, 'Europe and the Middle East Peace Process: Emerging from the Sidelines,' in Stavridis, T., Couloumbis, T., Veremis, N. Waites (eds.) 1999, *The Foreign Policies of the European Union's Mediterranean States and Applicant Countries in the 1990s*, MacMillan Press, London, pp.295-316.

Said Aly, A. 1997, 'The Political Role of the EU in the Middle East: an Arab Perspective,' in *The Political Role of the European Union in the Middle East*, Working papers presented at the workshop of the Bertelsmann Foundation on 'The Political Role of the European Union in the Middle East,' Frankfurt, October 26-28, pp.51-62.

Salem, P. E. 1997, 'Arab Political Currents, Arab-European Relations and Mediterraneanism,' Guazzone, L. (ed.) 1997, *The Middle East in Global Change*, MacMillan Press, London, pp.23-42.

Waldenberg, M. 1994, *Le questioni nazionali nell'Europa centro-orientale*, Il Saggiatore, Milano. [Italian translation of *Kwestie Narodowe w Europie Srodkowo-Wshodniej. Dzieje. Idee*, Wydawnictwo Naukowe PWN, Warszawa (1992)].

Chapter 7 – The EU as global Actor: concepts and realities

Copenhagen Accession Criteria, Homepage of the European Commission: DG 1, Available: http://www.europa.eu.int/comm.

Agenda of the Presidencies of the Council of Ministers, Available: http://www.eu-praesidentschaft.de/01/frameset.htm.

Behrendt, S. 1998, 'Nahost und Mittelmeerpolitik,' in Weidenfeld, W., Wessels, W. 1998, *Jahrbuch der europäischen Integration*, IEP, Bonn.

Bull, H. 1977, *The Anarchical Society, A Study of Order in World Politics*, Columbia University Press, London.

Dehousse, R. 1997, *La Cour de Justice des Communautés européennes*, 2nd edn, Montchrestien, Paris.

Diedrichs, U. 1999, 'Die Lateinamerikapolitik der Europäischen Union,' in

Werner, W., Wessels, W. *1999, Jahrbuch der europäischen Integration*, Bonn, IEP, pp.289-294.

Doutriaux, Y., Lequesne, C. 1998, *Les institutions de l'Union européenne* (nouvelle édition mise à jour), Refléxe Europe, Paris.

Dumond, J-M., Setton, P. 1999, *La politique étrangère et de sécurité commune* (PESC), Refléxe Europe, Paris.

Duchêne, F. 1973, 'Die Rolle Europas im Weltsystem: Von der regionalen zur planetarischen Interdependenz,' in Kohnstamm, M., Hager, W. (ed.), *Zivilmacht Europa-Supermacht oder Partner?*, Suhrkamp, Franfurt a. Main, pp.19-26.

Edwards, G., Regelsberger, E. 1990, *Europe's Global Links: The European Community and Interregional Cooperation*, Pinter, London.

European Commission 1993, Europe agreement with Hungary, Homepage of the European Commission, available http//:www.europa.eu.int/comm/eurlex/en/lif/dat/ 1993/en_293A1231_13.html.

Fallik, A. (ed.) 1996, *The European Public Affairs Directory*, Landmark, Bruxelles.

The European Council 1999, June 11-last updated, *The European Council Presidency Conclusions* [Homepage of the European Council, [Online]. Available: http://www.europa.eu.int/council/off/conclu/june99/june99_en.htm [2002, 8 March].

Galtung, J. 1973, *Kapitalistische Großmacht Europa oder die Gemeinschaft der Konzerne?*, Reinbeck.

Gasteyger, C. 1996, *An Ambiguous Power. The European Union in a Changing World*, Brookings Institute, Washington.

The European Union 2001, January 2002-last updated, T*he General Report on the Activities of the European Union*, [Online]. Available: http://europa.eu.int/abc/doc/ off/rg/en/welcome.htm, [2002, 8 March].

General Secretariat of the European Council. 1993, *39ᵗʰ General Report on the Activities of the Council (Report of the general secretary)*, 1 January – 31 December 1991, Luxembourg.

General Report on the Activities of the European Union 1993, [Online]. Available: http://europa.eu.int/abc/doc/off/rg/en/welcome.htm, [2002, 8 March].

General Report on the Activities of the European Union 1996, [Online], Available: http://europa.eu.int/abc/doc/off/rg/en/welcome.htm, [2002, 8 March].

General Report on the Activities of the European Union 1998[Online]. Available: http://europa.eu.int/abc/doc/off/rg/en/welcome.htm, [2002, 8 March].

Guth, E. 1998, 'Haushaltspolitik,' in Weidenfeld, W., Wessels, W. 1998, *Jahrbuch der europäischen Integration*, IEP, Bonn, pp.155-162.

Hacke, C., 1988, *Die Außenpolitik der Bundesrepublik Deutschland: Weltmacht wider Willen*, Ullstein, Berlin.

Hill, C. 1993, 'The Capability Expectation Gap, or Conceptualising Europe's International Role,' *Journal of Common Market Studies*, Vol. 31, No. 3, pp.305.

Institut der Deutschen Wirtschaft (ed.), 1994, *Internationale Wirtschaftszahlen*, IDW, Köln.

Jachtenfuchs, M. 1993, *Ideen und Interessen: Weltbilder als Kategorien der politischen Analyse*, MZES, Mannheim.

Jachtenfuchs, M. 1995, 'Ideen und internationale Beziehungen,' in *Zeitschrift für internationale Beziehungen*, Vol 2, No 2, pp.417.

Oppenheimer, A. (ed.) 1993, *The Relationship between European Community Law and National Law: The Cases*, Cambridge University Press, Cambridge.

Kennedy, P. 1990, *The Rise and Fall of the Great Powers: Economic Change and Military Conflict from 1500 to 2000*, Vintage Books, London.

Kennedy, P. 1993, *Preparing for the Twenty-first Century*, Harper Collins, New York.

Kirste, K., Maull, H. W. 1996, Zivilmacht und Rollentheorie, in *Zeitschrift für internationale Beziehungen*, Vol 3, No 2, pp.283-312.

Kissinger, H. 1995, *Diplomacy*, Touchstone, New York.

Kohnstamm, M., Hager, W. (ed.) 1973, *Zivilmacht Europa-Supermacht oder Partner?*, Suhrkamp, Frankfurt.

Kommission der Europäischen Gemeinschaft, Generaldirektion Information, Kommunikation, Kultur, Audiovisuelle Medien, 1993: Europa im Wandel, Die Außenbeziehungen der Europäischen Gemeinschaft, Luxembourg.

Link, W. 1998, *Die Neuordnung der Weltpolitik: Grundprobleme globaler Politik an der Schwelle zum 21*, Jahrhundert, München.

Link, W. 1997, 'Die europäische Neuordnung und das Machtgleichgewicht,' in Jäger, T., Piepenschneider, M. (ed.) 1997, *Europa 2020: Szenarien politischer Entwicklung*, Leske+Budrich, Opladen, pp.9-32.

Lippert, B. 1994, 'Politik gegenüber Mittel-und Osteuropa sowie den GUS-Staaten,' in Werner, W., Wessels, W. (ed.) 1994, *Jahrbuch der Europäischen Integration*, pp.253-258.

Major, J. 1993, 'Raise Your Eyes: There is a Land Beyond,' *The Economist*, 25 September, pp.19-25.

Maull, H. W. 1992, 'Zivilmacht Bundesrepublik Deutschland: Vierzehn Thesen für eine neue deutsche Außenpolitik,' in *Europa-Archive*, No. 10, pp.269-278.

Maull, H. W. 1997, 'Europa als Weltmacht ? Perspektiven für die Gemeinsame Außen und Sicherheitspolitik,' in Thomas, J., Piepenschneider, M. (ed.), *Europa 2020: Szenarien politischer Entwicklung*, Leske+Budrich, Opladen, pp.81-95.

Meyers, R. 1994, *Begriff und Probleme des Friedens*, Leske+Budrich, Opladen.

Monar, J. 1994, 'Außenwirtschaftsbeziehungen,' in Werner, W., Wessels, W. (ed.), *Jahrbuch der Europäischen Integration*, IEP, Bonn.

Monar, J. 1996, 'Political Dialogue with Third Countries and Regional Political Groupings: The Fifteen as an Attractive Interlocutor,' in Elfriede, R., de Schoutheete, P., Wessels, W. (ed.) 1996, *Foreign Policy of the European Union. From EPC to CFSP and Beyond*, Lynne Reiner, London, pp.263-274.

Müller-Brandeck-Bocquet, 'Flexible Integration: Eine Chance für die europäische Umweltpolitik,' in *Integration*, Issue 4, October, pp.292-305.

Peterson, J., Bomberg, E. 1999, *Decision-Making in the European Union*, MacMillan, New York.

Quermonne, J-L. 1994, *Les systèmes politiques de l'Union européene*, 2nd edn, Montchrestien, Paris.

Regelsberger, E. 1994, 'Gemeinsame Außen- und Sicherheitspolitik,' in Werner, W., Wessels, W. (ed.) 1994, *Jahrbuch der Europäischen Integration*, IEP, Bonn.

German Ministry of Finance, *Annual Economic and Financial Report*s, Available: http://www.bundesfinanzministerium.de/finwiber/berichte/fpl2003.pdf.

Rittberger, V. 1994, *Internationale Organisationen: Politik und Geschichte*, Leske+Budrich, Opladen.

Rosecrance, R. N. 1986, *The Rise of the Trading State: Commerce and Conquest in the Modern World*, Basic Books, New York.

Schäuble/Lamers-Papier 1994, *Überlegungen zur europäischen Politik*, Bonn, 1 September 1994.

Schneider, H. 1977, 'Leitbilder der Europapolitik 1, Der Weg zur Integration,' Bonn.

Schneider, H. 1990, 'Vom KSZE-Prozeß zum gesamteuropäischen Kooperationssystem: Die europäische Architektur und ihr Architekturdilemma', in *Integration*, Vol. 4, pp.150-164.

Schneider, H. 1998, 'Ein Wandel europapolitischer Grundverständnisse? Grundsatzüberlegungen, Erklärungsansätze und Konsequenzen für die politische Bildungsarbeit,' in Jopp, M., Maurer, A., Schneider, H. (ed.) 1998, Europäische Grundverständnisse im Wandel. Analysen und Konsequenzen für die politische Bildung, Bonn, pp.19-147.

Schwarz, H. P. 1987, 'Der Faktor Macht im heutigen Staatensystem,' in Karl, K.,

Schwarz, H. P. (ed.) 1987, *Weltpolitik, Strukturen - Akteure - Perspektiven*, 2nd edn, Bonn.

Weidenfeld, W., Wolfgang, W. (ed.) 1994, *Jahrbuch der Europäischen Integration*, IEP, Bonn.

Weidenfeld, W., Wolfgang, W. (ed.) 1995, *Jahrbuch der Europäischen Integration*, IEP, Bonn.

Weidenfeld, W., Wolfgang, W. (ed.) 1996, *Jahrbuch der Europäischen Integration*, IEP, Bonn.

Weidenfeld, W., Wolfgang, W. (ed.) 1998, *Jahrbuch der Europäischen Integration*, IEP, Bonn.

Wessels, W. 1992, 'Staat und (westeuropäische) Integration. Die Fusionsthese,' in Kreile, M. (ed.) 1992, *Die Integration Europas, PVS: Sonderheft 23*, Leske+Budrich, Opladen, pp.36-61.

Wessels, W. 1992, 'The EC and the New European Architecture: The European Union as Trustee for a (Pan-)European Weal,' in Mario, T. (ed.) 1992, *Vers une nouvelle Europe?*, l'Université de Bruxelles, Bruxelles, pp.35-48.

Wessels, W. 1997, 'Der Amsterdamer Vertrag- Durch Stückwerksreformen zu einer effizienteren, erweiterten und föderalen Union ?,' in *Integration*, Vol 3, Bonn, pp.117-135.

Wessels, W. 1997, 'An Ever Closer Fusion ? A Dynamic Macropolitical View on Integration Processes,' *Journal of Common Market Studies*, Vol. 35, No. 2, June, pp.267-299.

Wessels, W.,Birke, J. 1997, 'Flexibilisierung: Die Europäische Union vor einer neuen Grundsatzdebatte ? Grundmodelle unter der Lupe,' in Rudolf, H. (ed.) 1997, *Die Reform der Europäischen Union*, Baden-Baden.

Wessels, W. 1999, 'Zentralmacht, Zivilmacht, Ohnmacht ?, Zur deutschen Außen- und Europapolitik nach 1989' Weilemann, in Peter, R., Küsters, H. J., Buchstab, G., (ed.) 1999, *Macht und Zeitkritik: Festschrift für Hans Peter Schwarz zum 65. Geburtstag*, Paderborn, pp.389-406.

Appendix B – Budgetary matters and policy reform

Falk, R., Szentes, T. (eds.) 1997, *A New Europe in the Changing Global System, United Nations*, United Nations University Press, New York.

Henderson, K. (ed.) 1999, *Back to Europe – CEE and the EU*, University College London Press, London.

Lachet, A., Pflüger, F. (eds.) 2000, *Amerika und Europa*.

Pelkmans J., Gros, D., Nunez Ferrer, J. 2000, *Long run economic aspects of the EU's Eastern Enlargement*, WRR, The Hague.

About TEPSA

The Trans European Policy Studies Association (TEPSA) is an independent network of institutes which promote international research on European integration in order to stimulate discussion on policies and political options for Europe. TEPSA links affiliated national institutes from all Union member states and from several candidate countries.

TEPSA projects include research and studies commissioned by the European institutions (Parliament, Commission, Economic and Social Committee), foundations and national or regional public and private authorities.

These studies address the functioning of the political systems of the Union and its institutions and relations with national and regional structures. Research is also carried out on several Common policies, such as Economic and Monetary Union, Economic and Social Cohesion, External Relations, Common Foreign and Security Policy, and Justice and Home Affairs.

TEPSA's international conferences are its main vehicle to promote direct contact between politicians, academics, national and European civil servants, journalists and those active in the field of education. These conferences are prepared for TEPSA by the respective member institute and based on research carried out by that institute or by an ad hoc TEPSA study group.

The most important conferences are those preceding the change of EU Presidency. TEPSA organises such conferences twice a year in co-operation with the government about to assume the next Presidency. These presidential conferences bring elements of TEPSA's planning and analysis to bear on the draft programme of the designated country, so as to enhance the overall policy potential of the Union.